Mastering Assembly Programming

From instruction set to kernel module with Intel processor

Alexey Lyashko

BIRMINGHAM - MUMBAI

Mastering Assembly Programming

First published: September 2017

Production reference: 1220917

Published by Packt Publishing Ltd.
Livery Place
35 Livery Street
Birmingham
B3 2PB, UK.

ISBN 978-1-78728-748-8

www.packtpub.com

Credits

Author
Alexey Lyashko

Reviewer
Tomasz Grysztar

Commissioning Editor
Merint Mathew

Acquisition Editor
Karan Sadawana

Content Development Editor
Zeeyan Pinheiro

Technical Editor
Vivek Pala

Copy Editor
Pranjali Chury

Project Coordinator
Vaidehi Sawant

Proofreader
Safis Editing

Indexer
Francy Puthiry

Graphics
Abhinash Sahu

Production Coordinator
Nilesh Mohite

About the Author

Alexey Lyashko is an Assembly language addict, independent software reverse engineer, and consultant. At the very beginning of his career, when he was a malware researcher at Aladdin Knowledge Systems, he invented and developed a generic code recognition method known as HOFA™. After spending a few years in the anti-malware industry and gaining sufficient experience in low-level development and reverse engineering, Alexey switched to content protection and worked as a reverse engineering consultant with Irdeto's BD+ department, actively participating in content protection technology development. Since 2013, he has worked with several software development companies providing reverse engineering and low-level software development consultancy.

I would like to express my endless gratitude to everyone who made this book a reality--the current and former members of the team at Packt Publishing: Sonali Vernekar, Kinnari Sanghvi, Angad Singh, Zeeyan Pinheiro, Vivek Pala, and many others, who devoted their time and effort. To Mr. Tomasz Grysztar, the author of the Flat Assembler, who agreed to be the technical reviewer for the book--thank you and I hope you did not suffer much reading my stream of consciousness.

A special thank you to my darling wife, Yulia, for her patience and support, and to my 3 years old son, Yaakov, for helping with the cover design selection. This book would never have happened without the support from you all. Thank you!

About the Reviewer

Tomasz Grysztar is a self-employed programmer and systems designer, with a focus on machine languages. He is the author of FASM, one of the assemblers for the x86 architecture of processors, and he has been continuously developing it for nearly 20 years.

www.PacktPub.com

For support files and downloads related to your book, please visit www.PacktPub.com.

Did you know that Packt offers eBook versions of every book published, with PDF and ePub files available? You can upgrade to the eBook version at www.PacktPub.com and as a print book customer, you are entitled to a discount on the eBook copy. Get in touch with us at service@packtpub.com for more details.

At www.PacktPub.com, you can also read a collection of free technical articles, sign up for a range of free newsletters and receive exclusive discounts and offers on Packt books and eBooks.

https://www.packtpub.com/mapt

Get the most in-demand software skills with Mapt. Mapt gives you full access to all Packt books and video courses, as well as industry-leading tools to help you plan your personal development and advance your career.

Why subscribe?

- Fully searchable across every book published by Packt
- Copy and paste, print, and bookmark content
- On demand and accessible via a web browser

Customer Feedback

Thanks for purchasing this Packt book. At Packt, quality is at the heart of our editorial process. To help us improve, please leave us an honest review on this book's Amazon page at https://www.amazon.com/dp/1787287483.

If you'd like to join our team of regular reviewers, you can e-mail us at customerreviews@packtpub.com. We award our regular reviewers with free eBooks and videos in exchange for their valuable feedback. Help us be relentless in improving our products!

Table of Contents

Preface

The Assembly language is the lowest-level human readable programming language on any platform. Knowing the way things are on the Assembly level will help developers design their code in a much more elegant and efficient way.

Unfortunately, the modern world of software development does not require deep understanding of how programs are executed on the low level, not to mention the number of scripting languages and different frameworks that are there to ease the process of software development, and which are often mistakenly treated as inefficient mostly because developers think that the framework/scripting engine should cope with the lameness of the code. The intent behind this book is to show how important it is to understand the basics, which are too often left behind a developer's learning curve.

The Assembly language is a powerful tool that developers may use in their projects to gain more efficiency with their code, not to mention that Assembly is the basis of computing even in today's world of high-level languages, software frameworks, and scripting engines. The core idea behind this book is to familiarize software developers with things that are often skipped or are not given enough attention by developers and, much worse, by those who teach them. It may be hard to believe that the Assembly language itself is only the tip of the iceberg (unfortunately, the part of the iceberg that is hidden in water falls outside the scope of this book), but even it alone may highly improve your ability to develop much cleaner, more elegant and, more importantly, much more efficient code.

What this book covers

Chapter 1, *Intel Architecture*, provides a brief insight into the Intel architecture, covering processor registers and their usage.

Chapter 2, *Setting Up a Development Environment*, contains detailed instructions on setting up a development environment for programming in Assembly.

Chapter 3, *Intel Instruction Set Architecture (ISA)*, introduces you to the instruction set of Intel processors.

Chapter 4, *Memory Addressing Modes*, gives an overview of the many memory addressing modes supported by Intel processors.

Chapter 5, *Parallel Data Processing*, is dedicated to the Intel architecture extensions that add support for parallel processing of multiple data.

Chapter 6, *Macro Instructions*, provides an introduction to one of the most powerful features of modern assemblers--their support for macro instructions.

Chapter 7, *Data Structures*, helps us organize data properly as there isn't much that we can do with it.

Chapter 8, *Mixing Modules Written in Assembly and Those Written in High-Level Languages*, gives a description of the various methods of interfacing our Assembly code with the outer world.

Chapter 9, *Operating System Interface*, gives you a way to discover how programs written in Assembly may interact with Windows and Linux operating systems.

Chapter 10, *Patching Legacy Code*, attempts to show the basics of patching existing executables, which is an art in itself.

Chapter 11, *Oh, Almost Forgot*, covers a few things that did not fit into any of the preceding chapters but are, nevertheless, interesting and may even be important.

What you need for this book

The requirements for this book are rather minimal. All you need is a computer running either Windows or Linux and the desire to learn new things.

Who this book is for

This book is primarily intended for developers wishing to enrich their understanding of low-level proceedings, but, in fact, there is no special requirement for much experience, although a certain level of experience is anticipated. Of course, anyone interested in Assembly programming should be able to find something useful in this book.

Conventions

In this book, you will find a number of text styles that distinguish between different kinds of information. Here are some examples of these styles and an explanation of their meaning.

Code words in text, database table names, folder names, filenames, file extensions, pathnames, dummy URLs, user input, and Twitter handles are shown as follows:

"If you decide to move it elsewhere, do not forget to put the INCLUDE folder and the FASMW.INI file (if one has already been created) into the same directory."

A block of code is set as follows:

```
fld      [radius]     ; Load radius to ST0
                      ; ST0 <== 0.2345
fldpi                 ; Load PI to ST0
                      ; ST1 <== ST0
                      ; ST0 <== 3.1415926
fmulp                 ; Multiply (ST0 * ST1) and pop
                      ; ST0 = 0.7367034
fadd     st0, st0     ; * 2
                      ; ST0 = 1.4734069
fstp     [result]     ; Store result
                      ; result <== ST0
```

Any command-line input or output is written as follows:

```
sudo yum install binutils gcc
```

New terms and **important words** are shown in bold.

Warnings or important notes appear like this.

Tips and tricks appear like this.

Reader feedback

Feedback from our readers is always welcome. Let us know what you think about this book-what you liked or disliked. Reader feedback is important for us as it helps us develop titles that you will really get the most out of. To send us general feedback, simply e-mail feedback@packtpub.com, and mention the book's title in the subject of your message. If there is a topic that you have expertise in and you are interested in either writing or contributing to a book, see our author guide at www.packtpub.com/authors.

Customer support

Now that you are the proud owner of a Packt book, we have a number of things to help you to get the most from your purchase.

Downloading the example code

You can download the example code files for this book from your account at http://www.packtpub.com. If you purchased this book elsewhere, you can visit http://www.packtpub.com/support and register to have the files e-mailed directly to you. You can download the code files by following these steps:

1. Log in or register to our website using your e-mail address and password.
2. Hover the mouse pointer on the **SUPPORT** tab at the top.
3. Click on **Code Downloads & Errata**.
4. Enter the name of the book in the **Search** box.
5. Select the book for which you're looking to download the code files.
6. Choose from the drop-down menu where you purchased this book from.
7. Click on **Code Download**.

Once the file is downloaded, please make sure that you unzip or extract the folder using the latest version of:

- WinRAR / 7-Zip for Windows
- Zipeg / iZip / UnRarX for Mac
- 7-Zip / PeaZip for Linux

The code bundle for the book is also hosted on GitHub at https://github.com/PacktPublishing/Mastering-Assembly-Programming. We also have other code bundles from our rich catalog of books and videos available at https://github.com/PacktPublishing/. Check them out!

Errata

Although we have taken every care to ensure the accuracy of our content, mistakes do happen. If you find a mistake in one of our books-maybe a mistake in the text or the code-we would be grateful if you could report this to us. By doing so, you can save other readers from frustration and help us improve subsequent versions of this book. If you find any errata, please report them by visiting http://www.packtpub.com/submit-errata, selecting your book, clicking on the **Errata Submission Form** link, and entering the details of your errata. Once your errata are verified, your submission will be accepted and the errata will be uploaded to our website or added to any list of existing errata under the Errata section of that title. To view the previously submitted errata, go to https://www.packtpub.com/books/content/support and enter the name of the book in the search field. The required information will appear under the **Errata** section.

Piracy

Piracy of copyrighted material on the Internet is an ongoing problem across all media. At Packt, we take the protection of our copyright and licenses very seriously. If you come across any illegal copies of our works in any form on the Internet, please provide us with the location address or website name immediately so that we can pursue a remedy. Please contact us at copyright@packtpub.com with a link to the suspected pirated material. We appreciate your help in protecting our authors and our ability to bring you valuable content.

Questions

If you have a problem with any aspect of this book, you can contact us at questions@packtpub.com, and we will do our best to address the problem.

1
Intel Architecture

-What languages do you usually use?
-C and Assembly. In fact, I love programming in Assembly.
-Hmmm... I would not have publicly admitted that...

When speaking about the Assembly language, people usually imagine a sort of unknown and dangerous beast, which obeys only the weirdest representatives of the programming community, or a gun that may only be used for shooting your own leg. Just as any prejudice, this one is rooted in ignorance and the primal fear of the unknown. The purpose of this book is not only to help you overcome this prejudice, but also to show how the Assembly language may become a powerful tool, a sharp lancet, that will help you perform certain tasks, even sophisticated ones, with elegance and relative simplicity, avoiding the unnecessary complications which are, sometimes, implied by high-level languages.

First of all, what is the Assembly language? To put it simply and precisely, we may safely define the Assembly language as symbolic or human readable machine code as each Assembly instruction translates into a single machine instruction (with a few exceptions). To be even more precise, there is no such thing as a single Assembly language as, instead, there are numerous Assembly languages--one per platform, where a platform is a programmable device. Almost any programmable device with a certain instruction set may have its own Assembly language, but this is not always so. Exceptions are devices such as, for example, NAND flash chips, which have their own command set, but have no means for fetching instructions from memory and executing them without implicitly being told to do so.

In order to be able to effectively use the Assembly language, one has to have a precise understanding of the underlying platform, as programming in the Assembly language means "talking" directly to the device. The deeper such understanding is, the more efficient is Assembly programming; however, we are not going to look at this in great detail, as this is beyond the scope of the book. One book would not be enough to cover each and every aspect of the specific architecture. Since we are going to concentrate on the Intel architecture during the course of this book, let's try to obtain at least a general understanding of Intel's x86/AMD64 architectures, and try to enrich it and make it deeper.

This chapter, in particular, covers processor registers and the functionality thereof and briefly describes memory organization (for example, segmentation and paging).

- **General purpose registers**: Despite the fact that some of them have special meanings under certain circumstances, these registers, as the name of the group states, may be used for any purpose.
- **Floating point registers**: These registers are used for floating point operations.
- **Segment registers**: These registers are hardly accessed by applications (the most common case is setting up structured exception handlers on Windows); however, it is important to cover them here so we may better understand the way the CPU percives RAM. The part of the chapter that discusses segment registers also addresses a few memory organization aspects, such as segmentation and paging.
- **Control registers**: This is a tiny group of registers of registers of high importance, as they control the behavior of the processor as well as enable or disable certain features.
- **Debug registers**: Although registers of this group are mainly used by debuggers, they add some interesting abilities to our code, for example the ability to set hardware breakpoints when tracing execution of a program.
- **EFlags register**: This is also known as the status register on some platforms. This one provides us with the information regarding the result of the latest **arithmetic logic unit** (**ALU**) operation performed, as well as some settings of the CPU itself.

Processor registers

Each programmable device, and Intel processors are not an exception, has a set of general purpose registers--memory cells located physically on the die, thus providing low latency access. They are used for temporary storage of data that a processor operates on or data that is frequently accessed (if the amount of general purpose registers allows this). The amount and bit size of registers on an Intel CPU vary in accordance with the current mode of operation. An Intel CPU has at least two modes:

- **Real mode**: This is the good old DOS mode. When the processor is powered up, it starts in the real mode, which has certain limitations, such as the size of the address bus, which is only 20 bits, and the segmented memory space.
- **Protected mode**: This was first introduced in 80286. This mode provides access to larger amount of memory, as it uses different memory segmentation mechanisms. Paging, introduced in 80386, allows even easier memory addressing virtualization.

Since about 2003, we also have the so-called long mode--64-bit registers/addressing (although, not all 64 bits are used for addressing yet), flat memory model, and RIP-based addressing (addressing relative to the instruction pointer register). In this book, we will work with 32-bit protected (there is such a thing as the 16-bit protected mode, but that is out of scope) and Long, which is a 64-bit mode of operation. The long mode may be considered a 64-bit extension of the protected mode, which evolved from 16-bit to 32-bit. It is important to know that registers accessible in the earlier mode are also accessible in the newer mode, meaning that the registers that were accessible in the real mode are also accessible in the protected mode, and that registers accessible in the protected mode would also be accessible in the long mode (if long mode is supported by the processor). There are a few exceptions regarding the bit width of certain registers and we will look at this soon in this chapter. However, since 16-bit modes (real and 16-bit protected modes) are no longer used by application developers (with minor possible exceptions), in this book, we will work on protected and long modes only.

General purpose registers

Depending on the mode of the operation (protected or long), there are 8 to 16 available general purpose registers in modern Intel processors. Each register is divided into subregisters, allowing access to data with a bit width lower than the width of the register.

The following table shows general purpose registers (further referred to as GPR):

Register encoding	Bits 32 – 63 (Zero-extended for 32 bit operands)	Bits 16 – 31 (not modified for 16 bit operands)	Bits 8 – 15 (not modified for 8 bit operands)	Bits 0 - 7
0	RAX			
		EAX		
			AX	
			AH	AL
3	RBX			
		EBX		
			BX	
			BH	BL
1	RCX			
		ECX		
			CX	
			CH	CL
2	RDX			
		EDX		
			DX	
			DH	DL
6	RSI			
		ESI		
			SI	
				SIL
7	RDI			
		EDI		
			DI	
				DIL
5	RBP			
		EBP		
			BP	
				BPL
4	RSP			
		ESP		
			SP	
				SPL

	R8			
8		R8D		
			R8W	
				R8B

	R9			
9		R9D		
			R9W	
				R9B

	R10			
10		R10D		
			R10W	
				R10B

	R11			
11		R11D		
			R11W	
				R11B

	R12			
12		R12D		
			R12W	
				R12B

	R13			
13		R13D		
			R13W	
				R13B

	R14			
14		R14D		
			R14W	
				R14B

	R15			
15		R15D		
			R15W	
				R15B

Table 1: x86/x86_64 registers

 All R* registers are only available in the long mode. Registers SIL, DIL, BPL, and SPL are only available in the long mode. Registers AH, BH, CH, and DH cannot be used in instructions that are not valid outside the long mode.

For convenience, we will refer to the registers by their 32-bit names (such as EAX, EBX, and so on) when we do not need to explicitly refer to a register of a certain bit width. The preceding table shows all general purpose registers available on the Intel platform. Some of them are only available in the long mode (all 64-bit registers, R* registers, and a few of the 8-bit registers) and certain combinations are not allowed. However, despite the fact that we can use those registers for any purpose, some of them do have a special meaning in certain circumstances.

Accumulators

The EAX register is also known as an **accumulator** and is used with multiplication and division operations, both as implied and target operands. It is important to mention that the result of a binary multiplication is twice the size of the operands and the result of a binary division consists of two parts (quotient and remainder), each of which has the same bit width as the operands. Since the x86 architecture began with 16-bit registers and for the sake of backward compatibility, the EDX register is used for storing partial results when the values of the operands are larger than could fit into 8 bits. For example, if we want to multiply two bytes, 0x50 and 0x04, we would expect the result to be 0x140, which cannot be stored in a single byte. However, since the operands were 8 bits in size, the result is stored into the AX register, which is 16 bits. But if we want to multiply 0x150 by 0x104, the result would need 17 bits to be stored (0x150 * 0x104 = 0x15540) and, as we have mentioned already, the first x86 registers were only 16 bits. This is the reason for using an additional register; in the case of the Intel architecture, this register is EDX (to be more precise, only the DX part would be used in this specific case). As a verbal explanation may sometimes be too generalized, it would be better to simply demonstrate the rule.

Operand size	Source 1	Source 2	Destination
8 bits (byte)	AL	8-bit register or 8-bit memory	AX
16 bits (word)	AX	16-bit register or 16-bit memory	DX:AX
32 bits (double word)	EAX	32-bit register or 32-bit memory	EDX:EAX
64 bits (quad word)	RAX	64-bit register or 64-bit memory	RDX:RAX

Division implies a slightly different rule. To be more precise, this is the inverted multiplication rule, meaning that the result of the operation is half the bit width of the dividend, which in turn means that the largest dividend in the long mode may be 128-bit wide. The smallest dividend value remains the same as in the smallest value of the source operand in the case of multiplication--8 bits.

Operand size	Dividend	Divisor	Quotient	Remainder
8/16 bits	AX	8-bit register or 8-bit memory	AL	AH
16/32 bits	DX:AX	16-bit memory or 16-bit register	AX	DX
32/64 bits	EDX:EAX	32-bit register or 32-bit memory	EAX	EDX
64/128 bits	RDX:RAX	64-bit register or 64-bit memory	RAX	RDX

Counter

ECX register - also known as counter register. This register is used in loops as a loop iteration counter. It is first loaded with a number of iterations, and then decremented each time the loop instruction is executed until the value stored in ECX becomes zero, which instructs the processor to break out of the loop. We can compare this to the `do{...}while()` clause in C:

```
int ecx = 10;
do
{
    // do your stuff
    ecx--;
}while(ecx > 0);
```

Another common usage of this register, actually the usage of its least significant part, CL, is in bitwise shift operations, where it contains the number of bits in which the source operand should be shifted. Consider the following code, for example:

```
mov eax, 0x12345
mov cl, 5
shl eax, cl
```

This would result in the register EAX being shifted 5 bits to the left (having the value of `0x2468a0` as a result).

Stack pointer

An ESP register is the stack pointer. This register, together with the SS register (the SS register is explained a bit later in this chapter), describes the stack area of a thread, where SS contains the descriptor of the stack segment and ESP is the index that points to the current position within the stack.

Source and destination indices

ESI and EDI registers serve as source and destination index registers in string operations, where ESI contains the source address and EDI, obviously, the destination address. We will talk about these registers a bit more in Chapter 3, *Intel Instruction Set Architecture (ISA)*.

Base pointer

EBP. This register is called the base pointer as its most common use is to point to the base of a stack frame during function calls. However, unlike the previously discussed registers, you may use any other register for this purpose if needed.

Another register worth mentioning here is EBX, which, in the good old days of 16-bit modes (when it was still just a BX register), was one of the few registers that we could use as a base for addressing. Unlike EBP, EBX was (in the case of the XLAT instruction, which by default uses DS:EBX, still is) intended to point to a data segment.

Instruction pointer

There is one more special register that cannot be used for data storage--EIP (IP in the real mode or RIP in the long mode). This is the instruction pointer and contains the address of the instruction after the instruction currently being executed. All instructions are implicitly fetched from the code segment by the CPU; thus the full address of the instruction following the one being executed should be described as CS:IP. Also, there is no regular way to modify its content directly. It is not impossible, but we can't just use a mov instruction in order to load a value into EIP.

All the other registers have no special meaning from the processor's perspective and may be used for any purpose.

Floating point registers

The CPU itself has no means for floating point arithmetic operations. In 1980, Intel announced the Intel 8087 - the floating point coprocessor for the 8086 line. 8087 remained as a separate installable device until 1989, when Intel came up with the 80486 (i486) processor, which had an integrated 8087 circuit. However, when talking about floating point registers and floating point instructions, we still refer to 8087 as a floating-point unit (FPU) or, sometimes, still as a floating-point coprocessor (however, the latter is becoming more and more rare).

8087 has eight registers, 80 bits each, arranged in a stack fashion, meaning that operands are pushed onto this stack from the memory and results are popped from the topmost register to the memory. These registers are named ST0 to ST7 (ST--stack) and the most used one, that is, the ST0 register, may be referred to as simply ST.

The floating-point coprocessor supports several data types:

- 80-bit extended-precision real
- 64-bit double-precision real
- 32-bit single-precision real
- 18-digit decimal integer
- 64-bit binary integer
- 32-bit binary integer
- 16-bit binary integer

The floating-point coprocessor will be discussed in more detail in `Chapter 3`, *Intel Instruction Set Architecture (ISA)*.

XMM registers

The 128-bit XMM registers are part of the SSE extension (where **SSE** is short for **Streaming SIMD Extension**, and **SIMD**, in turn, stands for **single instruction multiple data**). There are eight XMM registers available in non -64-bit modes and 16 XMM registers in long mode, which allow simultaneous operations on:

- 16 bytes
- eight words
- four double words

- two quad words
- four floats
- two doubles

We will pay much more attention to these registers and the technology behind them in `Chapter 5`, *Parallel Data Processing*.

Segment registers and memory organization

Memory organization is one of the most important aspects of CPU design. The first thing to note is that when we say "memory organization", we do not mean its physical layout on memory chips/boards. For us, it is much more important how the CPU sees memory and how it communicates with it (on a higher level, of course, as we are not going to dive into the hardware aspects of the architecture).

However, as the book is dedicated to application programming, rather than operating system development, we will further consider the most relevant aspects of memory organization and access in this section.

Real mode

Segment registers are a rather interesting topic, as they are the ones that tell the processor which memory areas may be accessed and how exactly they may be accessed. In real mode, segment registers used to contain a 16-bit segment address. The difference between a normal address and segment address is that the latter is shifted 4 bits to the right when stored in the segment register. For example, if a certain segment register was loaded with the `0x1234` value, it, in fact, was pointing to the address `0x12340`; therefore, pointers in real mode were rather offsets into segments pointed to by segment registers. As an example, let's take the DI register (as we are talking about a 16-bit real mode now), which is used with the DS (data segment) register automatically, and load it with, let's say, `0x4321` when the DS register is loaded with the `0x1234` value. Then the 20-bit address would be `0x12340 + 0x4321 = 0x16661`. Thus, it was possible to address at most 1 MB of memory in real mode.

There are in total six segment registers:

- **CS**: This register contains the base address of the currently used code segment.
- **DS**: This register contains the base address of the currently used data segment.
- **SS**: This register contains the base address of the currently used stack segment.
- **ES**: This is the extra data segment for the programmer's use.
- **FS** and **GS**: These were introduced with the Intel 80386 processor. These two segment registers have no specific hardware-defined function and are for the programmer's use. It is important to know that they do have specific tasks in Windows and Linux, but those tasks are operating system dependent only and have no connection to hardware specifications.

The CS register is used together with the IP register (the instructions pointer, also known as the program counter on other platforms), where the IP (or EIP in protected mode and RIP in long mode) points to the offset of the instruction in the code segment following the instruction currently being executed.

DS and ES are implied when using SI and DI registers, respectively, unless another segment register is implicitly specified in the instruction. For example, the `lodsb` instruction, although, it is written with no operands, loads a byte from the address specified by DS:SI into the AL register and the `stosb` instruction (which has no visible operands either) stores a byte from the AL register at the address specified by ES:DI. Using SI/DI registers with other segments would require explicitly mentioning those segments with the relevant segment register. Consider the following code, for example:

```
mov ax, [si]
mov [es:di], ax
```

The preceding code loads a double word from the location pointed by DS:SI and stores it to another location pointed by ES:DI.

The interesting thing about segment registers and segments at all is that they may peacefully overlap. Consider a situation where you want to copy a portion of code to either another place in the code segment or into a temporary buffer (for example, for decryptor). In such a case, both CS and DS registers may either point to the same location or the DS register may point somewhere into the code segment.

Protected mode - segmentation

While it was all fine and simple in real mode, things become a bit more complicated when it comes to protected mode. Unfortunately, memory segmentation is still intact, but the segment register no longer contain addresses. Instead, they are loaded with the so-called selectors, which are, in turn, the indices into the descriptor table multiplied by 8 (shifted 3 bits to the left). The two least significant bits designate the requested privilege level (0 for kernel space to 3 for user land). The third bit (at index 2) is the **TI** bit (**table indicator**), which indicates whether the descriptor being referred is in a global descriptor table (0) or in a local descriptor table (1). The memory descriptor is a tiny 8-byte structure, which describes the range of physical memory, its access rights, and some additional attributes:

Byte	Bits in byte	Meaning
0	0 – 7	First eight bits of segment limit (size).
1	0 – 7	Bits 8 – 15 of segment limit.
2	0 – 7	Bits 0 – 7 of segment base address.
3	0 – 7	Bits 8 – 15 of segment base address.
4	0 – 7	Bits 16 – 23 of segment base address.
5	0	Is set to '1' if segment has been accessed.
	1	Is set to '1' if segment is writeable.
	2	Is set to '1' if segment expands down (e.g. stack segment).
	3	Is set to '1' if segment contains executable code.
	4	Always '1'.
	5 – 6	'Descriptor Privilege Level' – describes the privilege level of the given segment, where DPL = 0 for most privileged segment (ring 0, also known as Kernel Space) and DPL = 3 for least privileged segment (ring 3, also known as User Land).
	7	'Present' – this bit is for use by operating system. The OS sets it to '1' if the content of the segment is loaded to memory or to '0', if the content has been temporarily stored to disk.
6	0 – 3	Bits 16 – 19 of segment limit
	4	'Available' – this bit is not used by the processor and is free for operating system use.
	5	This bit is set to '1' on Long mode, otherwise it is set to '0' (extension of bit D)
	6	'Default' (also known as 'D bit'). When set to '0' – use 16 bit addresses and operands, otherwise – 32 bit.
	7	'Granularity' bit. If this bit is set to zero, then the processor interprets segment limit as number of bytes, otherwise as number of 4Kb blocks and the size if a given segment is calculated as: segment_size = limit * 4096 + 4095
7	0 – 7	Bits 24 – 31 of segment base address.

Table 2: Memory descriptor structure

Descriptors are stored in at least two tables:

- **GDT**: Global descriptor table (used by the operating system)
- **LDT**: Local descriptor table (per task descriptor table)

As we may conclude, the organization of memory in protected mode is not that different from that in real mode after all.

There are other types of descriptors--interrupt descriptors (stored in the **interrupt description table (IDT)**) and system descriptors; however, since these are in use in kernel space only, we will not discuss them, as that falls out of the scope of this book.

Protected mode - paging

Paging is a more convenient memory management scheme introduced in 80386 and has been a bit enhanced since then. The idea behind paging is memory virtualization--this is the mechanism that makes it possible for different processes to have the same memory layout. In fact, the addresses we use in pointers (if we are writing in C, C++, or any other high-level language that compiles into native code) are virtual and do not correspond to physical addresses. The translation of a virtual address into a physical address is implemented in hardware and is performed by the CPU (however, some operating system interventions are possible).

By default, a 32-bit CPU uses a two-level translation scheme for the derivation of a physical address from the supplied virtual one.

The following table explains how a virtual address is used in order to find a physical address:

Address bits	Meaning
0 - 11	Offset into a 4 KB page
12 - 21	Index of the page entry in the table of 1024 pages
22 - 31	Index of the page table entry in a 1024-entries page directory

Table 3: Virtual address to physical address translation

Most, if not all, modern processors based on the Intel architecture also support **Page Size Extension** (**PSE**), which makes it possible to use the so-called large pages of 4 MB. In this case, the translation of a virtual address into a physical address is a bit different, as there is no page table any more. The following table shows the meaning of bits in a 32-bit virtual address:

Address bits	Meaning
0 - 21	Offset into a 4 MB page
22 - 31	Index of the corresponding entry in a 1024-entries page directory

Table 4: Virtual address to physical address translation with PSE enabled

Furthermore, the **Physical Address Extension** (**PAE**) was introduced, which significantly changes the scheme and allows access to a much bigger range of memory. In protected mode, PAE adds a page directory pointer table of four entries and the virtual to physical address conversion would be as per the following table:

Address bits	Meaning
0 - 11	Offset into a 4 KB page
12 - 20	Index of a page entry in the table of 512 pages
21 - 29	Index of a page table entry in a 512-entries page directory
30 - 31	Index of a page directory entry in a four-entries page directory pointer table

Table 5: Virtual to physical address translation with PAE enabled (no PSE)

Enabling PSE in addition to PAE forces each entry in the page directory to point directly to a 2 MB page instead of an entry in a page table.

Long mode - paging

The only address virtualization allowed in long mode is paging with PAE enabled; however, it adds one more table--the page map level 4 table as the root entry; therefore, the conversion of a virtual address to a physical address uses the bits of a virtual address in the way described in the following table:

Address bits	Meaning
0 - 11	Offset into a 4 KB page
12 - 20	Index of a page entry in the table of 512 pages
21 - 29	Index of a page table entry in the page directory
30 - 38	Index of a page directory entry in the page directory pointer table
39 - 47	Index of a page directory pointer table in the page-map level 4 table

Table 6: Virtual to physical address translation in long mode

It is, however, important to mention that despite the fact that it is a 64-bit architecture, the MMU only uses the first 48 bits of the virtual address (also called the linear address).

The whole process of address resolution is performed by the **memory management unit** (**MMU**) in the CPU itself, and the programmer is only responsible for actually building these tables and enabling PAE/PSE. However, this topic is much wider than may be covered in a single chapter and falls a bit out of the scope of this book.

Control registers

Processors based on the Intel architecture have a set of control registers that are used for configuration of the processor at run time (such as switching between execution modes). These registers are 32-bit wide on x86 and 64-bit wide on AMD64 (long mode).

There are six control registers and one **Extended Feature Enable Register (EFER)**:

- **CR0**: This register contains various control flags that modify the basic operation of the processor.
- **CR1**: This register is reserved for future use.

- **CR2**: This register contains the Page Fault Linear Address when a page fault occurs.
- **CR3**: This register is used when virtual addressing is enabled (paging) and contains the physical address of the page directory, page directory pointer table, or page map level 4 table, depending on the current mode of operation.
- **CR4**: This register is used in the protected mode for controlling different options of the processor.
- **CR8**: This register is new and is only available in long mode. It is used for prioritization of external interrupts.
- **EFER**: This register is one of the several model-specific registers. It is used for enabling/disabling SYSCALL/SYSRET instructions, entering/exiting long mode, and a few other features. Other model-specific registers are of no interest for us.

However, these registers are not accessible in `ring3` (user land).

Debug registers

In addition to control registers, processors also have a set of so-called debug registers, which are mostly used by debuggers for setting the so-called hardware breakpoints. These registers are in fact a very powerful tool when it comes to control over other threads or even processes.

Debug address registers DR0 - DR3

Debug registers 0 to 3 (DR0, DR1, DR2, and DR3) are used to store virtual (linear) addresses of the so-called hardware breakpoints.

Debug control register (DR7)

DR7 defines how the breakpoints set in **Debug Address Registers** should be interpreted by the processor and whether they should be interpreted at all.

The bits layout of this register is shown in the following table:

Bit	Name	Description
0	L0	Local enable for breakpoint in DR0
1	G0	Global enable for breakpoint in DR0
2	L1	Local enable for breakpoint in DR1
3	G1	Global enable for breakpoint in DR1
4	L2	Local enable for breakpoint in DR2
5	G2	Global enable for breakpoint in DR2
6	L3	Local enable for breakpoint in DR3
7	G3	Global enable for breakpoint in DR3
8	LE	These bits enable the "exact data breakpoint match" feature of the processor, slowing it down and allowing it to report the exact instruction that hit data breakpoint
9	GE	
10 - 15		These bits are reserved and should be set to 0
16 - 17	R/W0	DR0 breakpoint type
18 - 19	LEN0	DR0 breakpoint size in bytes
20 - 21	R/W1	DR1 breakpoint type
22 - 23	LEN1	DR1 breakpoint size in bytes
24 - 25	R/W2	DR2 breakpoint type
26 - 27	LEN2	DR2 breakpoint size in bytes
28 - 29	R/W3	DR3 breakpoint type
30 - 31	LEN3	DR3 breakpoint size in bytes

Table 3: DR7 bit layout

L* bits, when set to 1, enable breakpoint at the address which is specified in the corresponding Debug Address Register locally--within a task. These bits are reset by the processor on each task switch. G* bits, on the contrary, enable breakpoints globally--for all tasks, meaning that these bits are not reset by the processor.

The R/W* bits specify breakpoint conditions, as follows:

- 00: Break on instruction execution
- 01: Break when the specified address is accessed for writing only
- 10: Undefined
- 11: Break on either read or write access or when an instruction at the specified address is executed

The LEN* bits specify the size of a breakpoint in bytes, thus, allowing coverage of more than one instruction or more than one byte of data:

- 00: Breakpoint is 1-byte long
- 01: Breakpoint is 2-bytes long
- 10: Breakpoint is 8-bytes long (long mode only)
- 11: Breakpoint is 4-bytes long

Debug status register (DR6)

When an enabled breakpoint is triggered, the corresponding bit of the four low-order bits in DR6 is set to 1 before entering the debug handler, thus, providing the handler with information about the triggered breakpoint (bit 0 corresponds to the breakpoint in DR0, bit 1 to the breakpoint in DR1, and so on).

The EFlags register

It would have been impossible to write programs in any language for a given platform if the processor had no means to report its status and/or the status of the last operation. More than that, the processor itself needs this information from time to time. Try to imagine a processor unable to conditionally control the execution flow of a program--sounds like a nightmare, doesn't it?

The most common way for a program to obtain information on the last operation or on a certain configuration of an Intel-based processor is through the **EFlags** register (**E** stands for extended). This register is referred to as Flags in real mode, EFlags in protected mode, or **RFlags** in long mode.

Let's take a look at the meaning of the individual bits (also referred to as flags) of this register and its usage.

Bit #0 - carry flag

The **carry flag** (**CF**) is mostly used for the detection of carry/borrow in arithmetic operations and is set if the bit width result of the last such operation (such as addition and subtraction) exceeds the width of the ALU. For example, the addition of two 8-bit values, 255 and 1, would result in 256, which requires at least nine bits to be stored. In such a case, bit eight (the ninth bit) is placed into the CF, thus, letting us and the processor know that the last operation ended with carry.

Bit #2 - parity flag

The **parity flag** (**PF**) is set to 1 in case the number of 1s in the least significant byte is even; otherwise, the flag is set to zero.

Bit #4 - adjust flag

The **adjust flag** (**AF**) signals when a carry or borrow occurred in the four least significant bits (lower nibble) and is primarily used with **binary coded decimal** (**BCD**) arithmetics.

Bit #6 - zero flag

The **zero flag** (**ZF**) is set when the result of an arithmetic or bitwise operation is 0. This includes operations that do not store the result (for example, comparison and bit test).

Bit #7 - sign flag

The **sign flag** (**SF**) is set when the last mathematical operation resulted in a negative number; in other words, when the most significant bit of the result was set.

Bit #8 - trap flag

When set, the **trap flag** (**TF**) causes a single step interrupt after every executed instruction.

Bit #9 - interrupt enable flag

The **interrup enable flag** (**IF**) defines whether processor will or will not react to incoming interrupts. This flag is only accessible in real mode or at the Ring 0 protection level in other modes.

Bit #10 - direction flag

The **direction flag** (**DF**) controls the direction of string operations. An operation is performed from the lower address to the higher address if the flag is reset (is 0) or from the higher address to the lower address if the flag is set (is 1).

Bit #11 - overflow flag

The **overflow flag** (**OF**) is sometimes perceived as two's complement form of the carry flag, which is not really the case. OF is set when the result of the operation is either too small or too big a number to fit into the destination operand. For example, consider the addition of two 8-bit positive values, 0x74 and 0x7f. The resulting value of such an addition is 0xf3, which is still 8-bit, which is fine for unsigned numbers, but since we added two values that we considered to be signed, there has to be the sign bit and there are no more bits to store the 9-bit signed result. The same would happen if we try to add two negative 8-bit values, 0x82 and 0x81. The meaning of the addition of two negative numbers is in the fact subtraction of a positive number from a negative number, which should result in an even smaller number. Thus, 0x82 + 0x81 would result in 0x103, where the ninth bit, 1, is the sign bit, but it cannot be stored in an 8-bit operand. The same applies to larger operands (16, 32, and 64-bit).

Remaining bits

The remaining 20 bits of the EFlags register are not that important for us while in user-land except, probably, the ID bit (bit #21). The ID flag indicates whether we can or cannot use the CPUID instruction.

Bits 32 - 63 of the RFlags register in long mode would be all 0s.

Summary

In this chapter, we have briefly run through the basics of the internal structure of x86-based processors essential for the further understanding of topics covered in later chapters. Being a huge fan of Occam's Razor principle, yours truly had no intention to replicate Intel's programmer manual; however, certain topics covered in this chapter exceed the range of topics necessary for a successful start with Assembly language programming.

However, I believe that you would agree--we've had enough of dry information here and it is the right time to start doing something. Let's begin by setting up the development environment for Assembly language programming in `Chapter 2`, *Setting Up a Development Environment*.

2
Setting Up a Development Environment

We are slowly approaching the point where we will be able to begin to actually deal with Assembly language itself--writing code, examining programs, solving problems. We are just one step away, and the step is setting up a development environment for Assembly programming.

Despite the fact that the assembler used in this book is a **Flat Assembler (FASM)**, it is important to cover at least two other options and, therefore, in this chapter, you will learn how to configure three types of development environment:

- **Setting up a development environment for Windows-based applications using Visual Studio 2017 Community**: This will allow the direct integration of Assembly projects with existing solutions
- **Installing GNU Compilers Collection (GCC)**: Although it is possible to use GCC on both Windows and *nix platforms, we will emphasize GCC usage on Linux
- **Flat Assembler**: This one seems to be the simplest and most comfortable one to use for Assembly programming on either Windows or Linux

We will end each section with a short test program written in the Assembly language specifically for the assembler described in the section.

Microsoft Macro Assembler

As the name of this assembler states, it supports macros and has a nice set of built-in ones. However, it is hard to find a more or less valuable assembler without this feature today.

The first assembler I ever used was **Macro Assembler** (**MASM**) (I do not remember which version) on DOS installed on a Sony laptop with 4-MB RAM and a 100-MB hard disk (ah, good old times), and MS-DOS edit.exe was the only IDE. Needless to say, the compilation and linking was performed manually in the command line (as if DOS had any other interface).

In my opinion, this is the best way to learn Assembly or any other programming language-- just a simple editor with as few features as possible (however, syntax highlighting is a great advantage, as it helps in avoiding typos) and a set of command-line tools. Modern **integrated development environments** (**IDEs**) are very complex, yet very powerful tools, and I am not trying to underestimate them; however, it is much better to use them once you understand what happens behind this complexity.

However, the intent behind this book is to learn the language the CPU speaks, not a specific Assembly dialect or specific assembler command-line options. Not to mention the fact that the currently available Microsoft Visual Studio 2017 Community (the easiest way to get MASM is to install Visual Studio 2017 Community--free and convenient) comes with several assembler binaries:

- A 32-bit binary that produces 32-bit code
- A 32-bit binary that produces 64-bit code
- A 64-bit binary that produces 32-bit code
- A 64-bit binary that produces 64-bit code

Our goal is to know how the CPU thinks rather than how to make it understand our thoughts and how we can find the location of libraries and executables installed on the system. Therefore, if MASM is your choice, it's good to use Visual Studio 2017 Community, as it will save you a lot of time.

Installing Microsoft Visual Studio 2017 Community

You may safely skip this step if you already have Microsoft Visual Studio 2017 Community or any other version of Microsoft Visual Studio installed.

This is one of the easiest actions described in this book. Go to `https://www.visualstudio.com/downloads/` and download and run the installer for Visual Studio 2017 Community.

The installer has many options that you may want to select depending on your development needs; however, there is one that we need for Assembly development, and it is called **Desktop development with C++**.

If you insist on using the command line to build your Assembly programs, you can find MASM executables at the following locations:
`VS_2017_install_dir\VC\bin\amd64_x86\ml.exe`
`VS_2017_install_dir\VC\bin\amd64\ml64.exe`
`VS_2017_install_dir\VC\bin\ml.exe`
`VS_2017_install_dir\VC\bin\x86_amd64\ml64.exe`

Setting up the Assembly project

Unfortunately, Visual Studio, by default, has no template for Assembly language projects, therefore, we have to create one ourselves:

1. Launch Visual Studio and create an empty solution, as shown in the following screenshot:

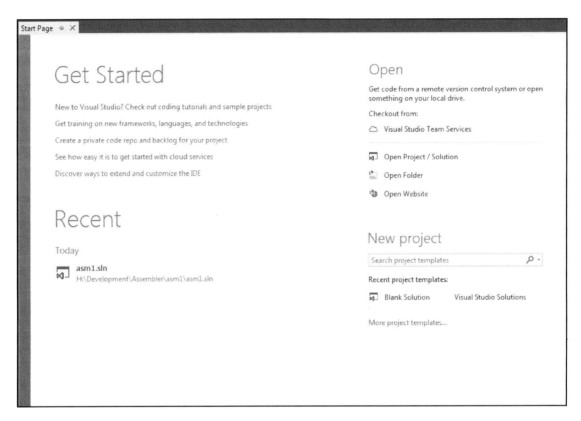

Creating blank VS2017 solution

Look at the bottom-right part of the **Start Page** window, where you will see the option to create a blank solution. If there is no such option, click on **More project templates...** and select **Blank Solution** from there.

2. Once the solution has been created for us, we may add a new project. Right-click on the name of the solution and go to **Add** | **New Project**:

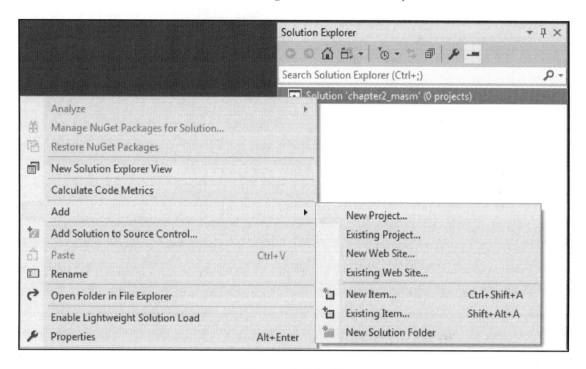

Adding a new project to the solution

As Visual Studio has no built-in template for an Assembly project, we will add an empty C++ project to our solution:

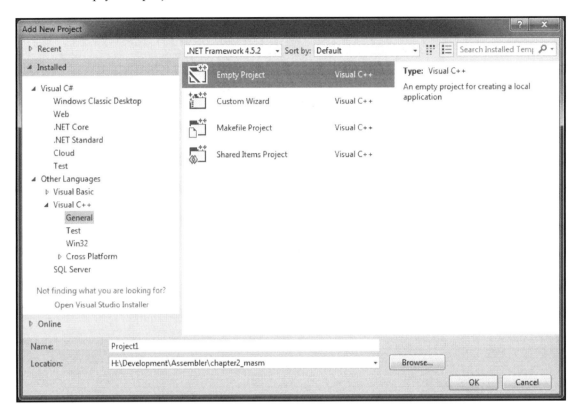

Creating an empty project

3. Choose a name for the project and click on **OK**. There are a two more things we have to do before we can add source files. To be more precise, we can add sources and then take care of these two things, as the order does not really matter. Just keep in mind that we will not be able to build (or, correctly build) our project before we take care of these.

4. The first thing to take care of is setting the subsystem for the project; otherwise, the linker will not know what kind of executable to generate.

   Right-click on the project name in the **Solution Explorer** tab and go to **Properties**. In the project properties window, we go to **Configuration Properties** | **Linker** | **System** and select **Windows (/SUBSYSTEM:WINDOWS)** under **SubSystem**:

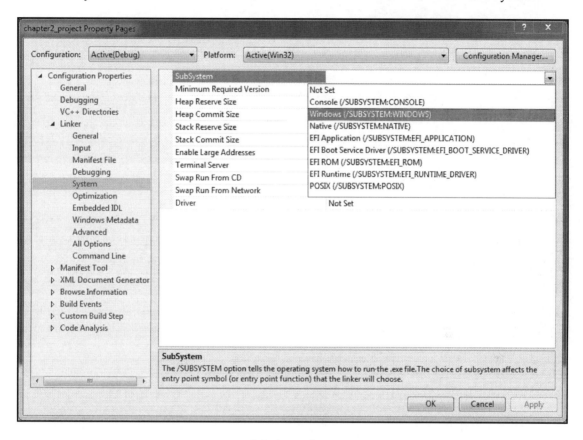

Setting the target subsystem

5. The next step is to tell Visual Studio that this is an Assembly language project:

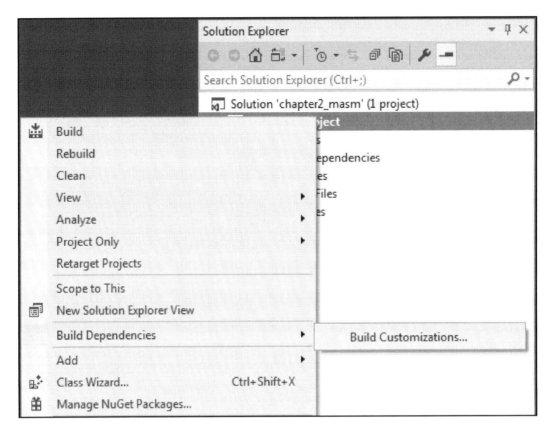

Opening the "Build Customizations" window

6. Right-click on the project name and go to **Build Dependencies** in the context menu, click on **Build Customizations...**, and from the build customizations window, select masm(.targets, .props):

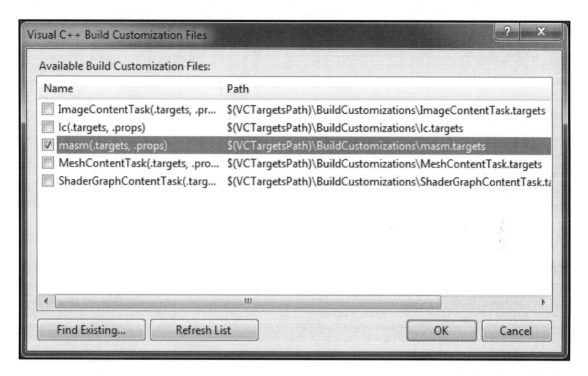

Setting proper targets

7. We are now ready to add the first Assembly source file:

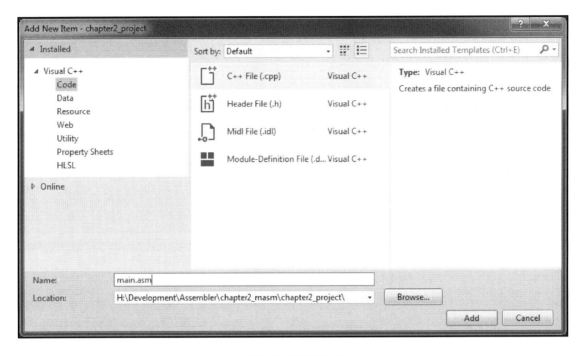

Adding a new Assembly source file

Unfortunately, Visual Studio does not seem to be prepared for Assembly projects and, therefore, has no built-in template for Assembly files. So, we right-click on **Source Files** in the **Solution Explorer**, select **New Item** under **Add**, and since there is no template for the Assembly source file, we select **C++ File (.cpp)**, but set the name of the file with the .asm extension. We click on **Add,** and voila! Our first Assembly source file is shown in the IDE.

8. Just for fun, let's add some code:

```
.686
.model flat, stdcall

; this is a comment
; Imported functions
ExitProcess proto uExitCode:DWORD
MessageBoxA proto hWnd:DWORD, lpText:DWORD, lpCaption:DWORD,
uType:DWORD

; Here we tell assembler what to put into data section
```

```
.data
    msg db 'Hello from Assembly!', 0
    ti db 'Hello message', 0

; and here what to put into code section
.code

; This is our entry point
main PROC
    push 0                  ; Prepare the value to return to the
                            ; operating system
    push offset msg         ; Pass pointer to MessageBox's text to
                            ; the show_message() function
    push offset ti          ; Pass pointer to MessageBox's title to
                            ; the show_message() function
    call show_message       ; Call it

    call ExitProcess        ; and return to the operating system
main ENDP

; This function's prototype would be:
; void show_message(char* title, char* message);
show_message PROC
    push ebp
    mov  ebp, esp
    push eax

    push 0                  ; uType
    mov  eax, [dword ptr ebp + 8]
    push eax                ; lpCaption
    mov  eax, [dword ptr ebp + 12]
    push eax                ; lpText
    push 0                  ; hWnd
    call MessageBoxA        ; call MessageBox()

    pop  eax
    mov  esp, ebp
    pop  ebp
    ret  4 * 2              ; Return and clean the stack
show_message ENDP
END main
```

Do not worry if the code does not "speak" to you yet; we will begin to get acquainted with the instructions and program structure in Chapter 3, *Intel Instruction Set Architecture (ISA).*

Right now, let's build the project and run it. The code does not do much, as it simply displays a message box and terminates the program:

Sample output

By now, we have a working setup for Assembly development on Windows.

GNU Assembler (GAS)

The GNU Assembler or GAS, or simply AS, is the most used assembler on *nix (Unix and Linux) platforms. While it is cross-platform (having the right build of GAS, we can compile Assembly code for a wide variety of platforms including Windows), flexible and powerful, it defaults to the AT&T syntax, which is, for those used to Intel syntax, weird, to say the least. GAS is free software released under the terms of GNU General Public License v3.

Installing GAS

GAS is distributed as part of the `binutils` package, but since it is the default backend for GCC (GNU Compilers Collection), it would be better if we install GCC. In fact, installing GCC instead of `binutils` alone will slightly simplify the creation of executables out of our Assembly code, as GCC would automatically handle a few tasks during the linking process. Despite having its roots in *nix systems, GAS is also available for Windows and may be downloaded from `https://sourceforge.net/projects/mingw-w64/` (just remember to add the `bin` subfolder in the installation folder to the `PATH` environment variable). Installation on Windows is quite straightforward--simply follow the steps in the GUI installation wizard.

Another option for those of us using Windows is "Bash on Windows;" however, this is only available on 64-bit Windows 10 with Anniversary/Creators Update installed. The installation steps for GAS would then be the same as those for running Ubuntu or Debian Linux.

As this book is intended for developers, it might be safe to assume that you already have it installed on your system, if you are on a *nix system, however, let's leave assumptions aside and install GAS.

Step 1 - installing GAS

Open your favorite terminal emulator and issue the following command:

```
sudo apt-get install binutils gcc
```

If you are on a Debian-based distribution or if it is RH based, then use the following command:

```
sudo yum install binutils gcc
```

Alternatively, you can use the following:

```
su -c "yum install binutils gcc"
```

Step 2 - let's test

Once ready, let's build our first Assembly program on Linux. Create an Assembly source file named, for example, test.S.

 Assembly source files on *nix platforms have the extension .S or .s instead of .asm.

Fill in the following code:

```
/*
 This is a multiline comment.
*/
// This is a single line comment.
# Another single line comment.

# The following line is not a necessity.
    .file "test.S"
```

```
# Tell GAS that we are using an external function.
    .extern printf

# Make some data - store message in data section 0
    .data
msg:
    .ascii "Hello from Assembly language!xaxdx0"

# Begin the actual code
    .text
# Make main() publicly visible
    .globl main
/*
 This is our main() function.
 It is important to mention,
 that we can't begin the program with
 'main()' when using GAS alone. We have then
 to begin the program with 'start' or '_start'
 function.
*/

main:
    pushl %ebp
    movl %esp, %ebp
    pushl $msg          # Pass parameter (pointer
                        # to message) to output_message function.
    call output_message # Print the message
    movl $0, %eax
    leave
    ret

# This function simply prints out a message to the Terminal
output_message:
    pushl %ebp
    movl %esp, %ebp
    subl $8, %esp
    movl 8(%ebp), %eax
    movl %eax, (%esp)
    call _printf        # Here we call printf
    addl $4, %esp
    movl $0, %eax
    leave
    ret $4
```

 Prepend `printf` and `main` with an underscore (_) if you are on Windows.

If on Linux, build the code with the following command:

```
gcc -o test test.S
```

In order for this code to be compiled correctly on a 64-bit system, as it is written for 32-bit assembler, you should install the 32-bit toolchain and libraries, as well as add the -m32 option, which tells GCC to generate code for a 32-bit platform, with this command:
```
gcc -m32 -o test test.S
```
Refer to the documentation of your Linux distro for instructions on how to install 32-bit libraries.

If you're on Windows, change the name of the output executable accordingly:

```
gcc -o test.exe test.S
```

Run the executable in the Terminal. You should see the message followed by a new line:

```
Hello from Assembly language!
```

As you may have noticed, the syntax of this Assembly source is different from that supported by MASM. While MASM supports what is called Intel syntax, GAS originally supported only the AT&T syntax. However, the support for Intel syntax was added at some point, thus making the life of new adepts significantly easier.

Flat Assembler

Now that we have seen the complexities introduced by MASM and GAS, whether it is syntax or setup complexity, let's take a look at Flat Assembler, a free, portable, self-compiling assembler for Windows and Linux with Intel syntax (very similar to that of MASM, but much less complicated and much more understandable). Exactly the tool we need for easier and faster understanding of Intel Assembly language and usage thereof.

In addition to support for various executable file formats (DOS COM files to begin with, through Windows PE (both 32 bit and 64 bit) and up to ELF (both 32 bit and 64 bit)), FASM has a very powerful macro engine, which we will definitely take advantage of. Not to mention the fact that FASM can be easily integrated into existing development environments for more complex projects.

Installing the Flat Assembler

Regardless of whether you are on Windows or on Linux, you can get the Flat Assembler in the same easy way:

1. First, visit `https://flatassembler.net/download.php` and select the proper package for your operating system:

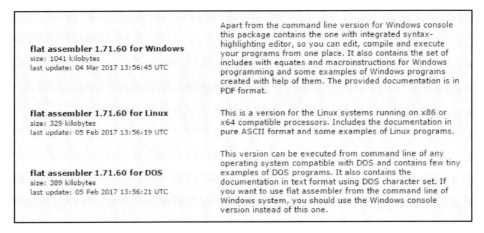

flat assembler 1.71.60 for Windows size: 1041 kilobytes last update: 04 Mar 2017 13:56:45 UTC	Apart from the command line version for Windows console this package contains the one with integrated syntax-highlighting editor, so you can edit, compile and execute your programs from one place. It also contains the set of includes with equates and macroinstructions for Windows programming and some examples of Windows programs created with help of them. The provided documentation is in PDF format.
flat assembler 1.71.60 for Linux size: 329 kilobytes last update: 05 Feb 2017 13:56:19 UTC	This is a version for the Linux systems running on x86 or x64 compatible processors. Includes the documentation in pure ASCII format and some examples of Linux programs.
flat assembler 1.71.60 for DOS size: 389 kilobytes last update: 05 Feb 2017 13:56:21 UTC	This version can be executed from command line of any operating system compatible with DOS and contains few tiny examples of DOS programs. It also contains the documentation in text format using DOS character set. If you want to use flat assembler from the command line of Windows system, you should use the Windows console version instead of this one.

Flat Assembler download page

2. Unpack the package. Both Windows and Linux packages come with FASM sources, documentation, and examples. As we see in the following screenshot, the Windows version comes with two executables: `fasm.exe` and `fasmw.exe`. The only difference between the two is that `fasmw.exe` is a GUI implementation of Flat Assembler, while `fasm.exe` is the command line only:

EXAMPLES	2/19/2017 6:51 PM	File folder	
INCLUDE	2/20/2017 1:10 AM	File folder	
SOURCE	2/20/2017 1:10 AM	File folder	
TOOLS	2/20/2017 1:10 AM	File folder	
FASM.EXE	2/20/2017 1:10 AM	Application	112 KB
FASM.PDF	2/20/2017 1:10 AM	Adobe Acrobat D...	514 KB
FASMW.EXE	2/20/2017 1:10 AM	Application	152 KB
FASMW.INI	3/16/2017 3:57 PM	Configuration sett...	1 KB
LICENSE.TXT	2/20/2017 1:10 AM	Text Document	2 KB
WHATSNEW.TXT	2/20/2017 1:10 AM	Text Document	21 KB

Content of the Flat Assembler package

Both executables may be run from the directory you unpacked the package to, as they have no external dependencies. If you decide to move it elsewhere, do not forget to put the INCLUDE folder and the FASMW.INI file (if one has already been created) into the same directory. If you copy FASMW.INI, then you will have to manually edit the Include path under the [Environment] section. Alternatively, you may skip copying FASMW.INI, as it will be automatically created the first time you launch FASMW.EXE.

The Linux version lacks the GUI part, but it still contains the fasm source code, documentation, and examples:

```
drwxr-xr-x 5 alexey alexey   4096 Dec  6  2015 examples
-rwxr-xr-x 1 alexey alexey 103455 Dec  6  2015 fasm
-rw-r--r-- 1 alexey alexey 265794 Dec  6  2015 fasm.txt
-rw-r--r-- 1 alexey alexey   1783 Dec  6  2015 license.txt
drwxr-xr-x 6 alexey alexey   4096 Dec  6  2015 source
drwxr-xr-x 5 alexey alexey   4096 Dec  6  2015 tools
-rw-r--r-- 1 alexey alexey  18514 Dec  6  2015 whatsnew.txt
```

The content of the Flat Assembler package for Linux

While the fasm executable for Linux, just like its Windows counterpart, has no external dependencies and may be executed directly from the folder you unpacked the package to, it is a matter of convenience to copy it to a more proper location, for example, to /usr/local/bin.

The first FASM program

Now that we have installed the Flat Assembler, we cannot move further on unless we build a tiny test executable for either Windows or Linux. Interestingly enough, both examples may be compiled with the same assembler, meaning that the Linux example may be compiled on Windows and vice versa. But let's get to the example itself.

Windows

If you are on Windows, launch fasmw.exe and enter the following code:

```
include 'win32a.inc'

format PE GUI
entry _start

section '.text' code readable executable
```

```
_start:
    push 0
    push 0
    push title
    push message
    push 0
    call [MessageBox]
    call [ExitProcess]

section '.data' data readable writeable
    message db 'Hello from FASM!', 0x00
    title db 'Hello!', 0x00

section '.idata' import data readable writeable
library kernel, 'kernel32.dll', \
        user, 'user32.dll'

import kernel, \
        ExitProcess, 'ExitProcess'

import user, \
        MessageBox, 'MessageBoxA'
```

Again, do not worry if you hardly understand anything in this code; it will begin to become clearer starting with the next chapter.

In order to run the preceding code, go to the **Run** menu and select **Run**.

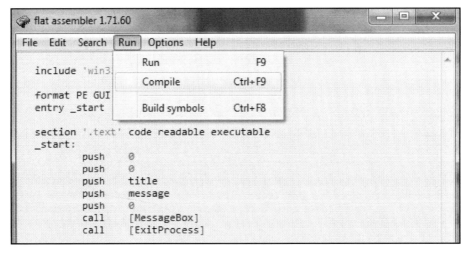

Compiling sources in FASMW

Admire the result for a few seconds.

Example output

Linux

If you are on Linux, the source code will be even shorter. Open your favorite source editor, whether it is nano, emacs, or vi, or whatever, and enter the following code:

```
format ELF executable 3
entry _start

segment readable executable
_start:
    mov eax, 4
    mov ebx, 1
    mov ecx, message
    mov edx, len
    int 0x80

    xor ebx, ebx
    mov eax, ebx
    inc eax
    int 0x80


segment readable writeable
    message db 'Hello from FASM on Linux!', 0x0a
    len = $ - message
```

The code is much more compact than that on Windows, as we are not using any high-level API functions; we'd rather use Linux system calls directly (this could turn into a nightmare on Windows). Save the file as fasm1lin.asm (this is not GAS or GCC, so we are free to give the Assembly source file its usual extension) and go to the terminal emulator. Issue the following command (assuming the fasm executable is in the place mentioned in the PATH environment variable) in order to build the executable out of this code:

```
fasm fasm1lin.asm fasm1lin
```

Then, try to run the file with the following:

```
./fasm1lin
```

You should see something like this:

```
alexey@main:~/Documents/Books/MasteringAssemblyProgramming/CH2$ fasm fasm1lin.asm fasm1lin
flat assembler  version 1.71.49  (16384 kilobytes memory)
3 passes, 171 bytes.
alexey@main:~/Documents/Books/MasteringAssemblyProgramming/CH2$ ./fasm1lin
Hello from FASM on Linux!
alexey@main:~/Documents/Books/MasteringAssemblyProgramming/CH2$ ▌
```

Building and running a Linux executable with Flat Assembler

As simple as that.

Summary

By now, we have reviewed three different assemblers: **Microsoft Macro Assembler** (**MASM**), this is an integral part of Visual Studio, **GNU Assembler** (**GAS**), this is the default backend for GNU Compilers Collection (GCC), **Flat Assembler** (**FASM**), this is a standalone, portable, flexible, and powerful assembler.

Although we will be using FASM, we may still refer to the other two from time to time, when the need arises (and it will).

Having an installed and working assembler, we are ready to proceed to Chapter 3, *Intel Instruction Set Architecture (ISA)*, and start working with the Assembly language itself. There is a long road ahead, and we have not made the first step yet. In Chapter 3, *Intel Instruction Set Architecture (ISA)*, we will go through the instruction set architecture of Intel processors, and you will learn how to write simple programs for both Windows and Linux, 32 and 64-bit.

3
Intel Instruction Set Architecture (ISA)

It may virtually be right to say that any digital device has a specific set of instructions. Even a transistor, the foundation stone of modern digital electronics, has two instructions, on and off, where each one is represented by 1 or 0 (which one of these represents on and off depends on whether the transistor is *n-p-n* or *p-n-p*). A processor is constructed from millions of transistors and is, as well, controlled by sequences of 1s and 0s (grouped into 8-bit bytes grouped into instructions). Fortunately, we do not have to take care of instruction encoding (it's the 21st century out there) as assemblers do that for us.

Each CPU instruction (and this is right for any CPU, not only Intel based) has a mnemonic designation (further simply mnemonic), which you need to learn about along with a few simple rules regarding operand sizes (and memory addressing, but we will take a deeper look at that in Chapter 4, *Memory Addressing Modes*), and this is exactly what we will do in this chapter.

We will begin by creating a simple Assembly template, which we will use throughout the book as a starting point for our code. Then, we will proceed to the actual CPU instruction set and get acquainted with the following types of instructions:

- Data transfer instructions
- Arithmetic instructions
- Floating point instructions
- Execution flow control instructions
- Extensions

Assembly source template

We will start with two 32-bit templates, one for Windows and one for Linux. 64-bit templates will be added very soon and we will see that they are not much different from 32-bit ones. The templates contain some macro instructions and directives that will be explained later in the book. As for now, these templates are provided with the sole purpose to give you the ability to write simple (and not so simple) snippets of code, compile them, and test them in a debugger.

The Windows Assembly template (32-bit)

A Windows executable consists of several sections (the structure of a PE executable/object file will be covered in more detail in Chapter 9, *Operating System Interface*); usually, one section for code, one for data, and one for import data (this contains information on external procedures, which are imported from dynamic link libraries). **Dynamic-link libraries (DLL)** also have an export section, which contains information on procedures/objects publicly available in the DLL itself. In our template, we simply define the sections and let the assembler do the rest of the work (write headers and so on).

Now, let's take a look at the template itself. See further explanation of PE specifics in the comments:

```
; File: srctemplate_win.asm

; First of all, we tell the compiler which type of executable we want it
; to be. In our case it is a 32-bit PE executable.
format PE GUI

; Tell the compiler where we want our program to start - define the entry
; point. We want it to be at the place labeled with '_start'.
entry _start

; The following line includes a set of macros, shipped with FASM, which
; are essential for the Windows program. We can, of course, implement all
; we need ourselves, and we will do that in chapter 9.
include 'win32a.inc'

; PE file consists of at least one section.
; In this template we only need 3:
;     1. '.text' - section that contains executable code
;     2. '.data' - section that contains data
;     3. '.idata' - section that contains import information
;
```

```
; '.text' section: contains code, is readable, is executable
section '.text' code readable executable
_start:
    ;
    ; Put your code here
    ;


    ; We have to terminate the process properly
    ; Put return code on stack
    push  0
    ; Call ExitProcess Windows API procedure
    call [exitProcess]

; '.data' section: contains data, is readable, may be writeable
section '.data' data readable writeable
    ;
    ; Put your data here
    ;

; '.idata' section: contains import information, is readable, is writeable
section '.idata' import data readable writeable

; 'library' macro from 'win32a.inc' creates proper entry for importing
; procedures from a dynamic link library. For now it is only
'kernel32.dll',
; library kernel, 'kernel32.dll'

; 'import' macro creates the actual entries for procedures we want to
import
; from a dynamic link library
import kernel,
    exitProcess, 'ExitProcess'
```

The Linux Assembly template (32-bit)

On Linux, although files on disc are divided into sections, executables in memory are divided into code and data segments. The following is our template for the ELF 32-bit executable for Linux:

```
; File: src/template_lin.asm

; Just as in the Windows template - we tell the assembler which type
; of output we expect.
; In this case it is 32-bit executable ELF
format ELF executable
```

```
; Tell the assembler where the entry point is
entry _start

; On *nix based systems, when in memory, the space is arranged into
; segments, rather than in sections, therefore, we define
; two segments:
; Code segment (executable segment)
segment readable executable

; Here is our entry point
_start:

    ; Set return value to 0
    xor ebx, ebx
    mov eax, ebx

    ; Set eax to 1 - 32-bit Linux SYS_exit system call number
    inc eax

    ; Call kernel
    int 0x80

; Data segment
segment readable writeable
    db 0

; As you see, there is no import/export segment here. The structure
; of an ELF executable/object file will be covered in more detail
; in chapters 8 and 9
```

As was mentioned in the preceding code, these two templates will be used as a starting point for any code we will write in this book.

Data types and their definitions

Before we start working with Assembly instructions, we have to know how to define data, or, to be more precise, how to tell the assembler which type of data we are using.

The Flat Assembler supports six built-in types of data and allows us to either define or declare variables. The difference between a definition and a declaration in this case is that when we define a variable we also assign a certain value to it, but when we declare, we simply reserve space for a certain type of data:

Variable definition format: `[label] definition_directive value(s)`

- `label`: This is optional, but addressing an unnamed variable is harder

Variable declaration format: `[label] declaration_directive count`

- `label`: This is optional, but addressing an unnamed variable is harder
- `count`: This tells the assembler how many entries of the type specified in `declaration_directive` it should reserve memory for

The following table shows definition and declaration directives for built-in data types, sorted by size thereof:

Size of data type in bytes	Definition directive	Declaration (reservation) directive
1	db file (includes binary file)	rb
2	dw du (defines unicode character)	rw
4	dd	rd
6	dp df	rp rf
8	dq	rq
10	dt	rt

The preceding table lists acceptable data types ordered by their size in bytes, which is in the leftmost column. The column in the middle contains the directives we use in the Assembly code for definition of data of a certain type. For example, if we want to define a byte variable named `my_var`, then we write the following:

```
my_var    db    0x5a
```

Here, `0x5a` is the value we assign to this variable. In cases where we do not need to initialize the variable with any specific value, we write this:

```
my_var db ?
```

Here, the question mark (?) means that the assembler may initialize the memory area occupied by this variable to any value (which would typically be 0).

There are two directives that require a bit more attention:

- `file`: This directive instructs the assembler to include a binary file during the compilation.
- du: This directive is used just like db is used to define characters or strings thereof, yet it produces unicode-like characters/strings instead of ASCII. The effect is the 0 extension of 8-bit values to 16-bit values. This is rather a convenience directive and has to be overridden when a proper transformation to unicode is required.

Directives shown in the rightmost column are used when we want to reserve space for a range of data entries of a certain type without specifying the values thereof. For example, if we want to reserve space for, let's say, 12 32-bit integers labeled my_array, then we would write the following:

```
my_array rd 12
```

The assembler would then reserve 48 bytes for this array, beginning at a place labeled my_array in the code.

Although you will use these directives in the data section most of the time, there is no limitation as to where they may be placed. For example, you may (for whatever purpose) reserve some space within a procedure, or between two procedures, or include a binary file containing precompiled code.

A debugger

We are almost ready to begin the process of instruction set exploration; however, there is one more thing that we have not touched yet, as there was no need for it--a debugger. There is a relatively wide choice of debuggers out there and you, being a developer, have most likely worked with at least one of them. However, since we are interested in debugging programs written in the Assembly language, I would suggest one of the following:

- **IDA Pro** (https://www.hex-rays.com/products/ida/index.shtml): Very convenient, but also very expensive. If you have it, good! If not, never mind, we have other options. Windows only.
- **OllyDbg** (http://www.ollydbg.de/version2.html): Free debugger/disassembler. More than enough for what we need. Windows only. Unfortunately, the 64-bit version of this tool was never finished, meaning that you would not be able to use it with 64-bit examples.

- **HopperApp** (`https://www.hopperapp.com`): Commercial, but very affordable disassembler with GDB frontend. macOS X and Linux.
- **GDB** (**GNU DeBugger**): Freely available, works on Windows, Linux, mac OS X, and others. Although GDB is a command-line tool, it is quite easy to use. The only limitation is that the disassembler's output is in AT&T syntax.

You are free to choose either one of these or a debugger that is not mentioned on the list (and there are relatively many). There is only one important factor to consider while selecting a debugger--you should feel comfortable with it, as running your code in a debugger, seeing everything that happens in registers of a processor or in memory, would greatly enhance your experience while writing code in Assembly.

The instruction set summary

We have finally got to the interesting part--the instruction set itself. Unfortunately, describing each and every instruction of a modern Intel-based processor would require a separate book, but since there is already such a book (`http://www.intel.com/content/dam/ www/public/us/en/documents/manuals/64-ia-32-architectures-software-developer- instruction-set-reference-manual-325383.pdf`), we will not multiply things without need and will concentrate on instruction groups rather than on individual instructions. At the end of the chapter, we will implement AES128 encryption for the sake of demonstration.

General purpose instructions

The general purpose instructions perform basic operations such as data movement, arithmetic, flow control, and so on. They are grouped by their purpose:

- Data transfer instructions
- Binary arithmetic instructions
- Decimal arithmetic instructions
- Logical instructions
- Shift and rotate instructions
- Bit/byte manipulation instructions
- Flow control instructions
- String manipulation instructions

- ENTER/LEAVE instructions
- Flag control instructions
- Miscellaneous instructions

The division of instructions into groups is the same as in the Intel Software Developer's Manual.

Data transfer instructions

Data transfer instructions, as the name of the group suggests, are used to transfer data between registers or between registers and memory. Some of them may have an immediate value as their source operand. The following example illustrates their usage.

```
push   ebx                 ; save EBX register on stack
mov    ax, 0xc001          ; move immediate value to AX register
movzx  ebx, ax             ; move zero-extended content of AX to EBX
                           ; register
                           ; EBX = 0x0000c001
bswap  ebx                 ; reverse byte order of EBX register
                           ; EBX = 0x01c00000
mov    [some_address], ebx ; move content of EBX register to
                           ; memory at 'some_address'
                           ; content of 'some_address' =
                           ; 0x01c00000
                           ; The above two lines of code could have
                           ; been replaced with:
                           ; movbe [some_address], ebx
pop    ebx                 ; restore EBX register from stack
```

Let's take a closer look at the instructions used with the example:

- **PUSH**: This instructs the processor to store the value of the operand onto a stack and decrements stack pointer (ESP register on 32-bit systems and RSP register on 64-bit ones).
- **MOV**: This is the most commonly used instruction for transferring data:
  - It moves data between registers of the same size
  - It loads a register with either an immediate value or a value read from memory
  - It stores the content of a register to memory
  - It stores the immediate value to memory

- **MOVZX**: This is less powerful than MOV by means of addressing modes, as it may only transfer data from register to register or from memory to register, but it has its special feature--the value being transferred is converted to a wider (one that uses more bits) one and is zero extended. As to the addressing modes supported by this instruction, it may only do the following:
    - It moves the byte value from register or memory to a word-sized register and extends the resulting value with zeroes (one byte would be added)
    - It moves byte value from register or memory to a double word-sized register, in which case three bytes would be added to the original value and the value itself would be extended with zeroes
    - It moves word-sized value from register or memory to a double word-sized register, adding two bytes and filling them with the extension value of 0
- **MOVSX** is similar to MOVZX; however, the extended bits are filled with the sign bit of the source operand.
- **BSWAP/MOVBE** The BSWAP instruction is the easiest way to switch the endianness of a value; however, it is not really a transfer instruction as it only rearranges data within a register. The BSWAP instruction only works on 32/64-bit operands. MOVBE is a more convenient instruction for swapping byte order as it also moves data between the operands. This instruction works on 16, 32, and 64-bit operands. It cannot move data from register to register.
- **POP**: This retrieves values previously stored on stack. The only operand of this instruction is the destination where the value should be stored, and it may be a register or a location in memory. This instruction increments the stack pointer register as well.

Binary Arithmetic Instructions

These instructions perform basic arithmetic operations. Operands may be byte, word, double-word or quad-word registers, memory locations, or immediate values. They all modify CPU flags according to the result of operation thereof, which, in turn, lets us change the execution flow depending on the values of certain flags.

Let us take a look at a few basic arithmetic instructions:

- **INC**: This is short for increment. This instruction adds 1 to the value of its operand. Obviously, the inc instruction, or its counterpart, the `dec` instruction, may not be used with immediate values. The `inc` instruction affects certain CPU flags. For example, consider that we take a register (let it be the EAX register for the sake of simplicity), set it to 0, and execute it, as follows:

  ```
  inc eax
  ```

  In this case, EAX would equal to 1 and ZF (zero flag, remember?) would be set to 0, meaning that the operation resulted in a non-zero value. On the other hand, if we load the EAX register with the `0xffffffff` value and increment it with the `inc` instruction, the register will become zero and, since zero is the result of the latest operation, ZF would be set then (will have value of 1).

- **ADD**: This performs simple addition, adding the source operand to the destination operand and storing the resulting value in the destination operand. This instruction affects several CPU flags as well. In the following example, we will add `0xffffffff` to the EBX register, which has been set to 1. The result of such an operation would be a 33-bit value, but as we only have 32 bits to store the result, the extra bit would go into the carry flag. Such a mechanism, in addition to being useful for control of the execution flow, may also be used when adding two big numbers (may be even hundreds of bits wide) as we can then process the numbers by smaller portions (of, for example, 32 bits).

- **ADC**: Talking about addition of big numbers, the adc instruction is the one that allows us to add the value of the carry flag, as set by a previous operation, to the summation of additional two values. For example, if we want to add `0x802597631` and `0x4fe013872`, we would then add `0x02597631` and `0xfe013872` first, resulting in `0x005aaea3` and a set carry flag. Then, we would add 8, 4 and, the value of the carry flag:

  ```
  ;Assuming EAX equals to 8 and EBX equals to 4
  adc eax, ebx
  ```

  This would result in $8 + 4 + 1$ (where 1 is the implicit operand--the value of the CF) = `0xd`, thus, the overall result would be `0xd005aaea3`.

The following example illustrates these instructions in more detail:

```
mov    eax, 0             ; Set EAX to 0
mov    ebx, eax           ; Set EBX to 0
inc    ebx                ; Increment EBX
                          ; EBX = 1
add    ebx, 0xffffffff ; add 4294967295 to EBX
                          ; EBX = 0 and Carry Flag is set
adc    eax, 0             ; Add 0 and Carry Flag to EAX
                          ; EAX = 1
```

Decimal arithmetic instructions

In about 15 years of Assembly development and reverse engineering software, I encountered these instructions exactly once, and that was in the college. However, it would be right to mention them, for a few reasons:

- Instructions like AAM and AAD may sometimes be used as a smaller variant of multiplication and division, since they allow immediate operand. They're smaller as they allow generation of smaller code due to their encoding.
- Sequences like AAD 0 (which is division by zero) may be used as an exception trigger in certain protection schemes.
- Not mentioning them would be historically wrong.

Decimal arithmetic instructions are illegal on 64-bit platforms.

First of all, what is BCD? It is **Binary coded decimal (BCD)** and is, in fact, an attempt to ease the conversion of binary representations of numbers to their ASCII equivalent and vice versa, as well as adding the ability to perform basic arithmetic operations on decimal numbers represented in a hexadecimal form (not their hexadecimal equivalents!).

There are two types of BCD: packed and unpacked. Packed BCD represents a decimal number using nibbles of a single byte. For example, the number 12 would be represented as 0x12. Unpacked BCD, on the other hand, uses bytes for representation of individual digits (for example, 12 converts to 0x0102).

However, given the fact that these instructions have not been changed since their first appearance, they only operate on values stored in a single byte, for packed BCD, or values stored in a single word, for unpacked BCD. More than this, these values should be stored only in the AL register for packed BCD and the AX register (or, to say it in a more precise way, in the AH:AL pair) for unpacked BCD.

There are only six BCD instructions:

- **Decimal Adjust after Addition (DAA)**: This instruction is specific to packed BCD. Since the addition of two packed BCD numbers would not necessarily result in a valid packed BCD number, the invocation of DAA fixes the problem by making the adjustments needed for converting a result into a proper packed BCD value. For example, let's add 12 and 18. Normally, the result would be 30, but if we add 0x12 and 0x18, the result would be 0x2a. The following example illustrates the procedure for such a calculation:

```
mov al, 0x12    ; AL = 0x12, which is packed BCD
                ; representation of 12
add al, 0x18    ; Add BCD representation of 18,
                ; which would result in 0x2a
daa             ; Adjust. AL would contain 0x30 after this
instruction,
                ; which is the BCD representation of 30
```

- **Decimal Adjust after Subtraction (DAS)**: This instruction performs similar adjustments after subtracting two packed BCD numbers. Let's add some more lines to the preceding code (AL still contains 0x30):

```
sub al, 0x03    ; We are subtracting 3 from 30, however,
                ; the result of 0x30 - 0x03
                ; would be 0x2d
das             ; This instruction sets AL to 0x27,
                ; which is the packed BCD
                ; representation of 27.
```

- **ASCII Adjust after Addition (AAA)**: This instruction is similar to DAA, yet it works on unpacked BCD numbers (meaning, the AX register). Let's look at the following example, where we still add 18 to 12, but we do that with the unpacked BCD:

```
mov ax, 0x0102   ; 0x0102 is the unpacked BCD representation of 12
add ax, 0x0108   ; same for 18
                 ; The result of the addition would be
                 ; 0x020a - far from being 0x0300
aaa              ; Converts the value of AX register to 0x0300
```

The resulting value may easily be converted to the ASCII representation by adding 0x3030.

- **ASCII Adjust after Subtraction (AAS)**: This instruction is similar to DAS, but operates on unpacked BCD numbers. We may continue to add code to the preceding example (The AX register still has the value of 0x0300). Let's subtract 3, which should, at the end, give us the value of 0x0207:

```
sub ax, 0x0003   ; AX now contains 0x02fd
aas              ; So we convert it to unpacked BCD
                 ; representation, but...
                 ; AX becomes 0x0107, but as we know,
                 ; 30 - 3 != 17...
```

What went wrong then? In fact, nothing went wrong; it is just that the internal implementation of the AAS instruction caused carry (and, as we may see in a debugger, the CF is in deed set) or, to be more precise, a borrow occurred. That is why it is better for our convenience to finalize this with the following:

```
adc ah, 0   ; Adds the value of CF to AH
```

We end up with 0x0207, which is the unpacked BCD representation of 27--exactly the result we were expecting.

- **ASCII Adjust AX after Multiply** (**AAM**): Result of the multiplication of two unpacked BCD numbers, as well, requires certain adjustments to be made in order to be in an unpacked BCD form. However, what we have to remember first of all is the size limitation implied by these operations. As we are limited to the AX register, the maximum value of a multiplicand is 9 (or 0x09), meaning that, being limited to AX with the resulting value, we are limited to one byte with multiplicands. Let's say we want to multiply 8 by 4 (which would be 0x08 * 0x04); naturally, the result would be 0x20 (the hexadecimal equivalent of 32), which is not even close to being an unpacked BCD represented number. The aam instruction solves this problem by converting the value of the AL register to the unpacked BCD format and stores it in AX:

```
mov al, 4
mov bl, 8
mul bl      ; AX becomes 0x0020
aam         ; Converts the value of AX to the
            ; corresponding unpacked BCD form. Now the AX
            ; register equals to 0x0302
```

As we see, the multiplication of two unpacked BCD bytes results in an unpacked BCD word.

- **ASCII Adjust AX before Division** (**AAD**): This is exactly as the name of the instruction suggests--it should adjust the value of the AX register before division. The size limitations are just the same as in AAM. The AX register still contains 0x0302 after the previous example, so let's divide it by 4:

```
mov bl, 4
aad         ; Adjust AX. The value changes from 0x0302 to 0x0020
div bl      ; Perform the division itself
            ; AL register contains the result - 0x08
```

As we see, although these instructions may seem to be somewhat convenient, there are better ways to convert numbers between their ASCII notation and their binary equivalents, not to mention the fact that regular arithmetic instructions are much more convenient to use.

Logical instructions

This group contains instructions for bitwise logical operations which you, being a developer, already know. These are NOT, OR, XOR, and AND operations. However, while high-level languages do make a difference between bitwise and logical operators (for example, bitwise AND (&) and logical AND (&&) in C), they are all the same on the Assembly level and are quite commonly used in conjunction with the EFlags register (or RFlags on 64-bit systems).

For example, consider the following simple snippet in C that checks for a specific bit being set and conditionally executes certain code:

```
if(my_var & 0x20)
{
    // do something if true
}
else
{
    // do something else otherwise
}
```

It may be implemented in Assembly like this:

```
and dword [my_var], 0x20   ; Check for sixth bit of 'my_var'.
                           ; This operation sets ZF if the result
                           ; is zero (if the bit is not set).
jnz do_this_if_true        ; Go to this label if the bit is set
jmp do_this_if_false       ; Go to this label otherwise
```

One of the many other applications of these instructions is the finite field arithmetic, where XOR stands for addition and AND stands for multiplication.

Shift and rotate instructions

Instructions of this group let us move bits within the destination operand, which is something we only partially have in high-level languages. We can shift, but we cannot rotate, neither can we implicitly specify arithmetic shifts (the selection of arithmetic or a logical shift is usually performed by high-level language implementation based on the type of data the operations are carried on).

Using shift instructions, in addition to their primary role of moving bits left or right a certain number of positions, is a simpler way to perform integer multiplication and division of the destination operand by powers of two. Additionally, two special shift instructions exist that let us move certain amount of bits from one location to another--to be more precise, from a register to another register or to a memory location.

Rotation instructions allow us, as the name suggests, to rotate bits from one end of the destination operand to another. It is important to mention that bits may be rotated through the CF (carry flag), meaning that the bit that is shifted out is stored in the CF while the value of the CF is shifted into the operand on the other side. Let's consider the following example, one of the simplest integrity control algorithms, CRC8:

```
        poly = 0x31        ; The polynomial used for CRC8 calculation
        xor   dl, dl       ; Initialise CRC state register with 0
        mov   al, 0x16     ; Prepare the sequence of 8 bits (may definitely
                           ; be more than 8 bits)
        mov   ecx, 8       ; Set amount of iterations
    crc_loop:
        shl   al, 1
        rcl   bl, 1
        shl   dl, 1
        rcl   bh, 1
        xor   bl, bh
        test  bl, 1
        jz    .noxor
        xor   dl, poly
    .noxor:
        loop crc_loop
```

The body of the loop in the preceding snippet was intentionally left without comments as we would like to take a closer look at what is happening there.

The first instruction of the loop `shl al, 1` shifts out the most significant bit of the value we are calculating CRC8 for and stores it into the CF. The next instruction `rcl bl, 1` stores the value of the CF (the bit we shifted out of our bit stream) into the BL register. The following two instructions do the same for the DL register, storing the most significant bit into BH. The side effect of the `rcl` instruction is that the most significant bits of the first BL and then the BH register are moved to the CF. Although it is of no importance in this specific case, we should not forget about this when rotating through the CF. At the end, this means after 8 iterations, the preceding code provides us with the CRC8 value for `0x16` (which is `0xE5`) in the DL register.

The two shift and rotate instructions mentioned in the example have their right-sided counterparts:

- **SHR**: This shifts bits to the right, while saving the last bit shifted out in the CF
- **RCR**: This rotates bits to the right through the carry flag

There are a few additional instructions in this group that we cannot skip:

- **SAR**: This shifts bits to the right while "dragging" the sign bit instead of simply filling the "vacant" bits with zeroes.
- **SAL**: This is an arithmetic shift to the left. It is not truly an instruction, rather a mnemonic used for a programmer's convenience. The assembler generates the same encoding as for SHL.
- **ROR**: This rotates bits to the right. Each bit being shifted out to the right and shifted in to the left is also stored in the CF.

Finally, as it was mentioned earlier, the two special shift instructions are as follows:

- **SHLD**: This shifts a certain number of left-side (most significant) bits from a register into another register or into a memory location
- **SHRD**: This shifts a certain number of right-side (least significant) bits from a register into another register or into a memory location

Another new instruction in the previous example is TEST, but it will be explained in the next section.

Bit and byte instructions

Instructions of this group are those that let us manipulate individual bits within an operand and/or set bytes in accordance with the sate of flags in the EFlags/RFlags register.

With high-level languages that implement bit fields, it is quite easy to access individual bits even if we want to perform more complex operations than just scan, test, set or reset, as provided by Intel Assembly. However, with high-level languages having no bit fields we have to implement certain constructs in order to have access to individual bits and that is where Assembly is more convenient.

While bit and byte instructions may have a variety of applications, let's consider them (just a few of them) in the context of the CRC8 example. It would not be completely right to say that using these instructions in that example would have significantly optimized it; after all, it would let us get rid of a single instruction, making the implementation of the algorithm look a bit clearer. Let's see how `crc_loop` would have changed:

```
crc_loop:
    shl  al, 1      ; Shift left-most bit out to CF
    setc bl         ; Set bl to 1 if CF==1, or to zero otherwise
    shl  dl, 1      ; shift left-most bit out to CF
    setc bh         ; Set bh to 1 if CF==1, or to zero otherwise
    xor  bl, bh     ; Here we, in fact, are XOR'ing the previously left-most
bits of al and dl
    jz   .noxor     ; Do not add POLY if XOR result is zero
    xor  dl, poly
.noxor:
    loop crc_loop
```

The preceding code is quite self-explanatory, but let's take a closer look at the set of bit instructions:

- **BT**: This stores a bit from the destination operand (bit base) to the CF. The bit is identified by the index specified in the source operand.
- **BTS**: This is the same as BT, but it also sets the bit in the destination operand.
- **BTR**: This is the same as BT, but it also resets the bit in the destination operand.
- **BTC**: This is the same as BT, but it also inverts (complements) the bit in the destination operand.
- **BSF**: This stands for **bit scan forward**. It searches the source operand for the least significant bit that is set. The index of the bit, if found, is returned in the destination operand. If the source operand is all zeros, then the value for the destination operand is not defined and ZF is set.
- **BSR**: This stands for **bit scan reverse**. It searches the source operand for the most significant bit that is set. The index of the bit, if found, is returned in the destination operand. If the source operand is all zeros, then the value of the destination operand is not defined and ZF is set.
- **TEST**: This instruction makes it possible to check for several bits being set at the same time. To put it simply, the TEST instruction performs the logical AND operation, sets flags accordingly, and discards the result.

Byte instructions are all of a form SETcc, where **cc** stands for **condition code**. The following are the condition codes on the Intel platform, as specified in section B.1 Condition Codes of *Appendix B EFlags Condition Codes* of Intel 64 and IA-32 Architectures Software Developer's Manual Volume 1:

Mnemonic (cc)	Condition tested for	Status flags setting
O	Overflow	OF = 1
NO	No overflow	OF = 0
B NAE	Below Neither above nor equal	CF = 1
NB AE	Not below Above or equal	CF = 1
E Z	Equal Zero	ZF = 1
NE NZ	Not equal Not zero	ZF = 0
BE NA	Below or equal Not above	(CF or ZF) = 1
NBE A	Neither below nor equal Above	(CF or ZF) = 0
S	Sign	SF = 1
NS	No sign	SF = 0
P PE	Parity Parity even	PF = 1
NP PO	No parity Parity odd	PF = 0
L NGE	Less Neither greater nor equal	(SF xor OF) = 1
NL GE	Not less Greater or equal	(SF xor OF) = 0
LE NG	Less or equal Not greater	((SF xor OF) or ZF) = 1
NLE G	Not less or equal Greater	((SF xor OF) or ZF) = 0

So, as we may conclude using the preceding table and the `setc` instruction from the CRC8 example, it instructs the processor to set `bl` (and `bh`) to 1 if the C condition is true, which means CF == 1.

Execution flow transfer instructions

Instructions of this group make it possible to easily branch the execution, whether in accordance to a specific condition designated by the EFlags/RFlags register or completely unconditionally, and may, therefore, be divided into two groups:

- Unconditional execution flow transfer instructions:
  - **JMP**: Perform unconditional jump to an explicitly specified location. This loads the instruction pointer register with the address of the specified location.
  - **CALL**: This instruction is used to call a procedure. This pushes the address of the next instruction onto the stack and loads the instruction pointer with the address of the first instruction in the called procedure.
  - **RET**: This instruction performs a return from procedure. It pops the value stored on the stack into the instruction pointer register. When used at the end of a procedure, it returns the execution to instruction following the CALL instruction.
    The RET instruction may have a two-bytes value as its operand, in which case the value defines the amount of bytes occupied by the operands that were passed to the procedure on stack. The stack pointer is then automatically adjusted by adding the amount of bytes.
  - **INT**: This instruction causes a software interrupt.
    The use of this instruction on Windows while programming in ring 3 is quite rare. It may even be safe to assume that the only usage is INT3--software breakpoint. On 32-bit Linux, however, it is used for invocation of system calls.
- Conditional execution flow transfer instructions:
  - **Jcc**: This is the conditional variant of the JMP instruction, where **cc** stands for **condition code**, which may be one of the condition codes listed in the preceding table. For example, look at the `jz` `.noxor` line from the CRC8 example.
  - **JCXZ**: This is a special version of the conditional jump instruction, which uses the CX register as a condition. The jump is only executed if the CX register contains 0.
  - **JECXZ**: This is the same as above, but it operates on the ECX register.
  - **JRCXZ**: This is the same as above, but it operates on the RCX register (long mode only).

- **LOOP**: A loop with ECX as a counter, this decrements ECX and, if the result is not 0, loads the instruction pointer register with the address of the loop label. We have already used this instruction in the CRC8 example.
- **LOOPZ/LOOPE**: This is the loop with ECX as a counter while ZF = 1.
- **LOOPNZ/LOOPNE**: This is the loop with ECX as a counter while ZF = 0.

Let's, for the sake of example, implement the CRC8 algorithm as a procedure (insert the following into the code section of the relevant 32-bit template):

```
;
; Put your code here
;
    mov al, 0x16            ; In this specific case we pass the
                            ; only argument via AL register
    call crc_proc           ; Call the 'crc_proc' procedure

    ; For Windows
    push 0                  ; Terminate the process if you are on Windows
    call [exitProcess]

    ; For Linux               ; Terminate the process if you are on Linux
    xor   ebx, ebx
    mov   eax, ebx
    inc   eax
    int   0x80

crc_proc:                   ; Our CRC8 procedure
    push ebx ecx edx        ; Save the register we are going to use on stack
    xor dl, dl              ; Initialise the CRC state register
    mov ecx, 8              ; Setup counter
.crc_loop:
    shl al, 1
    setc bl
    shl dl, 1
    setc bh
    xor bl, bh
    jz .noxor
    xor dl, 0x31
.noxor:
    loop .crc_loop
    mov al, dl              ; Setup return value
    pop edx ecx ebx         ; Restore registers
    ret                     ; Return from this procedure
```

String instructions

This is an interesting group of instructions that operate on strings of bytes, words, double words, or quad words (long mode only). These instructions have implicit operands only:

- The source address should be loaded into the ESI (RSI for long mode) register
- The destination address should be loaded into the EDI (RDI for long mode) register
- One of the EAX (for example, AL and AX) register variations is used with all of them except the MOVS* and CMPS* instructions
- The number of iterations (if any) should be in ECX (only used with the REP* prefix)

 ESI and/or EDI registers are automatically incremented by one for byte, two for word, and four for double word data. The direction of these operations (whether they increment or decrement ESI/EDI) is controlled by the direction flag (DF) in the EFlags register: DF = 1 : decrement ESI/EDI DF = 0 : increment ESI/EDI.

These instructions may be divided into five groups. In fact, to put it in a more precise manner, there are five instructions supporting four data sizes each:

- **MOVSB/MOVSW/MOVSD/MOVSQ**: These move byte, word, double word, or quad word in memory from the location pointed by ESI/RSI to the location pointed by EDI/RDI. The instruction's suffix specifies the size of data to be moved. Setting ECX/RCX to the amount of data items to be moved and prefixing it with the REP* prefix instructs the processor to execute this instruction ECX times or while the condition used with the REP* prefix (if any) is true.
- **CMPSB/CMPSW/CMPSD/CMPSQ**: These compare the data pointed by the ESI/RSI register to the data pointed by the EDI/RDI register. The iteration rules are the same as for MOVS* instruction.
- **SCASB/SCASW/SCASD/SCASQ**: These scan sequences of data items (size thereof is specified by the instruction's suffix) pointed by the EDI/RDI register for a value specified in AL, AX, EAX, or RAX, depending on the mode (protected or long) and the instruction's suffix. Iterations rules are the same as those for the MOVS* instruction.
- **LODSB/LODSW/LODSD/LODSQ**: These load AL, AX, EAX, or RAX (depending on operation mode and instruction's suffix) with a value from memory, pointed by the ESI/RSI register. The iteration rules are the same as those for the MOVS* instruction.

- **STOSB/STOSW/STOSD/STOSQ**: These store the value of the AL, AX, EAX, or RAX registers to the memory location pointed by the EDI/RDI register. These iteration rules are the same as those for the MOVS* instruction.

All of the preceding instructions have the explicit-operands form without a suffix, but in such a case, we need to specify the size of the operands. While the operands themselves may not be changed and therefore would always be ESI/RSI and EDI/RDI, all we may change is the size of the operand. The following is an example of such case:

```
scas byte[edi]
```

The following example shows typical usage of the SCAS* instruction--scanning a sequence of, in this particular case, bytes for specific value, which is stored in the AL register. The other instructions are similar in their usage.

```
; Calculate the length of a string
    mov    edi, hello
    mov    ecx, 0x100    ; Maximum allowed string length
    xor    al, al        ; We will look for 0
    rep scasb            ; Scan for terminating 0
    or     ecx, 0         ; Check whether the string is too long
    jz     too_long
    neg    ecx           ; Negate ECX
    add    ecx, 0x100    ; Get the length of the string
                          ; ECX = 14 (includes terminating 0)
too_long:
    ; Handle this

hello db "Hello, World!", 0
```

The `rep` prefix, used in the preceding example, indicates to the processor that it should execute the prefixed command using the ECX register as a counter (in the same manner as it is used by the LOOP* instructions). However, there is one more optional condition designated by ZF (zero flag). Such a condition is specified by the condition suffix attached to REP. For example, using it with the E or Z suffix would instruct the processor to check ZF for being set before each iteration. Suffixes NE or NZ would instruct the processor to check ZF for being reset before each iteration. Consider the following example:

```
repz cmpsb
```

This would instruct the processor to keep comparing two sequences of bytes (pointed by the EDI/RDI and ESI/RSI registers) while they are equal and ECX is not zero.

ENTER/LEAVE

According to the Intel manual for developers, *these instructions provide machine-language support for procedure calls in block-structured languages;* however, they are very useful for Assembly developers as well.

When we implement a procedure, we have to take care of the creation of the stack frame where we store the procedure's variables, storing the value of ESP and then restoring all that before we leave a procedure. These two instructions can do all that work for us:

```
; Do something here
call    my_proc
; Do something else here

my_proc:
    enter 0x10, 0    ; Save EBP register on stack,
                     ; save ESP to EBP and
                     ; allocate 16 bytes on stack for procedure variables
    ;
    ; procedure body
    ;
    leave            ; Restore ESP and EBP registers (this automatically
                     ; releases the space allocated on stack with ENTER)
    ret              ; Return from procedure
```

The preceding code is equivalent to the following code:

```
; Do something here
call    my_proc
; Do something else here

my_proc:
    push    ebp      ; Save EBP register on stack,
    mov     ebp, esp ; save ESP to EBP and
    sub     esp, 0x10 ; allocate 16 bytes on stack for procedure variables
    ;
    ; procedure body
    ;
    mov     esp, ebp ; Restore ESP and EBP registers (this automatically
    pop     ebp      ; releases the space allocated on stack with ENTER)
    ret              ; Return from procedure
```

Flag control instructions

The EFlags register contains information on certain aspects of the last ALU operation as well as certain settings of the CPU (for example, the direction of string instructions); however, we have the mechanism for controlling the content of this register, up to the level of a single flag, with the following instructions:

- **Set/clear carry flag (STC/CLC)**: We may want to have the CF set or reset prior to certain operations.
- **Complement the carry flag (CMC)**: This instruction inverts the value of the CF.
- **Set/clear direction flag (STD/CLD)**: We may use these instructions to set or reset the DF in order to define whether ESI/EDI (RSI/RDI) should increment or decrement with string instructions.
- **Load flags into the AH register (LAHF)**: There are certain flags, for example, ZF, that do not have associated instructions for direct modification, therefore, we may load the Flags register into AH, modify the corresponding bit, and reload the Flags register with the modified value.
- **Store the AH register into flags (SAHF)**: This instruction stores the value of AH register into the Flags register.
- **Set/clear the interrupt flag (STI/CLI)** (not in user land): These instructions are used on the operating system-level to enable/disable interrupts.
- **Push Flags/EFlags/RFlags register onto the stack (PUSHF/PUSHFD/PUSHFQ)**: LAHF/SAHF instructions may not be sufficient for inspection/modification of certain flags in the Flags/EFlags/RFlags register. With the PUSHF* instruction, we gain access to other bits (flags).
- **Retrieve Flags/EFlags/RFlags register from the stack (POPF/POPFD/POPFQ)**: These reload Flags/EFlags/RFlags register with the new value from the stack.

Miscellaneous instructions

There are a few instructions without any particular category assigned to them, which are as follows:

- **Load effective address** (**LEA**): This instruction calculates the effective address specified with one of the processor's addressing modes in the source operand and stores it in the destination operand. It is also frequently used instead of the ADD instruction when terms are specified as parts of the addressing mode. The following example code shows both cases:

```
lea eax, [some_label] ; EAX will contain the address of some_label
lea eax, [ebx + edi] ; EAX will contain the sum of EBX and EDI
```

- **No operation** (**NOP**): As the name states, this instruction performs no operation and is often used for filling the gaps between aligned procedures.
- **Processor identification** (**CPUID**): Depending on the value of the operand (in EAX), this instruction returns CPU identification information. This instruction is available only if the ID flag in the EFlags register (bit 21) is set.

FPU instructions

FPU instructions are executed by the x87 **floating-point unit** (**FPU**) and operate on floating point, integer, or binary coded decimal values. These instructions are grouped by their purpose:

- FPU data transfer instructions
- FPU basic arithmetic instructions
- FPU comparison instructions
- FPU load constant instructions
- FPU control instructions

Another important aspect of the FPU operation is the fact that, unlike the registers of the processor, floating point registers are organized in the form of a stack. Instructions like `fld` are used to push the operand onto the top of the stack, instructions like `fst` are used for reading a value from the top of the stack, and instructions like `fstp` are used for popping the value from the top of the stack and moving other values toward the top.

The following example shows the calculation of the circumference for a circle with radius of 0.2345:

```
; This goes in '.text' section
fld     [radius]      ; Load radius to ST0
                      ; ST0 <== 0.2345
fldpi                 ; Load PI to ST0
                      ; ST1 <== ST0
                      ; ST0 <== 3.1415926
fmulp                 ; Multiply (ST0 * ST1) and pop
                      ; ST0 = 0.7367034
fadd    st0, st0      ; * 2
                      ; ST0 = 1.4734069
fstp    [result]      ; Store result
                      ; result <== ST0

; This goes in '.data' section
radius  dt  0.2345
result  dt  0.0
```

Extensions

Since the first Intel microprocessor, technology has significantly evolved and so has the complexity of the processor architecture. The initial set of instructions, although it was and still is quite powerful, is not enough for some tasks (and here we have to admit that the number of such tasks is growing as time goes by). The solution adopted by Intel is nice and quite user friendly: **Instruction Set Architecture Extensions (ISA Extensions)**. Intel has gone a long way from **MMX** (unofficially, **MultiMedia eXtension**) to SSE4.2, AVX, and AVX2 extensions, which introduced support for 256-bit data processing and AVX-512, which allows the processing of 512-bit data and extends the number of usable SIMD registers to 32. All of these are SIMD extensions, where SIMD stands for single instruction multiple data. In this section, we will particularly pay attention to the AES-NI extension and partially to SSE (which will be covered in more detail in Chapter 5, *Parallel Data Processing*).

AES-NI

AES-NI stands for **Advanced Encryption Standard New Instructions**, an extension initially proposed by Intel in 2008 for speeding up AES algorithm implementations.

The following code checks whether AES-NI is supported by the CPU:

```
mov   eax, 1      ; CPUID request code #1
cpuid
```

```
test ecx, 1 shl 25   ; Check bit 25
jz not_supported     ; If bit 25 is not set - CPU does not support AES-NI
```

Instructions in this extension are rather simple and few:

- **AESENC**: This performs one round of AES encryption on 128-bit data using a 128-bit round key for all encryption rounds except the last round
- **AESENCLAST**: This performs the last round of AES encryption on 128-bit data
- **AESDEC**: This performs one round of AES decryption on 128-bit data using a 128-bit round key for all decryption rounds except the last round
- **AESDECLAST**: This performs the last round of AES decryption on 128-bit data
- **AESKEYGENASSIST**: This assists in the generation of an AES round key using an 8-bit round constant (RCON)
- **AESIMC**: This performs the inverse mix column transformation on a 128-bit round key

SSE

SSE stands for Streaming SIMD Extension, which allows, as the name suggest, processing of multiple data with a single instruction, which is best seen in the following example code:

```
lea   esi, [fnum1]
movq  xmm0, [esi]    ; Load fnum1 and fnum2 into xmm0 register
add   esi, 8
movq  xmm1, [esi]    ; Load fnum3 and fnum4 into xmm1 register
addps xmm0, xmm1     ; Add two floats in xmm1 to another two floats in xmm0
                     ; xmm0 will then contain:
                     ; 0.0  0.0  1.663  12.44


fnum1  dd 0.12
fnum2  dd 1.24
fnum3  dd 12.32
fnum4  dd 0.423
```

Example program

As you have noticed, the previous two sections (AES-NI and SSE) were left without proper examples. The reason is that the best way to demonstrate the abilities of both extensions would be to mix them in a single program. In this section, we will implement a simple AES-128 encryption algorithm with the help of the two. AES encryption is one the classic examples of an algorithm that would definitely benefit from parallel processing of data offered by SSE.

We will use the templates we prepared in the beginning of this chapter, thus, all we have to do is write the following code in place of this comment:

```
;
; Put your code here
;
```

The code runs equally well on both Windows and Linux, so no other preparations required:

```
; First of all we have to expand the key
; into AES key schedule.
lea esi, [k]
movups xmm1, [esi]
lea edi, [s]

; Copy initial key to schedule
mov ecx, 4
rep movsd
; Expand the key
call aes_set_encrypt_key

; Actually encrypt data
lea esi, [s] ; ESI points to key schedule
lea edi, [r] ; EDI points to result buffer
lea eax, [d] ; EAX points to data we want
             ; to encrypt
movups xmm0, [eax] ; Load this data to XMM0

; Call the AES128 encryption procedure
call aes_encrypt

; Nicely terminate the process
push 0
call [exitProcess]


; AES128 encryption procedure
aes_encrypt: ; esi points to key schedule
             ; edi points to output buffer
             ; xmm0 contains data to be encrypted
   mov ecx, 9
   movups xmm1, [esi]
   add esi, 0x10
   pxor xmm0, xmm1            ; Add the first round key

.encryption_loop:
   movups xmm1, [esi]         ; Load next round key
   add esi, 0x10
```

```
    aesenc xmm0, xmm1          ; Perform encryption round
    loop .encryption_loop

    movups xmm1, [esi]         ; Load last round key
    aesenclast xmm0, xmm1      ; Perform the last encryption round

    lea edi, [r]
    movups [edi], xmm0         ; Store encrypted data
    ret

; AES128 key setup procedures
; This procedure creates full
; AES128 encryption key schedule
aes_set_encrypt_key: ; xmm1 contains the key
                     ; edi points to key schedule
    aeskeygenassist xmm2, xmm1, 1
    call key_expand
    aeskeygenassist xmm2, xmm1, 2
    call key_expand
    aeskeygenassist xmm2, xmm1, 4
    call key_expand
    aeskeygenassist xmm2, xmm1, 8
    call key_expand
    aeskeygenassist xmm2, xmm1, 0x10
    call key_expand
    aeskeygenassist xmm2, xmm1, 0x20
    call key_expand
    aeskeygenassist xmm2, xmm1, 0x40
    call key_expand
    aeskeygenassist xmm2, xmm1, 0x80
    call key_expand
    aeskeygenassist xmm2, xmm1, 0x1b
    call key_expand
    aeskeygenassist xmm2, xmm1, 0x36
    call key_expand
    ret

key_expand: ; xmm2 contains key portion
            ; edi points to place in schedule
            ; where this portion should
            ; be stored at
    pshufd xmm2, xmm2, 0xff     ; Set all elements to 4th element
    vpslldq xmm3, xmm1, 0x04    ; Shift XMM1 4 bytes left
                               ; store result to XMM3
    pxor xmm1, xmm3
    vpslldq xmm3, xmm1, 0x04
    pxor xmm1, xmm3
    vpslldq xmm3, xmm1, 0x04
```

```
pxor xmm1, xmm3
pxor xmm1, xmm2
movups [edi], xmm1
add edi, 0x10
ret
```

The following should be placed in the data section/segment:

```
; Data to be encrypted
d db 0, 1, 2, 3, 4, 5, 6, 7, 8, 9, 0xa,0xb, 0xc, 0xd, 0xe, 0xf

; Encryption key
k db 1, 1, 1, 1, 1, 1, 1, 1, 1, 1, 1, 1, 1, 1, 1, 1

; AES key schedule (11 round keys, 16 bytes each)
s rb 16 * 11

; Result will be placed here
r rb 16
```

Summary

We began this chapter with creation of two templates--one for a 32-bit Windows executable and the other for a 32-bit Linux executable. While there are certain parts of both templates that may still be unclear, let that bother you not, as we will cover each and every aspect thereof when the time comes. You may use these templates as a skeleton for your own code.

The most significant part of the chapter, however, was dedicated to the Intel Instruction Set Architecture itself. It was, of course, a very brief overview as there was no need to describe each and every instruction--Intel did the job releasing their Programmer's Manual, which contains over three thousand pages. Instead, a decision was made to provide only the basic information and help us achieve certain level of acquaintance with Intel instruction set.

We ended the chapter by implementing the AES128 encryption algorithm with the aid of AES-NI extension, which makes the process of AES128 encryption/decryption significantly simpler and easier.

Now, when we understand the instructions, we are ready to proceed further to the memory organization and data and code addressing modes.

4
Memory Addressing Modes

Thus far, we have gained some acquaintance with certain basic aspects of Assembly programming. We have covered the Intel Architecture basics, setting up the development environment of your choice, and the **instruction set architecture (ISA)**.

We know what operations we are able to perform over different types of data, but all this is of very little value as long as we don't know how to retrieve and store data. Of course, we are familiar with the mov instruction, but without knowing how to address the data in memory, this instruction is quite useless.

Fortunately for us, Intel provides a very flexible mechanism for addressing data or code in memory. In this chapter, we will cover the following modes of memory addressing:

- Sequential addressing
- Direct addressing
  - Via an immediate address
  - Via an address stored in a register
- Indirect addressing
  - Via an address pointed by immediate
  - Via an address pointed by a register
- Base relative addressing
  - Base + index
  - Base + index * scale
- IP/RIP-based addressing
- Far pointers

The preceding categorization has nothing to do with the way Intel categorizes addressing modes as we are not paying attention to address encoding within an instruction. Knowing the ways to address memory and being able to use them appropriately is what we are after. It is worth mentioning that the preceding list represents addressing modes for both data and code. Additionally, we will use 64-bit examples in this chapter in order to be able to cover all of the modes listed here.

Addressing code

When we say "addressing code," we mean the way CPU interprets the address of the next instruction to be executed, and that depends on the logic of the code itself, which tells the processor whether it should execute instructions sequentially or jump to another location.

Sequential addressing

The default addressing mode for code is **sequential addressing**, when the **instruction pointer** (**IP**) register (IP for 32-bit systems and RIP for 64-bit) contains the address of the instruction following the one being currently executed. There is nothing we need to do in order to put processor into this mode. The instruction pointer is set to the next instruction automatically by the CPU.

For example, when executing the first instruction of the following code, the IP is already set to the address of the next one, labeled as `next_instruction`. As the first instruction is `call`, which, as we know, causes the return address to be pushed onto the stack--which, in this particular case, is also the address of `next_instruction`--the second one (the `pop` instruction) retrieves the value of the return address from the stack:

```
    call next_instruction
next_instruction:
    pop rax
    ; the rest of the code
```

The preceding example (or its variations) could be met in the code of different packers and protectors very often and is also used by shellcode writers as a mean of creation of position-independent code, where addresses of procedures and variables can be calculated by adding their offsets from `next_instruction` to the address of `next_instruction`.

Direct addressing

The term *direct addressing* implies the address to be directly included in the instruction is an operand. One of the examples may be a *far call/jmp*. Most of Windows, executables are loaded at address 0x00400000 with the first section, which is by default the code section being loaded at address `0x00401000`. For the sake of the example, let us imagine that we have an executable which, we are sure, is loaded at the aforementioned address, with its code section being located at offset 0x1000 from the base address (the address our executable is loaded at), and we have some sort of a special code right in the beginning of the first section. Let it be an error handler that would terminate the execution of our program in the right way. In such a case, we may direct the execution flow to that code by using either a far call or a far jump:

```
; The following call would be encoded as (address is underlined):
; 0xff 0x1d 0x00 0x10 0x40 0x00
call far [0x00401000]

; or as
; 0xff 0x2d 0x00 0x10 0x40 0x00
jmp far [0x00401000]
```

However, the more common example would be the register call, where the target address is stored in a register:

```
lea rax, [my_proc]
call rax
```

In the preceding code, we loaded the RAX register with the address of the `my_proc` procedure that we want to call on the first line, and the second line is the call itself. Such a mode is used, for example, by compilers when translating the `switch` clause to Assembly, when the address of the code corresponding to a specific case is either loaded from the jump table or calculated using some hardcoded base (it may well be relocated at execution time) and an offset taken from the jump table.

Indirect addressing

The term "indirect addressing" is quite self-explanatory. As the name of the mode suggests, the address is somewhere in there, but is not used directly. Instead, it is referenced by a pointer, which may be a register or certain base address (immediate address). For example, the following code calls the same procedure twice. In the first call, the address is retrieved using a pointer stored in the `rax` register, while in the second call we use a variable that stores the address of the procedure we want to call:

```
; This goes into code section
push my_proc
lea    rax, [rsp]
call   qword [rax]
add   rsp, 8
call   qword [my_proc_address]
;
;
my_proc:
     ret

; This goes into data section
my_proc_address dq my_proc
```

As we can see, in both cases, the operand of the `call` instruction is a pointer to a location in memory, where the address of the `my_proc` procedure is stored. This addressing mode may be used in order to harden the obfuscation of the execution flow of a code fragment.

RIP based addressing

IP or RIP (depending on whether we are on a 32-bit or a 64-bit platform) means addressing relative to the instruction pointer register.

The best example of this addressing mode would be the `call` and `jmp` instructions. For example, consider the following code:

```
call my_proc
 ; or
 jmp some_label
```

This will not contain the addresses of `my_proc` or `some_label`. Instead, the `call` instruction would be encoded in such a way that its parameter would be the offset from the following instruction to `my_proc`. As we know, the instruction pointer register contains the address of the following instruction at the time the processor executes the current one; therefore, we may surely say that the target address is calculated relative to the value of the instruction pointer (IP on 32-bit or RIP on 64-bit platform).

The same rule applies to the `jmp` instruction in the preceding example--the target address is calculated relative to the current value of the instruction pointer, which contains the address of the following instruction.

Addressing data

Data addressing modes are the same as those for code addressing, with the exception of IP-based addressing on 32-bit systems.

Sequential addressing

Yes, this is not a typo, there is sequential addressing when it comes to addressing data as well, although it does require certain setup.

Remember the RSI/RDI pair (or ESI/EDI for 32-bit systems), which we have mentioned in both Chapter 1, *Intel Architecture*, and Chapter 3, *Intel Instruction Set Architecture (ISA)*. This pair is a good example of sequential data addressing, where the source and/or target addresses are incremented or decremented (depending on the value of the direction flag) automatically after each instruction that uses these registers (either one of them or both) has been executed.

The following example illustrates this mode by copying a text string from its location in the data section to a buffer allocated on the stack:

```
; This portion goes into the code section.
; Assuming the RBP register contains the stack frame address
; and the size of the frame is 0x50 bytes.
lea rdi, [rbp - 0x50]
lea rsi, [my_string]
mov ecx, my_string_len
rep movsb

; And this portion goes into the data section
my_string db 'Just some string',0
my_string_len = $ - my_string
```

As we see, the RDI register is loaded with the lowest address in the stack frame, the RSI register is loaded with the address of the string, and the RCX register is loaded with the length of the string, including the terminating zero. After that, each time the `rep movsb` line is executed, both the RSI and the RDI are sequentially incremented (the size of increment is dependent, as we remember, on the `movs*` variant--1 for `movsb`, 2 for `movsw`, 4 for `movsd`, and 8 for `movsq` on a 64-bit platform).

Direct addressing

Just as in the case of code addressing, this mode implies that the address of either the source or destination operand (depending on the instruction and intention) is explicitly specified. However, unlike code addressing, we are able to specify the address itself, except when loading it into a register first. Consider the example of loading the value of a variable into a register or storing it from register to memory:

```
mov al, [name_of_variable]
; or
mov [name_of_another_variable], eax
```

In both cases, `name_of_variable` and `name_of_another_variable` are translated by the assembler into the addresses of those variables. Of course, we may also use registers for this purpose. The following example illustrates an `if...else` clause:

```
; This goes into code section.
    xor  rax, rax
    ; inc rax                          ; Increment RAX in order to call the
second procedure
    lea  rbx, [indices]
    add  rax, rbx
    lea  rbx, [my_proc_address]
    add  bl, [rax]
    mov  rbx, [rbx]
    call qword rbx
    ; The rest of the code

  align 8
my_proc0:
    push rbp
    mov  rbp, rsp
    xor  eax, eax
    mov  rsp, rbp
    pop  rbp
    ret

  align 8
my_proc1:
    push rbp
    mov  rbp, rsp
    xor  eax, eax
    inc  eax
    mov  rsp, rbp
    pop  rbp
    ret

; And the following goes into data section
indices             db 0, 8
  align 8
  my_proc_address       dq my_proc0, my_proc1
```

The first line of the code sets the `rax` register to zero, which, when the second line is commented out, causes the code to call `my_proc0`. On the other hand, if we uncomment the `inc rax` instruction, then `my_proc1` would be called instead.

Scale, index, base, and displacement

This is a very flexible addressing mode as it allows us to address memory in a manner similar to addressing data within arrays, which we are all familiar with. Despite the fact that this addressing mode is often referred to as scale/index/base (omitting the displacement part), we are not forced to make use of all of its elements at once, and we will further see that the scale/index/base/displacement scheme often gets reduced to base, base + index, or displacement + index. The latter two may come with or without scale. But, first of all, let's see who is who and which part represents what:

- **Displacement**: Technically, this is an integer offset relative to a certain segment base (DS by default).
- **Base**: This is a register containing the offset to data relative to the displacement, or the address of the start of the data if no displacement was specified (in fact, when we do not specify displacement, the assembler adds a displacement of zero).
- **Index**: This is a register containing the offset into the data relative to base + displacement. This is similar to an index or an array member.
- **Scale**: The CPU has no concept of type of data; it only understands sizes. Therefore, if we are operating on values larger than 1 byte, we have to scale the index value appropriately. The scale may be 1, 2, 4, or 8 for bytes, words, double words, or quad words, respectively. Obviously, there is no reason to explicitly specify the scale of 1, as it is the default value if no scale is specified.

It is possible to explicitly specify another segment by prepending the segment prefix to the address (for example, `cs:` for CS, `es:` for ES, and so on).

In order to calculate the final address, the processor takes the segment's base address (the default is DS), adds displacement, adds base and finalizes the calculation by adding the index times scale:

*segment base address + displacement + base + index * scale*

In theory, all of this looks nice and easy, so let's advance toward practice, which is nicer and much easier too. If we take another look at the example code for direct addressing, we may see that it contains a few completely redundant lines. The following would be the first one for us to deal with:

```
mov rbx, [rbx]
```

Although it provides a good example of register-based direct addressing, it may be safely removed, and the following instruction (`call`) should then be changed to (remember the indirect call?):

```
call qword [rbx]
```

However, even this line may be omitted just like most of the caller code. Taking a closer look at the problem, we see that there is an array of procedure pointers (in fact, an array of two). In terms of a high-level language, C for example, what the preceding code is intended to do is as follows:

```c
int my_proc0()
{
    return 0;
}

int my_proc1()
{
    return 1;
}

int call_func(int selector)
{
    int (*funcs[])(void) = {my_proc0, my_proc1};
    return funcs[selector]();
}
```

The Intel architecture provides a similar interface for addressing data/code in an array-like fashion of base + index, yet it introduces another member of the equation--scale. As the assembler and, especially, the processor do not care about types of data we are operating, we have to help them with it ourselves.

While the base part (whether it is a label or a register holding an address) is treated by the processor as an address in memory, and index is simply a number of bytes to add to that base address, in this particular case, we may, of course, scale the index ourselves, as the algorithm is fairly simple. We only have two possible values for the selector (which is the `rax` register in the preceding Assembly code), 0 and 1, so we load, for example, the `rbx` register with the address of `my_proc_address`:

```
lea rbx, [my_proc_address]
```

Then, we shift the `rax` register three times left (doing this is equivalent to multiplying by 8 as we are on 64-bit and addresses are 8 bytes long, and as we would point into the second byte of address of `my_proc0` otherwise) and add the result to the `rbx` register. This may be good for a single iteration, but not very convenient for a code that gets executed very frequently. Even if we use an additional register to store the sum of `rbx` and `rax`--what if we need that other register for something else?

This is where the scale part comes into play. Rewriting the calling code from the Assembly example would result in the following:

```
xor rax, rax
; inc rax                     ; increment RAX to call the second procedure
lea rbx, [my_proc_address]
call qword [rbx + rax * 8]

; or even a more convenient one

xor rax, rax
; inc rax
call qword[my_proc_address + rax * 8]
```

Of course, the base/index/scale mode may be used for addressing any type of array, not necessarily an array of function pointers.

RIP addressing

RIP-based (instruction pointer register on a 64-bit platform) addressing of data was introduced with the 64-bit architecture and allows generation of a more compact code. This addressing mode follows the same idea as the base/index/scale mode, while the instruction pointer is used as the base.

For example, if want to load a certain register with the address of a variable, we would write the following line in Assembly:

```
lea rbx, [my_variable]
```

The assembler would then do all the adjustments automatically, and the result encoding of the instruction would be equivalent to this:

```
lea rbx, [rip + (my_variable - next_instruction)]
```

Loading the `rbx` register with the value of the `rip` register (the address of the following instruction) plus the offset in bytes of a variable from the address of the following instruction.

Far pointers

It may be relatively safe to say that far pointers belong to the past when it comes to the application development level; however, it would not be right not to mention them here, as, after all, there are a few useful things we can do with it. Putting it simply, a far pointer combines a segment selector and an offset into the segment. Originating in the era of 16-bit modes of operation, surviving the 32-bit protected mode, far pointers have made it to the long mode, although they are hardly relevant, as, especially in long mode, all memory is considered to be a flat array and we are hardly going to use them.

The instructions used (some are obsolete) for loading a far pointer into the segment register: general-purpose register pairs are as follows:

- **LDS**: This loads the selector part of the far pointer into the DS
- **LSS**: This loads the selector part of the far pointer into the SS
- **LES**: This loads the selector part of the far pointer into the ES
- **LFS**: This loads the selector part of the far pointer into the FS
- **LGS**: This loads the selector part of the far pointer into the GS

However, let's see how we can make use of them anyway. For the sake of simplicity, we will consider a short 32-bit example for Windows, where we are obtaining the address of the **Process Environment Block (PEB)**:

```
; This goes into the code section
mov    word [far_ptr + 4], fs    ; Store FS selector to the selector part of
the far_ptr
lgs    edx, [far_ptr]            ; Load the pointer
mov    eax, [gs:edx]             ; Load EAX with the address of the TIB
mov    eax, [eax + 0x30]         ; Load EAX with the address of the PEB

; This goes into the data section
far_ptr    dp 0                  ; Six bytes far pointer:
                                 ;     four bytes offset
                                 ;     two bytes segment selector
```

As you may see, the code in this example is quite redundant as we already have the proper selector loaded into the FS register, but it still illustrates the mechanism. In the real world, no one would've gone this way in order to obtain the address of PEB; instead, the following instruction would have been issued:

```
mov    eax, [fs:0x30]
```

This would have loaded the `eax` register with the address of the PEB, as `fs:0x00000000` is already the far pointer pointing to TIB.

 The instructions LDS and LES (for use with the DS and ES registers, respectively) are obsolete.

Summary

In this chapter, we had a brief introduction to addressing modes on the modern Intel CPU. Some resources define more addressing modes, but, let me reiterate that as a huge fan of Occam's Razor, I do not see any reason to multiply things without need, as most of those additional modes are just variations of the modes already explained above.

Thus far, we saw how both code and data may be addressed, which is mostly the essence of programming in the Assembly language. As you will witness while reading this book and trying the code yourself, at least 90% of writing a program in Assembly is writing how you want some data to be moved, where from and where to (the remaining 10% are actual operations on data).

By getting this far, we are ready to dive deeper into Assembly programming and try to actually write working programs, rather than typing a few lines into a template and watching registers change in the debugger.

The next section of this book, the *Practical Assembly* section, begins with a chapter dedicated to parallel data processing. Then, you will learn the basics of macros and get acquainted with data structures manipulation mechanisms, and we will see how our Assembly code can interact with the surrounding operating system, which is quite important.

5
Parallel Data Processing

I remember sitting in front of my ZX Spectrum with 64 KB of memory (16 KB ROM + 48 KB RAM) with an old tape recorder plugged in, and a newly bought cassette inserted. Among the relatively large amount of programs on the cassette, there was one that specifically drew my attention. Not that it was able to do anything special; after all, it simply computed personal biorhythm graphs based on the date of birth (in fact, I had to enter the current date too) and plotted them on the screen. There wasn't even any sophistication in the algorithm (how ever sophisticated an algorithm may be when it is all about calculation of sine over some value). What seemed to be interesting was the **Wait while results are being processed** message, which had some kind of a progress bar that appeared for for almost half a minute (yes, I was naive enough to think that some calculations were really taking place "behind" the message), and the three graphs being plotted simultaneously. Well, it looked as if they were being plotted simultaneously.

The program was written in BASIC, so reversing it was a fairly easy task. Easy but disappointing. Of course, there was no parallel processing when plotting the graphs, simply the same function, sequentially called for each graph on each point.

Obviously, the ZX Spectrum was not the right platform to look for parallel processing capabilities. Intel architecture, on the other hand, provides us with such a mechanism. In this chapter, we will examine a few capabilities provided by the **Streaming SIMD Extension (SSE)**, which allows simultaneous computations on the so-called packed integers, the packed single precision or packed double precision floating point numbers that are contained in 128-bit registers.

We will begin the chapter with a brief introduction to the SSE technology, reviewing available registers and access modes thereof. Later, we will proceed to the implementation of the algorithm itself, which involves parallel operations of single precision floating point values related to all three biorhythms.

Some steps, which are essential for biorhythmic graph calculation and are trivial when implemented in high-level languages, like calculation of sine, exponentiation, and factorial, will be covered in more detail, as we do not have access (at this moment) to any math library; hence, we have no ready-to-use implementation of the procedures involved in the aforementioned calculations. We will make our own implementation for each step.

SSE

The Intel Pentium II processor brought along the **MMX** technology (unofficially called the **MultiMedia eXtension**, however, such an alias has never been used in Intel documentation), which provided us with the possibility of working with packed integer data using 64-bit registers. Despite the obvious benefit, there were at least two disadvantages:

- We could process integer data only
- The MMX registers were mapped onto the registers of the **floating-point unit (FPU)**

While being better than nothing, the MMX technology still did not provide enough computational power.

The situation changed a lot with the introduction of the Pentium III processor with its Streaming SIMD Extension with its own set of 128-bit registers and instructions, allowing a wide range of operations to be performed on scalar or packed bytes, 32-bit integers, 32-bit single precision floating-point values, or 64-bit double precision floating point values.

Registers

Intel-based processors have 8 XMM registers for use with SSE, which are named XMM0 to XMM7 on 32-bit platforms, and 16 XMM registers, named XMM0 to XMM15, on 64-bit platforms. It is important to note that only 8 XMM registers are available on 64-bit platforms while not in long mode.

The content of each of the XMM registers may be considered to be one of the types below:

- 16 bytes (which we saw in the AES-NI implementation)
- Eight 16-bit words
- Four 32-bit double words

- Four 32-bit single precision floating-point numbers (we will use the registers this way throughout the chapter)
- Two 64-bit quad words
- Two 64-bit double precision floating point numbers

SSE instructions are able to operate on the same parts of registers that are used as operands and on different parts of the operands (for example, they can move the lower part of the source register to the higher part of the destination register).

Revisions

There are, at the moment, five revisions of the SSE instruction set (and hence of the technology), which are as follows:

- **SSE**: This was introduced in 1999 and contained the initial design of the technology and instructions thereof
- **SSE2**: This revision came out with Pentium 4 and brought 144 new instructions with it
- **SSE3**: Although only 13 new instructions were added with SSE3, they introduced the ability to perform the so-called "horizontal" operations (operations performed on a single register)
- **SSSE3**: This introduced 16 new instructions, including the instructions for horizontal integer operations
- **SSE4**: This brought another 54 instructions, thus making life significantly easier for developers

Biorhythm calculator

I have mentioned it before and I would like to reiterate that, in my eyes, the best way to understand and learn things is by example. We began this chapter by mentioning an old program for biorhythm level calculation and it seems that this program, when implemented using the SSE architecture, may be a simple yet good example of how parallel calculations may be performed. The code in the next section demonstrates biorhythms calculations for my humble self for the period between May 9, 2017 and May 29, 2017, storing results into a table. All calculations (including exponentiation and sine) are implemented using SSE instructions and, obviously, XMM registers.

The idea

The word "biorhythm" originates from two Greek words; "bios", meaning life and "rhythmos", meaning rhythm. The idea itself was developed by Wilhelm Fliess, a German otolaryngologist, who lived in the late nineteenth and the beginning of the twentieth centuries. He believed that our life is influenced by biological cycles, which affect the mental, physical, and emotional aspects.

Fliess derived three major biorhythmic cycles:

- **Physical cycle**
  Duration: 23 days
  Denotes:
    - Coordination
    - Strength
    - Well-being

- **Emotional cycle**
  Duration: 28 days
  Denotes:
    - Creativity
    - Sensitivity
    - Mood
    - Awareness

- **Intellectual cycle**
  Duration: 33 days
  Denotes:
    - Alertness
    - Analytical and logical abilities
    - Communication

The theory itself may be quite arguable, especially since it is considered pseudoscience by most of scientific public; however, it is scientific enough to, at least, serve for an example of a parallel data processing mechanism.

The algorithm

The algorithm of biorhythm calculation is fairly simple, not to say trivial.

Variable values, used to specify the rate of each biorhythm at specific date, are in the (-1.0, 1.0) range and are calculated using this formula:

$$x = sin((2 * PI * t) / T)$$

Here, *t* is the number of days that have passed since the date of the person's birth till the date we want to know the biorhythms' values for (most likely, the current date), and *T* is the period of a given biorhythm.

There aren't too many things we may optimize with the aid of the SSE technology. What we definitely can do is calculate data for all three types of biorhythms at once, which in turn is sufficient to demonstrate the abilities and power of the Streaming SIMD Extension.

Data section

As there is no specific order of sections in the source file, we will begin with a quick look at the data section in order to better comprehend the code. The data section or, to be more precise, the arrangement of data in a data section, is quite self-explanatory. The emphasis was made on data alignment, allowing faster access with aligned SSE instructions:

```
section '.data' data readable writeable
    ; Current date and birth date
    ; The dates are arranged in a way most suitable
    ; for use with XMM registers
    cday    dd 9                ; Current day of the month
    cyear   dd 2017             ; Current year
    bday    dd 16               ; Birth date day of the month
    byear   dd 1979             ; Birth year

    cmonth  dd 5                ; 1-based number of current month
            dd 0
    bmonth  dd 1                ; 1-based number of birth month
            dd 0


    ; These values are used for calculation of days
    ; in both current and birth dates
    dpy     dd 1.0
            dd 365.25
```

```
        ; This table specifies number of days since the new year
        ; till the first day of specified month.
        ; Table's indices are zero based
monthtab:
        dd 0   ; January
        dd 31  ; February
        dd 59  ; March
        dd 90  ; April
        dd 120 ; May
        dd 151 ; June
        dd 181 ; July
        dd 212 ; August
        dd 243 ; September
        dd 273 ; October
        dd 304 ; November
        dd 334 ; December


  align 16
  ; Biorhythmic periods
  T       dd 23.0 ; Physical
          dd 28.0 ; Emotional
          dd 33.0 ; Intellectual


  pi_2    dd 6.28318 ; 2xPI - used in formula


  align 16
  ; Result storage
  ; Arranged as table:
  ; Physical : Emotional : Intellectual : padding
  output  rd 20 * 4


; '.idata' section: contains import information,
; is readable, is writeable
section '.idata' import data readable writeable

; 'library' macro from 'win32a.inc' creates
; proper entry for importing
; functions from a dynamic link library.
; For now it is only 'kernel32.dll'.
library kernel, 'kernel32.dll'

; 'import' macro creates the actual entries
; for functions we want to import from a dynamic link library
import kernel,\
 exitProcess, 'ExitProcess'
```

The code

We will begin with the standard template for 32-bit Windows (if you are on Linux, you may safely use the Linux template instead).

Standard header

First of all, we tell the assembler what kind of output we expect, which is the GUI executable (although, it would be without any GUI), what our entrypoint is, and, of course, we include the `win32a.inc` file in order to be able to call the `ExitProcess()` Windows API. Then, we create the code section:

```
format PE GUI                              ; Specify output file format
entry _start                               ; Specify entry point
include 'win32a.inc'                       ; Include some macros
section '.text' code readable executable   ; Start code section
```

The main() function

The following is the analog of the C/C++ `main()` function, which controls the whole algorithm and is responsible for performing all the needed preparations as well as for the execution of the forecast calculation loop.

Data preparation steps

First of all, we need to make some tiny corrections to the dates (months are specified by their number). We are interested in the number of days since January 1 until the first day of a month. The easiest and fastest way to perform such correction would be using a small table with 12 entries, containing the number of days between January 1 and the first day of a month. The table is called `monthtab` and is located in the data section.

```
;;;;;;;;;;;;;;;;;;;;;;;;;;;;;;;;;;;;;;;;;;;;;;;;;;;;;;;;
;
; Entry point
;
;-------------------------------------------------------
_start:
    mov ecx, 20                    ; Length of biorhythm data to
                                   ; produce

    mov eax, [bmonth]              ; Load birth month
    dec eax                        ; Decrement it in order to address
                                   ; 0-based array
```

```
    mov eax, [monthtab + eax * 4]    ; Replace month with number of days
                                     ; since New Year
    mov [bmonth], eax                ; Store it back

    mov eax, [cmonth]                ; Do the same for current month
    dec eax
    mov eax, [monthtab + eax * 4]
    mov [cmonth], eax

    xor eax, eax                     ; Reset EAX as we will use it as counter
```

The preceding code illustrates this very fix being applied:

- We read the month number from the birth date
- Decrement it as the table we are using is in fact a 0-based array of values
- Replace the original month number with the value read from the table

 By the way, the addressing mode used when reading a value from the table is a variation of the scale/index/base/displacement. As we may see, `monthtab` is the displacement, `eax` register holds the index and 4 is the scale.

The day/month/year of the two dates are specifically pre-arranged to fit properly in the XMM registers and to ease calculations. It may seem that the first line of the following code loads the value of `cday` into XMM0, but, in fact, the instruction being used loads `xmmword` (128-bit data type) starting from the address of `cday`, meaning that it loads four values into XMM0:

bits 96 - 127	bits 64 - 95	bits 32 - 63	bits 0 - 31
byear	bday	cyear	cday
1979	16	2017	9

Data representation in the XMM0 register

Similarly, the second `movaps` loads XMM1 register with four double words starting at address of `cmonth`:

bits 96 - 127	bits 64 - 95	bits 32 - 63	bits 0 - 31
0	bmonth	0	cmonth
0	0	0	120

Data representation in the XMM1 register

As we can see, placing the two tables directly one above the other and thinking of them as XMM registers 0 and 1, we have `cmonth`/`cday` and `bmonth`/`bday` loaded to the same double words in both XMM0 and XMM1. We will see why such an arrangement of the data was so important in a few moments.

The `movaps` instruction is only able to move data between two XMM registers or an XMM register and a 16 bytes aligned memory location. You should use `movups` for accessing unaligned memory locations.

In the last two lines of the following code fragment, we convert the values we have just loaded from double words to single precision float numbers:

```
    movaps xmm0, xword[cday]     ; Load the day/year parts of both dates
    movapd xmm1, xword[cmonth]   ; Load number of days since Jan 1st for both
dates
    cvtdq2ps xmm0, xmm0          ; Convert loaded values to single precision
floats
    cvtdq2ps xmm1, xmm1
```

We still have not finished conversion of dates into the amount of days, as years are still, well, years, and the number in days of a month and the number of days since January 1st for both dates are still stored separately. All we have to do before summation of the days for each date is multiply each year by 365.25 (where 0.25 is a compensation for leap years). However, parts of the XMM registers cannot be accessed separately, as with parts of general purpose registers (for example, there is no analog to AX, AH, AL in EAX). We can, however, manipulate parts of XMM registers by using special instructions. In the first line of the following code fragment we load the lower 64-bit part of XMM2 register with two float values stored at `dpy` (days per year). The aforementioned values are `1.0` and `365.25`. What does 1.0 have to do with it, you may ask, and the answer is shown in the following table:

bits 96 - 127	bits 64 - 95	bits 32 - 63	bits 0 - 31	register name
1979.0	16.0	2017.0	9.0	XMM0
0.0	0.0	0.0	120.0	XMM1
0.0	0.0	365.25	1.0	XMM2

Content of XMM0 - XMM2 registers

Packed operations on XMM registers (packed means operations on more than one value) are, most of the time, performed in columns. Thus, in order to multiply `2017.0` by `365.25`, we need to multiply XMM2 by XMM0. However, we must not forget about `1979.0` either, and the easiest way to multiply both `2017.0` and `1979.0` by `365.25` with a single instruction is to copy the content of the lower part of XMM2 register to its upper part with the `movlhps` instruction.

```
movq xmm2, qword[dpy]    ; Load days per year into lower half of XMM2
movlhps xmm2, xmm2       ; Duplicate it to the upper half
```

After these instructions the content of the XMM0 - XMM2 registers should look like this:

bits 96 - 127	bits 64 - 95	bits 32 - 63	bits 0 - 31	register name
1979.0	16.0	2017.0	9.0	XMM0
0.0	0.0	0.0	120.0	XMM1
365.25	1.0	365.25	1.0	XMM2

Content of XMM0 - XMM2 registers after movlhps

Use `pinsrb`/`pinsrd`/`pinsrq` instructions for insertions of individual bytes/double words/quad words into an XMM register when needed. They are not used in our code for the purpose of demonstration of horizontal operations.

Now we are safe to proceed with multiplication and summation:

```
addps xmm1, xmm0       ; Summation of day of the month with days since
January 1st
mulps xmm2, xmm1       ; Multiplication of years by days per year
haddps xmm2, xmm2      ; Final summation of days for both dates
hsubps xmm2, xmm2      ; Subtraction of birth date from current date
```

The preceding code first calculates the total number of days since January 1 up to the day of the month for both dates on the first line. On the second line, at last, it multiplies the years of both dates by the number of days per year. This line also explains why the days per year value was accompanied by `1.0`--as we are multiplying XMM1 by XMM2 and we do not want to lose the previously calculated number of days, we simply multiply the number of days since January 1st by `1.0`.

At this moment the content of the three XMM registers should be like this:

bits 96 - 127	bits 64 - 95	bits 32 - 63	bits 0 - 31	register name
1979.0	16.0	2017.0	9.0	XMM0
1979.0	16.0	2017.0	129.0	XMM1
722829.75	16.0	736709.25	129.0	XMM2

Content of XMM0 - XMM2 registers after addition of days and multiplication by days per year of relative parts of XMM2 and XMM1 registers

There are two remaining operations to perform:

- Finalize calculation of the total number of days for each date
- Subtract the earlier date from the later one

By this time, all of the values that we need to use in our calculations are stored in a single register, XMM2. Luckily, SSE3 introduced two important instructions:

- `haddps`: Horizontal addition of single-precision values
  Adds the single-precision floating-point values in the first and second and in third and fourth dwords of the destination operand, and stores the results in the first and second dwords of the destination operand respectively. The third and fourth dwords are overwritten with the results too, where the third dword contains the same value as the first dword and the fourth dword the same value as the second dword.
- `hsubps`: Horizontal subtraction of single-precision values
  Subtracts the single-precision floating-point value in the second dword of the destination operand from the first dword of the destination operand and the value of the fourth dword of the destination operand from the third dword, and stores the results into the first and second dwords and third and fourth dwords of the destination operand respectively.

Upon completion of `hsubps` instruction, the content of the registers should be:

bits 96 - 127	bits 64 - 95	bits 32 - 63	bits 0 - 31	register name
1979.0	16.0	2017.0	9.0	XMM0
1979.0	16.0	2017.0	129.0	XMM1
13992.5	13992.5	13992.5	13992.5	XMM2

Content of XMM0 - XMM2 registers after addition and later subtraction of values

As we see, the XMM2 register contains the number of days between the two dates (the date of birth and the current date) minus 1, as the day of birth itself is not included (this problem will be solved in the calculation loop);

```
movd xmm3, [dpy]         ; Load 1.0 into the lower double word of XMM3
movlhps xmm3, xmm3       ; Duplicate it to the third double word of XMM3
movsldup xmm3, xmm3      ; Duplicate it to the second and fourth double words
of XMM3
```

The preceding three lines set up the step value for our forecast by loading the double word stored at `dpy`, which is `1.0`, and propagate this value throughout the XMM3 register. We will be adding XMM3 to XMM2 for each new day of the forecast.

The following three lines are logically similar to the previous three; they set all four single precision floats of the XMM4 register to *2*PI*:

```
movd xmm4, [pi_2]
movlhps xmm4, xmm4
movsldup xmm4, xmm4
```

And the last step before entering the calculation loop: we load XMM1 with the lengths of the biorhythmic cycles and set the `eax` register to point to the location in the memory where we are going to store our output data (the forecast). Given the arrangement of data in the data section, the fourth single of the XMM1 register will be loaded with *2*PI*, but, since the fourth single is not going to be used in our calculations, we simply leave it as is. We could, however, zero it out with the value of `eax` by using the `pinsrd xmm1, eax, 3` instruction:

```
movaps xmm1, xword[T]
lea eax, [output]
```

At last we have all the data set up and ready for actual calculation of biorhythmic values for a given range of dates. The registers XMM0 to XMM4 should now have the following values:

bits 96 - 127	bits 64 - 95	bits 32 - 63	bits 0 - 31	register name
1979.0	16.0	2017.0	9.0	XMM0
6.2831802	33.0	28.0	23.0	XMM1
13992.5	13992.5	13992.5	13992.5	XMM2
1.0	1.0	1.0	1.0	XMM3
6.2831802	6.2831802	6.2831802	6.2831802	XMM4

Calculation loop

Once all the preparations are done, the calculation loop in which we generate our forecast is fairly simple. First of all we increment the number of days value, which has a dual purpose--during the first iteration, it solves the problem of the day of birth not being included and advances the current date one day during the remaining iterations.

The second instruction copies the XMM4 register to XMM0, which will be used for most of our calculations, and multiplies it with the number of days in XMM2 by the execution of the third instruction--which actually calculates the $(2*PI*t)$ part of the formula.

The fourth instruction completes the calculation of the value we need the sine of, by division of XMM0 by lengths of biorhythmic periods:

```
.calc_loop:
    addps xmm2, xmm3     ; Increment the number of days by 1.0
    movaps xmm0, xmm4    ; Set XMM0 to contain 2*PI values
    mulps xmm0, xmm2     ; Actually do the 2*PI*t
    divps xmm0, xmm1     ; And complete by (2*PI*t)/T
```

Now we need to calculate the sine for the resulting values, which is a bit problematic due to the algorithm we are going to use for sine computation and the relatively large numbers. The solution is simple--we need to normalize the values so they fit the $(0.0, 2*PI)$ range. This is implemented by the adjust() procedure:

```
    call adjust          ; Adjust values for sine computations
```

Having adjusted the values in XMM0 (ignore the value of the fourth part of XMM0 as it is irrelevant), we may now compute sine for each of the first three single-precision float parts of the register:

```
    call sin_taylor_series  ; Compute sine for each value
```

We store computed sine values to a table pointed by the eax register (since the table is aligned on a 16-bytes boundary, we are safe to use the movaps instruction, which is slightly faster than its movups counterpart). Then, we advance the table pointer by 16 bytes, decrement ECX, and keep looping while ECX is not 0 with the loop instruction.

When ECX reaches 0, we simply terminate the process:

```
movaps [eax], xmm0      ; Store the result of current iteration

add eax, 16
loop .calc_loop


push 0
call [exitProcess]
```

The table, by the end of the loop, should contain the following values:

Date	Physical (P)	Emotional (S)	Intellectual (I)	Irrelevant
May 9th, 2017	0.5195959	-0.9936507	0.2817759	-NAN
May 10th, 2017	0.2695642	-0.9436772	0.4582935	-NAN
May 11th, 2017	-8.68E-06	-0.8462944	0.6182419	-NAN
May 12th, 2017	-0.2698165	-0.7062123	0.7558383	-NAN
May 13th, 2017	-0.5194022	-0.5301577	0.8659862	-NAN
May 14th, 2017	-0.7308638	-0.3262038	0.9450649	-NAN
May 15th, 2017	-0.8879041	-0.1039734	0.9898189	-NAN
May 16th, 2017	-0.9790764	0.1120688	0.9988668	-NAN
May 17th, 2017	-0.9976171	0.3301153	0.9718016	-NAN
May 18th, 2017	-0.9420508	0.5320629	0.909602	-NAN
May 19th, 2017	-0.8164254	0.7071083	0.8145165	-NAN
May 20th, 2017	-0.6299361	0.8467072	0.6899831	-NAN
May 21st, 2017	-0.3954292	0.9438615	0.5407095	-NAN
May 22nd, 2017	-0.128768	0.9937283	0.3714834	-NAN
May 23rd, 2017	0.1362932	0.9936999	0.1892722	-NAN
May 24th, 2017	0.3983048	0.9438586	-8.68E-06	-NAN
May 25th, 2017	0.6310154	0.8467024	-0.18929	-NAN
May 26th, 2017	0.8170633	0.7069295	-0.371727	-NAN
May 27th, 2017	0.9422372	0.5320554	-0.5407244	-NAN
May 28th, 2017	0.9976647	0.3303373	-0.6901718	-NAN

Adjustment of sine input values

As we have seen, using SSE instructions is quite convenient and effective; although, as we were mostly loading data from memory to registers and moving it within the registers, we have not been able to see its actual effectiveness yet. There are two procedures called from the calculation loop that perform the actual computations. One of them is the adjust() procedure.

Due to the overall simplicity of the algorithm, and since each of the two procedures is called from exactly one place, we are not following any specific calling convention; instead, we're using the XMM0 register for passing the floating point values and the ECX register for passing integer parameters.

In the case of the `adjust()` procedure, we only have one parameter, which is already loaded into the XMM0 register, so we simply call the procedure:

```
;;;;;;;;;;;;;;;;;;;;;;;;;;;;;;;;;;;;;;;;;;;;;;;;;;;;;;;;
;
; Value adjustment before calculation of SIN()
; Parameter is in XMM0 register
; Return value is in XMM0 register
;-----------------------------------------------------
adjust:
    push ebp
    mov ebp, esp
    sub esp, 16 * 2        ; Create the stack frame for local variables
```

This is a standard way to create a stack frame for local variables and temporary storage of non-general-purpose registers used in the procedure by saving the stack pointer ESP/RSP in EBP/RBP registers (we are free to use other general-purpose registers). General-purpose registers may be saved on stack by issuing a push instruction right after the allocation of space for local variables. The allocation of space for local variables is performed by subtracting the overall size of variables from the ESP/RSP register.

Addressing the allocated space is shown in the following code:

```
        movups [ebp - 16], xmm1        ; Store XMM1 and XMM2 registers
        movups [ebp - 16 * 2], xmm2
```

In the preceding two lines, we temporarily store the content of the XMM1 and XMM2 registers as we are going to use them, but we need to preserve their values.

The adjustment of the input values is very simple and may be expressed by the following code in C:

```
    return v - 2*PI*floorf(v/(2*PI));
```

However, in C, we would have to call this function for every value (unless we use intrinsic functions), while in Assembly, we may adjust all three simultaneously with a few simple SSE instructions:

```
    movd xmm1, [pi_2]              ; Load singles of the XMM1 register with 2*PI
    movlhps xmm1, xmm1
    movsldup xmm1, xmm1
```

We are already familiar with the above sequence, which loads a double word into an XMM register and duplicates it to every single-precision float part of it. Here, we load *2*PI* into XMM1.

The following algorithm performs the actual calculations:

- We duplicate the input parameter into the XMM2 register
- Divide its singles by *2*PI*
- Round down the result (SSE has no floor or ceiling instructions, instead we may use `roundps` and specify the rounding mode in the third operand; in our case, we instruct the processor to, roughly speaking, round down)
- Multiply rounded down results by *2*PI*
- Subtract them from the initial value and get results that fit into the *(0.0, 2*PI)* range

and the Assembly implementation thereof is:

```
movaps xmm2, xmm0            ; Move the input parameter to XMM2
divps xmm2, xmm1             ; Divide its singles by 2*PI
roundps xmm2, xmm2, 1b       ; Floor the results
mulps xmm2, xmm1             ; Multiply floored results by 2*PI
subps xmm0, xmm2             ; Subtract resulting values from the
                            ; input parameter

movups xmm2, [ebp - 16 * 2] ; Restore the XMM2 and XMM1 registers
movups xmm1, [ebp - 16]

mov esp, ebp                 ; "Destroy" the stack frame and return
pop ebp
ret
```

The result of the last operation is already in XMM0, so we simply return from procedure to our calculation loop.

Computing sine

We hardly ever think about how sine or cosine are calculated without actually having a right-angled triangle with known lengths of each of the cathetus and the hypotenuse. There are at least two approaches to make those computations in a fast and efficient way:

- **CORDIC algorithm**: This stands for **COordinate Rotation DIgital Computer**. This one is implemented in simple calculators or primitive hardware devices.

- **Taylor series**: A fast approximation algorithm. It does not provide the exact value, but is definitely enough for our needs.

LIBC on the other hand uses a different algorithm, which we could implement here, but it would be much more than a simple example. Therefore, what we are using in our code is a simple implementation of the simplest approximation algorithm, which provides us with a nice precision (much nicer than we need in this program) of up to the sixth digit after the point--the Taylor series for trigonometric functions (also known as Maclaurin series).

The formula for sine computation using the Taylor series is as follows:

$$sin(x) = x - x^3/3! + x^5/5! - x^7/7! + x^9/9! \ldots$$

Here, the ellipsis denote an infinite function. However, we do not need to run it forever to obtain values of satisfactory precision (after all, we are only interested in 2 digits after the point), instead, we will run it for 8 iterations.

Just as with the `adjust()` procedure, we will not follow any specific calling convention and, since the parameter we need to compute sine for is already in XMM0, we will simply leave it there. The head of the the `sin_taylor_series` procedure does not contain anything new for us:

```
;;;;;;;;;;;;;;;;;;;;;;;;;;;;;;;;;;;;;;;;;;;;;;;;;;;;;;;
;
; Calculation of SIN() using the Taylor Series
; approximation:
; sin(x) = x - x^3/3! + x^5/5! - x^7/7! + x^9/9! ...
; Values to calculate the SIN() of are in XMM0 register
; Return values are in XMM0 register
;------------------------------------------------------
sin_taylor_series:
    push ebp                        ; Create stack frame for 5 XMM registers
    mov ebp, esp
    sub esp, 5 * 16
    push eax ecx                    ; Temporarily store EAX and ECX
    xor eax, eax                    ; and set them to 0
    xor ecx, ecx

    movups [ebp - 16], xmm1         ; Temporarily store XMM1 to XMM5 on stack
or, to be more
    movups [ebp - 16 * 2], xmm2     ; precise, in local variables.
    movups [ebp - 16 * 3], xmm3
    movups [ebp - 16 * 4], xmm4
    movups [ebp - 16 * 5], xmm5
```

```
    movaps xmm1, xmm0                ; Copy the parameter to XMM1 and XMM2
    movaps xmm2, xmm0

    mov ecx, 3                       ; Set ECX to the first exponent
```

The following computation loop is simple and does not contain any instructions that we have not met yet. However, there are two procedure calls taking two parameters each. Parameters are passed with the XMM0 register (three single-precision floating-point numbers) and the ECX register containing the currently used value of the exponent:

```
.l1:
    movaps xmm0, xmm2      ; Exponentiate the initial parameter
    call pow
    movaps xmm3, xmm0

    call fact              ; Calculate the factorial of current exponent
    movaps xmm4, xmm0

    divps xmm3, xmm4       ; Divide the exponentiated parameter by the
factorial of the exponent
    test eax, 1            ; Check iteration for being odd number, add the
result to accumulator
                          ; subtract otherwise
    jnz .plus
    subps xmm1, xmm3
    jmp @f
.plus:
    addps xmm1, xmm3
@@:                       ; Increment current exponent by 2
    add ecx, 2
    inc eax
    cmp eax, 8            ; and continue till EAX is 8
    jb .l1

    movaps xmm0, xmm1     ; Store results into XMM0
```

All computations have completed and we now have sine values for the three inputs. For the first iteration, the inputs in XMM0 would be as follows:

bits 96 - 127	bits 64 - 95	bits 32 - 63	bits 0 - 31	register name
(irrelevant)	0.28564453	4.8244629	2.5952148	XMM0

Also, the result of our `sin()` approximation with eight iterations of Taylor series is as follows:

bits 96 - 127	bits 64 - 95	bits 32 - 63	bits 0 - 31	register name
(irrelevant)	0.28177592	-0.99365967	0.51959586	XMM0

This shows a perfect (at least for our needs) level of approximation. Then, we restore the previously saved XMM registers and return to caller procedure:

```
movups xmm1, [ebp - 16]
movups xmm2, [ebp - 16 * 2]
movups xmm3, [ebp - 16 * 3]
movups xmm4, [ebp - 16 * 4]
movups xmm5, [ebp - 16 * 5]

pop ecx eax
mov esp, ebp
pop ebp
ret
```

Exponentiation

We make use of exponentiation in our `sin_taylor_series` procedure, an algorithm which is not as trivial as it may seem when it comes to real numbers used as exponents; however, we are quite lucky because the Taylor series only uses natural numbers for that purpose, but, it is worth mentioning that, should we need larger exponents, the algorithm would have been too slow. Therefore, our implementation of an exponentiation algorithm is as basic as it gets--we simply multiply the parameter in XMM0 by itself ECX-1 times. ECX is decremented once because there is no need to calculate x^1:

```
;;;;;;;;;;;;;;;;;;;;;;;;;;;;;;;;;;;;;;;;;;;;;;;;;;;;;;;;;
;
; Trivial exponentiation function
; Parameters are:
; Values to exponentiate in XMM0
; Exponent is in ECX
; Return values are in XMM0
;-------------------------------------------------------
pow:
    push ebp
    mov ebp, esp
    sub esp, 16

    push ecx
    dec ecx                         ; The inputs are already x1 so we decrement
```

```
the exponent
    movups [ebp - 16], xmm1

    movaps xmm1, xmm0            ; We will be mutliplying XMM0 by XMM1
.l1:
    mulps xmm0, xmm1
    loop .l1

    movups xmm1, [ebp - 16]
    pop ecx
    mov esp, ebp
    pop ebp
    ret
```

Factorials

We also make use of factorials as we divide exponentiated values by a factorial of exponents thereof. The factorial of a given number n is the product of all positive integers less than or equal to the given number n:

```
;;;;;;;;;;;;;;;;;;;;;;;;;;;;;;;;;;;;;;;;;;;;;;;;;;;;;;
;
; Simple calculation of factorial
; Parameter is in ECX (number to calculate the factorial of)
; Return value is in XMM0 register
;-----------------------------------------------------
fact:
    push ebp
    mov ebp, esp
    sub esp, 16 * 3

    push ecx
    movups [ebp - 16], xmm1
    movups [ebp - 16 * 2], xmm2
    mov dword[ebp - 16 * 3], 1.0
    movd xmm2, [ebp - 16 * 3]
    movlhps xmm2, xmm2
    movsldup xmm2, xmm2
    movaps xmm0, xmm2
    movaps xmm1, xmm2

.l1:
    mulps xmm0, xmm1
    addps xmm1, xmm2
    loop .l1
```

```
movups xmm2, [ebp - 16 * 2]
movups xmm1, [ebp - 16]
pop ecx
mov esp, ebp
pop ebp
ret
```

AVX-512

This chapter would not have been complete without mentioning AVX-512 - Advanced Vector Extensions 512-bit. It, in fact, consists of multiple extensions, while only the core one - AVX-512F ("F" stands for foundation) is mandatory for all processors. AVX-512 does not only add new instructions, but greatly enhances the implementation of parallel (vectored) computations, allowing calculations to be performed over vectors of single or double-precision floating point values up to 512 bits long. Also, 32 new 512-bit registers are introduced (ZMM0 - ZMM31) and with its ternary logic it resembles dedicated platforms.

Summary

The example code in this chapter was designed for the demonstration of the parallel data processing capabilities of modern Intel-based processors. Of course, the technology being used herein is far from able to provide the power of architectures such as CUDA, but it is definitely able to significantly speed up certain algorithms. While the algorithm we worked on here is very simple and hardly requires any optimization at all, as it could be implemented with FPU instructions alone and we would hardly notice any difference, it still illustrates the way in which multiple data may be processed simultaneously. A much better application could be solving an n-body problem, as SSE allows simultaneous computation of all vectors in a 3 dimensional space or even the implementation of a multilayer perceptron (one of many types of artificial neural networks) as it could have made it possible to process several neurons at once or; if the network is small enough, host them all in available XMM registers without the need to move data from/to memory. Especially keeping in mind the fact that sometimes procedures that seem to be quite complex, when implemented with SSE, may still be faster than a single FPU instruction.

Now that we know about at least one technology that may make our life easier, we will learn about the way assemblers can, if not simplify, then definitely ease the work of Assembly developer--macro instructions. Similar to macros in C or any other programming language supporting such features, macro instructions can have a significantly positive impact, allowing the replacement of a series of instructions with a single macro instruction, iteratively and/or conditionally assemble or skip certain sequences, or even create new instructions if the assembler is not supporting instructions we need (never happened to me yet, but "never say never").

6
Macro Instructions

Using Assembly language for the implementation of your ideas is fun (I surely have said that already and, probably, even more than once). However, it may become quite annoying when it comes to certain operations, which have to be re-implemented in different parts of your program. One possible solution may be implementing those operations in the form of a procedure and calling it when needed. However, this may quickly become a nuisance as well, once you have a procedure; which receives more than zero parameters. While in high-level languages you simply "pass" the parameters to a function, in Assembly, you have to actually pass them to a procedure in accordance with the calling convention of your choice, which, in turn, may imply additional headache with management of registers (if parameters are passed via certain registers) or accessing the stack. Sometimes, this complication is worth it, but that is not always the case, especially when it comes to a short set of recurring instructions. This is exactly the case where macro instructions may save us from a lot of headaches and redundant efforts, not to mention the amount of CPU time spent on calls (parameter preparations and procedure prolog and epilog), tiny fractions of a millisecond which may, at the end, aggregate into quite substantial delays.

In this chapter, we will cover the following:

- Macro instructions and the mechanisms behind them
- How macro instructions may be parameterized
- Learning variadic macro instructions and power thereof
- Getting acquainted with common calling conventions
- Examining additional assembler directives and conditional assembly

All of this is essential for our future work with this book, as the methods and algorithms we will explore would be too cumbersome otherwise.

What are macro instructions?

First of all, before we submerge into the world of macro instructions, we have to understand what they actually are. Putting it the simplest way, macro instructions are aliases for sequences of instructions. You may be familiar with the term from high-level languages (we say "may be" because not all high-level languages implement this feature), but we'll still explain it here. Remember the following sequence from the previous chapter?

```
movd xmm3, [dpy]
movlhps xmm3, xmm3
movsldup xmm3, xmm3
```

This sequence loads all four singles of an XMM register (in this specific case, it was XMM3) with a single precision floating point value from memory pointed by dpy. We used such sequences several times in our code, so it would be natural to try and replace it with a single macro instruction. Thus, defining the following macro would make our code look more elegant and readable:

```
macro load_4 xmmreg, addr
{
    movd xmmreg, [addr]
    movlhps xmmreg, xmmreg
    movsldup xmmreg, xmmreg
}
```

We use it in our code like this:

```
load_4 xmm3, dpy
load_4 xmm4, pi_2
```

This would make the code look more elegant and much more readable.

Parentheses are a great feature of FASM and are present neither in MASM nor in GAS. Instead, you would write the following code for MASM:
```
MACRO macro_name
; macro body
ENDM
```

And the following code for GAS:
```
.macro macro_name
; macro_body
.endm
```

How it works

The logic behind macro instructions is quite simple. The preprocessor parses the code for the definitions of macro instructions and stores them, simply speaking, in the form of a dictionary, where the name of the macro instruction is the key and its content is the value. Of course, in reality, it is more complicated, as macro instructions may have (and most of the time, they do have) parameters, not to mention the fact that they may also be variadic (have an undefined number of parameters).

When the assembler processes the code and encounters unknown instructions, it checks this dictionary for a macro instruction with the corresponding name. Once such an entry is found, the assembler replaces the macro instruction with its value--expands macro. Consider that the assembler sees the following:

```
load_4 xmm3, dpy
```

Then, it refers to the collected macro instruction definitions and replaces this line with the actual code:

```
movd xmm3, [dpy]
movlhps xmm3, xmm3
movsldup xmm3, xmm3
```

If the assembler finds no relevant macro definition, we are notified of this via the error reporting mechanism.

Macro instructions with parameters

Although you definitely can define a macro instruction that receives no parameters at all, you would rarely need to do this. Most of the time, you would define macro instructions that need at least one parameter. Let us take, for example, a macro instruction that implements the procedure prolog:

```
macro prolog frameSize
{
    push ebp
    mov  ebp, esp
    sub  esp, frameSize
}
```

The `frameSize` property in the preceding macro instruction is a macro parameter which, in this case, is used to specify the size of the stack frame in bytes. The usage of such a macro instruction would be as follows:

```
my_proc:
    prolog 8
    ; body of the procedure
    mov esp, ebp
    pop ebp
    ret
```

The preceding code is logically equivalent to (and is expanded by the preprocessor into) the following:

```
my_proc:
    push ebp
    mov   ebp, esp
    sub   esp, 8
    ; body of the procedure
    mov   esp, ebp
    pop   ebp
    ret
```

In addition, we may define the `return` macro, which would implement the destruction of the stack frame and return from the procedure:

```
macro return
{
    mov   ebp, esp
    pop   ebp
    ret
}
```

This would make our procedure even shorter:

```
my_proc:
    prolog 8
    ; body of the procedure
    return
```

Here, the `return` macro is also a good example of parameterless macro instruction.

Variadic macro instructions

In certain cases, we do not know how many parameters would be passed to the same macro instruction used in different places in our code, and FASM provides a great and easy solution for such a problem--support for variadic macro instructions. The term *variadic* means that an operator, a procedure, or a macro can take a varying number of operands/parameters.

Syntactically, variadic macro instructions are very simple. We begin with the macro keyword, then the name of the macro followed by a comma-separated list of parameters, if any. The variadic portion of the list of parameters is enclosed in square brackets. For example, should we have a macro instruction that expands to the `printf()` function or invokes it, and we want it to have a similar declaration, then the macro declaration would start like this:

```
macro printf fmt, [args]
```

Here, `fmt` stands for the format argument of the `printf()` function and `args` represents all optional parameters.

Let's consider a very simple example of the reworked `prolog` macro, which, in addition to the size of a stack frame, receives the list of registers that need to be stored on the stack as they would be altered in the body of a procedure:

```
macro prolog frameSize, [regs]
{
    common
    push    ebp
    mov     ebp, esp
    sub     esp, frameSize
    forward
    push regs
}
```

Here, you've definitely noticed the `common` and `forward` keywords, which are essential for the correctness of the expansion of this macro instruction. The interesting feature of variadic macro instructions is that the content thereof is expanded for each and every variadic parameter (parameters specified in square brackets). As the creation of the stack frame after each and every register (specified by the `regs` parameter) is pushed onto stack would look weird, we have to instruct the preprocessor to expand a specific portion of the macro instruction only once, and this is what the `common` keyword does.

The `forward` keyword (and its counterpart, the `reverse` keyword) instructs the preprocessor about the order the variadic parameters should be processed in. The line `push regs` expands into the `push` instruction for each parameter specified in `regs` and the preceding `forward` keyword instructs the preprocessor to process parameters in exactly the order they were written in. For example, consider the following code:

```
my_proc:
    prolog 8, ebx, ecx, edx
    ; body of the procedure
```

This piece of code would expand to the following:

```
my_proc:
    push ebp
    mov  ebp, esp
    sub  esp, 8
    push ebx
    push ecx
    push edx
```

Let's apply proper fixes to the `return` macro instruction for the sake of completeness:

```
macro return [regs]
{
    reverse
    pop   regs
    common
    mov   esp, ebp
    pop   ebp
    ret
}
```

Here, for the sake of an example, we use the `reverse` keyword, as we specify registers that should be retrieved from stack in exactly the same order in which they were passed to the `prolog` macro instruction. The procedure would then look like this:

```
my_proc:
    prolog 8, ebx, ecx, edx
    ; body of the function
    return ebx, ecx, edx
```

An introduction to calling conventions

When writing code in Assembly language, it's preferable to stick to certain calling conventions (the way parameters are passed to procedures) when invoking procedures because, first of all, this minimizes the occurrence of annoying and hard to find errors and, of course, help you link your Assembly modules to high-level languages. There are quite a few calling conventions for Intel Architecture, but we will only consider some of them, which we will use later in this book.

We already know about procedures and we have even mentioned the term "calling convention" in the previous chapter, so you may wonder why it is now that we cover the mechanism itself. The answer is quite simple--invocation of a procedure is a process that requires certain preparations, and, as such preparations would logically be the same with every procedure call, it is obvious to implement these preparations in the form of macro instruction.

First, let's see the calling conventions that we will cover in this part of the chapter:

Platform	Calling Convention Name	Register Parameters	Order of Parameters on Stack	Stack Cleanup
32-bit	cdecl	none	parameters are pushed in reverse order	stack cleanup is performed by the caller
	stdcall (Microsoft specific)	none	parameters are pushed in reverse order	stack cleanup is performed by the callee
64-bit	Microsoft x64	RCX, RDX, R8, R9 (floating point values are passed in XMM0 - XMM3)	stack parameters are stored in reverse order	stack cleanup is performed by the caller
	AMD64	RDI, RSI, RDX, RCX, R8, R9 (floating point values are passed in XMM0 - XMM7)	stack parameters are stored in reverse order	stack cleanup is performed by the caller

cdecl (32-bit)

The cdecl calling convention is the standard convention in C and C++ high-level languages. Parameters are stored on a stack with the rightmost parameter pushed onto stack first and the leftmost parameter pushed onto stack last. It is the caller's responsibility to restore the stack once it regains control.

The simplest macro that emulates the cdecl procedure invocation would be as follows:

```
macro ccall procName, [args]
{
    common
    a = 0
    if ~args eq
        forward
        a = a + 4
        reverse
        push args
    end if
    common
    call procName
    if a > 0
        add  esp, a
    end if
}
```

The if clauses here are self-explanatory; however, you may simply ignore them for now as they will be covered a bit later in this chapter.

stdcall (32-bit)

The stdcall calling convention is almost identical to cdecl in that parameters are passed on to the stack in the same manner--the rightmost is pushed first and leftmost is pushed last. The only difference is that the caller does not have to take care of stack cleanup:

```
macro stdcall procName, [args]
{
    if ~args eq
        reverse
        push args
    end if
    common
    call procName
}
```

Let's consider a simple example that uses both the calling conventions:

```
cdecl_proc:
    push ebp
    mov  ebp, esp
    ; body of the procedure
    mov  esp, ebp
    pop  ebp,
    ret

stdcall_proc:
    push ebp
    mov  ebp, esp
    ; body of the procedure
    mov  esp, ebp
    pop  ebp
    ret  8                          ; Increments the stack pointer by 8 bytes after
                                    ; return, thus releasing the space occupied
                                    ; by procedure parameters

main:
    ccall   cdecl_proc, 128  ; 128 is a numeric parameter passed to
                             ; the procedure
    stdcall stdcall_proc, 128, 32
```

While all is clear with the `cdecl_proc` and `stdcall_proc` procedures, let's take a closer look at what the `main` procedure expands to:

```
main:
    push 128
    call cdecl_proc
    add  esp, 4
    ;
    push 32
    push 128
    call stdcall_proc
```

In the preceding example, the `stdcall` macro invocation also illustrates what happens when there is more than one parameter--the rightmost parameter is pushed first. Such mechanisms allow easier and more intuitive addressing of parameters within the function. Given the nature of a stack frame, we could access them as follows:

```
mov   eax, [ebp + 8]   ; Would load EAX with 128
mov   eax, [ebp + 12]  ; Would load EAX with 32
```

We are using an EBP register as the base pointer. The first (leftmost) parameter is located at offset 8 from the value stored in EBP, as the procedure's return address and the previously pushed value of EBP register occupy exactly 8 bytes. The following table shows the content of the stack after the creation of the stack frame:

Offset from EBP	Content
+12	rightmost parameter (32)
+8	leftmost parameter (128)
+4	procedure return address
EBP points here	previous value of EBP
-4	first stack frame variable
....	other stack frame variables
....	saved registers
ESP points here	current stack position

Microsoft x64 (64-bit)

Microsoft uses its own calling convention in the 64-bit mode (long mode) using a mixed register/stack paradigm for passing procedure parameters. This means that only the first four parameters may be passed via registers and the rest (if any) should be pushed onto the stack. The following table illustrates which registers are used and in what manner:

Parameter index (zero based)	Integer/pointer	Floating point
0	RCX	XMM0
1	RDX	XMM1
2	R8	XMM2
3	R9	XMM3

All of this looks quite clear, yet there are two things that we need to pay special attention to:

- The stack must be aligned on a 16-bytes boundary
- A 32-bytes shadow space on the stack is required--32 bytes between the last pushed stack parameter (if any) and the return address

The following macro instruction (`ms64_call`) is simplistic; it is a primitive implementation of this calling convention. This specific macro does not support stack parameters:

```
macro ms64_call procName, [args]
{
   a = 0
   if ~args eq
      forward
      if a = 0
         push rcx
         mov rcx, args
      else if a = 1
         push rdx
         mov rdx, args
      else if a = 2
         push r8
         mov r8, args
      else if a = 3
         push r9
         mov r9, args
      else
         display "This macro only supports up to 4 parameters!",10,13
         exit
      end if
      a = a + 1
      end if
   common
   sub rsp, 32              ; Allocate shadow space
   call procName           ; Call procedure
   add rsp, 32             ; Free shadow space
   forward
   if ~args eq
      if a = 4
         pop r9
      else if a = 3
         pop r8
      else if a = 2
         pop rdx
      else if a = 1
         pop rcx
      end if
      a = a - 1
   end if
}
```

Consider an example of calling the procedure labeled `my_proc` in the 64-bit code, using Microsoft x64 calling convention:

```
ms64_call my_proc, 128, 32
```

Such a macro instruction would be expanded to the following:

```
push rcx            ;Save RCX register on stack
mov   rcx, 128      ;Load it with the first parameter
push rdx            ;Save RDX register on stack
mov   rdx, 32       ;Load it with the second parameter
sub   rsp, 32       ;Create 32 bytes shadow space
call my_proc        ;Call the my_proc procedure
add   rsp, 32       ;Destroy shadow space
pop   rdx           ;Restore RDX register
pop   rcx           ;Restore RCX register
```

AMD64 (64-bit)

The AMD64 calling convention is used on 64-bit Unix-like systems by default. The idea is very similar except that a different set of registers is used and there is no shadow space requirement. Another difference is that the AMD64 calling convention allows up to 6 integer parameters and up to 8 floating point values to be passed via registers:

Parameter index (zero based)	Integer/pointer	Floating point
0	RDI	XMM0
1	RSI	XMM1
2	RDX	XMM2
3	RCX	XMM3
4	R8	XMM4
5	R9	XMM5
6	on stack	XMM6
7	on stack	XMM7

The following macro instruction is a primitive implementation of such a mechanism. Just as in the case of the Microsoft x64 example, this one does not handle stack parameters:

```
macro amd64_call procName, [args]
{
    a = 0
    if ~args eq
        forward
        if a = 0
            push rdi
            mov rdi, args
        else if a = 1
            push rsi
            mov rsi, args
        else if a = 2
            push rdx
            mov rdx, args
        else if a = 3
            push rcx
            mov rcx, args
        else if a = 4
            push r8
            mov r8, args
        else if a = 5
            push r9
            mov r9, args
        else
            display "This macro only supports up to 4 parameters", 10, 13
            exit
        end if
        a = a + 1
    end if
    common
    call procName
    forward
    if ~args eq
        if a = 6
            pop r9
        else if a = 5
            pop r8
        else if a = 4
            pop rcx
        else if a = 3
            pop rdx
        else if a = 2
            pop rsi
        else if a = 1
            pop rdi
```

```
        end if
        a = a - 1
    end if
}
```

Using such a macro in 64-bit code intended to run on a Unix-like system for calling the procedure my_proc like this:

```
amd64_call my_proc, 128, 32
```

Would expand it into:

```
push rdi         ;Store RDI register on stack
mov  rdi, 128    ;Load it with the first parameter
push rsi         ;Store RSI register on stack
mov  rsi, 32     ;Load it with the second parameter
call my_proc     ;Call the my_proc procedure
pop  rsi         ;Restore RSI register
pop  rdi         ;Restore RDI register
```

A note on Flat Assembler's macro capabilities

One of the huge advantages of Flat Assemblers over other assemblers for the Intel platform is its macro engine. In addition to being able to perform its original task--substituting macro instructions with their definitions--it is able to perform relatively complex computations, and I would dare to call it an additional programming language. The preceding examples only utilize a tiny fraction of what FASM's macro processor is capable of. While we only used a set of if clauses and a variable, we may, in necessary cases, use loops (with while or repeat statements). For example, imagine a string of characters that you want to keep encrypted:

```
my_string  db 'This string will be encrypted',0x0d, 0x0a, 0x00
my_string_len = $ - my_string
```

Here, my_string_len is the length of the string.

$ is a special symbol denoting the current address. Thus, $-my_string means the current address minus the address of my_string, which is the length of the string.

A simplistic XOR encryption may be applied with just a four-line macro:

```
repeat my_string_len
    load b byte from my_string + % - 1
    store byte b xor 0x5a at my_string + % - 1
end repeat
```

The % symbol here denotes the current iteration and the -1 value is needed because the count of iterations starts at 1.

This is just a short and primitive example of what the macro engine of FASM is able to do, and there is a lot more. However, this book, though it uses FASM as a primary assembler, is dedicated to Intel Assembly language rather than to specific dialect, so this additional information goes beyond its scope. I strongly recommend that you refer to the FASM documentation available at http://flatassembler.net.

Macro instructions in MASM and GAS

Although the core idea behind the macro instruction mechanism is the same across all assemblers, the syntax of macro instructions and the capabilities of the engine vary. The following are two examples of simple macros for MASM and GAS.

Microsoft Macro Assembler

Remember our test program for MASM in Chapter 2, *Setting Up a Development Environment*? We can replace the code that invokes the show_message procedure with the following macro instruction:

```
MSHOW_MESSAGE MACRO title, message ;macro_name MACRO parameters
    push message
    push title
    call show_message
ENDM
```

This may make the code a bit more readable as we may then call the show_message procedure this way:

```
MSHOW_MESSAGE offset ti, offset msg
```

The GNU Assembler

The macro engine of the GNU Assembler is quite similar to that of Microsoft's MASM, yet there are a few syntactic differences (not taking into account the overall syntax difference) that we have to pay attention to. Let us take the `output_message` procedure from the Linux test program in Chapter 2, *Setting Up a Development Environment*, and replace the call to `printf()` with a simple macro for demonstration purposes.

```
.macro print message      ; .macro macro_name parameter
   pushl \message         ; Put the parameter on stack
                          ; parameters are prefixed with '\'
   call  printf           ; Call printf() library function
   add   $4, %esp         ; Restore stack after cdecl function call
.endm

output_message:
   pushl %ebp
   movl  %esp, %ebp
   print 8(%ebp)          ; This line would expand to the above macro
   movl  $0, %eax
   leave
   ret   $4
```

Other assembler directives (FASM Specific)

Up until now, we mostly considered macro instructions to be some sort of replacement for procedure calls, although I believe it would be correct to refer to them as convenience instruments for simplifying the writing and maintenance of the code. In this part of the chapter, we will see some so to say built-in macro instructions--assembler directives--which may virtually be divided into three categories:

- Conditional assembly
- Repeat directives
- Inclusion directives

Additional categories may be present depending on assembler implementation. You should refer to the documentation of the assembler you are using for more information.

The conditional assembly

Sometimes we may want a macro instruction or a code fragment to be assembled differently depending on certain conditions. Both MASM and GAS provide this functionality too, but let's get back to FASM (as the most convenient one) and consider the following macro instruction:

```
macro exordd p1, p2
{
    if ~p1 in <eax, ebx, ecx, edx, esi, edi, ebp, esp> &\
       ~p2 in <eax, ebx, ecx, edx, esi, edi, ebp, esp>
       push eax
       mov  eax, [p2]
       xor [p1], eax
       pop  eax
    else
       if ~p1 in <eax, ebx, ecx, edx, esi, edi, ebp, esp>
          xor [p1], p2
       else if ~p2 in <eax, ebx, ecx, edx, esi, edi, ebp, esp>
          xor p1, [p2]
       else
          xor p1, p2
       end if
    end if
}
```

It may appear a bit complicated at first, but the purpose of the macro is rather simple. We extend an XOR instruction so that we may specify two memory locations as operands, which cannot be done with the original instruction. For simplicity, we only operate on double word values.

In the beginning, we check whether both parameters are labels of memory locations and if they are, we load the value from one of them to a register and perform a XOR operation, as we would when the first operand is a memory location and the second operand is a register.

If this condition is not true, we move to the second part of the macro instruction, where we perform a XOR operation appropriately depending on whether the first operand is a memory location or the second one, or whether they are both general purpose registers.

As an example, let's take two variables named `my_var1` and `my_var2` containing values `0xCAFECAFE` and `0x02010201`, respectively, and swap them with XOR:

```
exordd my_var1, my_var2    ; a = a xor b
mov    ebx, [my_var2]
exordd ebx, my_var1        ; b = b xor a
mov    [my_var2], ebx
exordd my_var1, ebx        ; a = a xor b
exordd ebx, ebx            ; Reset EBX register for extra fun
```

Once processed, the preceding code would expand to this:

```
push eax                   ; exordd my_var1, my_var2
mov   eax, [my_var2]
xor   [my_var1], eax
pop   eax
mov   ebx, [my_var2]
xor   ebx, [my_var1]       ; exordd ebx, my_var1
mov   [my_var2], ebx
xor   [my_var1], ebx       ; exordd [my_var1], ebx
xor   ebx, ebx             ; exordd ebx, ebx
```

As we see, the `exordd` macro instruction is expanded differently depending on its parameters.

Repeat directives

There may be a need to repeat the same portion of code with minor differences or even without them. Assemblers have directives (sometimes referred to as built-in macro instructions) that allow us exactly this. There are three such statements common to all three assemblers--FASM, MASM and GAS:

- `rept count`: The `rept` directive followed by the `count` parameter simply makes `count` copies of the code defined in the block. In case of Flat Assembler, we may declare the second parameter, which will equal the number of the current iteration (1 based). For example, the following code:

```
hex_chars:
rept 10 cnt {db '0' + cnt - 1}
rept 6  cnt {db 'A' + cnt - 1}
```

This would generate an array of hexadecimal characters named `hex_chars`, and is equivalent to:

```
hex_chars db "0123456789ABCDEF"
```

- `irp arg, a, b, c, ...`: The `irp` directive is followed by an argument and a list of parameters. The argument (here `arg`) represents a single parameter during each iteration. For example, this code:

```
irp reg, eax, ebx, ecx {inc reg}
```

Sequentially increments registers EAX, EBX then ECX.

- **`irps arg, a b c ...`**: The `irps` directive is the same as `irp`, except that parameters in the list are not separated with commas.

Inclusion directives

There are two directives that we have hardly touched upon in previous chapters, which appear to be very useful. These directives are:

- `include 'filename'`
- `file 'filename'`

The include directive

The syntax of the `include` directive is very simple. It is the directive itself followed by a quoted name of a source file we want to include. Logically, the operation is the same as of `#include` keyword in C or C++. Programming in Assembly is not always simple and it is a very good idea to split your code into several source files (for example, put all your definitions of macro instructions in a separate file), then combine them all by including them in the main source.

File directive

While syntactically `include` and `file` directives are similar and both cause a file to be included in source processing, logically they are very different. Unlike the `include` directive, the `file` directive does not cause any processing of a file being included. This allows inclusion of binary data into the data section or into any place you need.

Summary

In this chapter, we have very briefly covered the numerous abilities of the macro instructions in Assembly language programming. Unfortunately, it may require an entire book to mention everything that may be done with macro instructions, especially when it comes to the Flat Assembler, which has an exceptional preprocessor.

An example from my own practice: I once had to implement a heavily obfuscated version of the AES128 decryption algorithm, which took 2175 lines in total, having only a few procedures, and almost half of that (1064 lines) was occupied by the definition of different macro instructions. As you may safely assume, about 30% to 60% of each procedure contained the invocation thereof.

In the next chapter, we will continue to dive deeper into the preprocessor and deal with different data structures, and the creation and management thereof.

7
Data Structures

As it has been stated more than once in this book, Assembly is about moving and performing certain basic operations on data, and Assembly programming is about knowing what to move where and which operations to apply to it on the way. Until now, we have primarily dedicated all our attention to operations that we are able to perform on different types of data, and it is now time to talk about the data itself.

The least data item that is accessible on Intel architecture-based processors is bit, and the least addressable item is byte (which is 8 bits on Intel architecture). We already know how to work with such data and even words, double words, and single-precision floating-point values. Data, however, may be much more complex than that, and I do not mean quad words and/or double-precision floating points.

In this chapter, we will see how to declare, define, and manipulate simple and complex data structures and how this may make our lives as Assembly developers much easier. Starting with simple data structures, such as arrays, we will proceed to more complex ones containing different types of data and go through linked lists and trees toward more complex and powerful methods of data arrangement. The intention here, given that you as a developer are familiar with different data structures, is to show how easy it may be to work with them in Assembly, especially using FASM with its powerful features as an assembler.

The following are the data structures (data arrangement schemes) covered in this chapter:

- Arrays
- Structures
- Arrays of structures
- Linked lists and special cases thereof
- Binary Search Trees and balancing thereof
- Sparse matrices
- Graphs

Arrays

By now, we have come a long way, dealing primarily with basic data types ranging from bytes to quad words, preparing ourselves for more complex data-related concepts. Let's continue by looking into arrays, which may be characterized as the sequential storage of data of the same type. Theoretically, there is no limitation to the size of array members, but practically we are limited to, for example, the size of a register. However, workarounds exist and we will see that later in this chapter.

Simple byte arrays

A good example of a widely used, yet simple, array would be a forward substitution table and/or a reverse substitution table used with the AES algorithm:

```
aes_sbox:
db 0x63, 0x7c, 0x77, 0x7b, 0xf2, 0x6b, 0x6f, 0xc5
db 0x30, 0x01, 0x67, 0x2b, 0xfe, 0xd7, 0xab, 0x76
db 0xca, 0x82, 0xc9, 0x7d, 0xfa, 0x59, 0x47, 0xf0
db 0xad, 0xd4, 0xa2, 0xaf, 0x9c, 0xa4, 0x72, 0xc0
db 0xb7, 0xfd, 0x93, 0x26, 0x36, 0x3f, 0xf7, 0xcc
db 0x34, 0xa5, 0xe5, 0xf1, 0x71, 0xd8, 0x31, 0x15
db 0x04, 0xc7, 0x23, 0xc3, 0x18, 0x96, 0x05, 0x9a
db 0x07, 0x12, 0x80, 0xe2, 0xeb, 0x27, 0xb2, 0x75
db 0x09, 0x83, 0x2c, 0x1a, 0x1b, 0x6e, 0x5a, 0xa0
db 0x52, 0x3b, 0xd6, 0xb3, 0x29, 0xe3, 0x2f, 0x84
db 0x53, 0xd1, 0x00, 0xed, 0x20, 0xfc, 0xb1, 0x5b
db 0x6a, 0xcb, 0xbe, 0x39, 0x4a, 0x4c, 0x58, 0xcf
db 0xd0, 0xef, 0xaa, 0xfb, 0x43, 0x4d, 0x33, 0x85
db 0x45, 0xf9, 0x02, 0x7f, 0x50, 0x3c, 0x9f, 0xa8
db 0x51, 0xa3, 0x40, 0x8f, 0x92, 0x9d, 0x38, 0xf5
db 0xbc, 0xb6, 0xda, 0x21, 0x10, 0xff, 0xf3, 0xd2
```

```
db 0xcd, 0x0c, 0x13, 0xec, 0x5f, 0x97, 0x44, 0x17
db 0xc4, 0xa7, 0x7e, 0x3d, 0x64, 0x5d, 0x19, 0x73
db 0x60, 0x81, 0x4f, 0xdc, 0x22, 0x2a, 0x90, 0x88
db 0x46, 0xee, 0xb8, 0x14, 0xde, 0x5e, 0x0b, 0xdb
db 0xe0, 0x32, 0x3a, 0x0a, 0x49, 0x06, 0x24, 0x5c
db 0xc2, 0xd3, 0xac, 0x62, 0x91, 0x95, 0xe4, 0x79
db 0xe7, 0xc8, 0x37, 0x6d, 0x8d, 0xd5, 0x4e, 0xa9
db 0x6c, 0x56, 0xf4, 0xea, 0x65, 0x7a, 0xae, 0x08
db 0xba, 0x78, 0x25, 0x2e, 0x1c, 0xa6, 0xb4, 0xc6
db 0xe8, 0xdd, 0x74, 0x1f, 0x4b, 0xbd, 0x8b, 0x8a
db 0x70, 0x3e, 0xb5, 0x66, 0x48, 0x03, 0xf6, 0x0e
db 0x61, 0x35, 0x57, 0xb9, 0x86, 0xc1, 0x1d, 0x9e
db 0xe1, 0xf8, 0x98, 0x11, 0x69, 0xd9, 0x8e, 0x94
db 0x9b, 0x1e, 0x87, 0xe9, 0xce, 0x55, 0x28, 0xdf
db 0x8c, 0xa1, 0x89, 0x0d, 0xbf, 0xe6, 0x42, 0x68
db 0x41, 0x99, 0x2d, 0x0f, 0xb0, 0x54, 0xbb, 0x16
```

As we may clearly see, all values have a size of 1 byte and are stored sequentially one after the other. Accessing such arrays is very simple and may even be performed with the XLAT instruction. For example, imagine that we are in the middle of an AES-128 calculation and we have a value in which we need to substitute each byte with a byte from the preceding table. Let the following be the value:

```
needs_substitution db 0, 1,  2,  3,  4,  5,  6,  7\
                       8, 9, 10, 11, 12, 13, 14, 15
```

The following code would do the substitution:

```
    lea   ebx, [aes_sbox]
    lea   esi, [needs_substitution] ; Set the source pointer (ESI) and
    mov   edi, esi                  ; destination pointer (EDI) as we
                                    ; will be storing substituted
                                    ; byte back
    mov   ecx, 0x10                 ; Set the counter
@@:
    lodsb                           ; Load byte from the value
    xlatb                           ; Substitute byte from the s-box
    stosb                           ; Store new byte to the value
    loop @b                         ; Loop while ECX != 1
```

The first thing we do is load the base address of the table (of the s-box) into the EBX register, as the XLAT instruction uses exactly this register for addressing the substitution/lookup table. Then, we load the address of the array of values requiring substitution into the ESI register in order to not bother with index computations, as the ESI register is automatically incremented by the `lodsb` instruction. Duplicate the address into the EDI register, as we will be storing data back.

You may as well process the 16 byte value from the last byte to the first by loading ESI and EDI with `lea esi, [needs_substitution + 0x0f]`, duplicating the address to EDI and setting the direction flag with the `std` instruction. Do not forget to clear the direction flag with the `cld` instruction when done.

We then sequentially read each byte of the value, substitute it with a byte form the s-box with the XLAT instruction, and store the result back. As an alternative to the XLAT instruction (which is limited to 256 byte tables and may only operate on byte values depending on the AL register), we can write the following:

```
mov al, [aes_sbox + eax] ; aes_sbox is the base and EAX is the index
```

However, we would have needed to set the whole EAX register to 0 prior to entering the loop, while XLAT allows the upper 24 bits of the EAX register to remain unchanged throughout the whole operation.

Arrays of words, double words, and quad words

The previous simple example illustrates a trivial byte array and how we can access its members. The same would apply to arrays of words, double words, or quad words with a few additions:

- We cannot use XLAT on arrays bigger than 256 bytes, nor if members of an array are bigger than 8 bits
- We would need to use SIB addressing (scale index base) in order to access array members bigger than one byte
- On 32-bit systems we would not be able to read a quad word into a single register

For the sake of a simple example, let's consider using a lookup table for the calculation of the factorial for numbers in the range of 0 to 12 (this code is for 32-bit and factorials of larger numbers would not fit into a double word). Although the algorithm of factorial calculation is rather simple, using a lookup table even for such a short range is much more convenient.

First, put the following into the data section (you may put this into the code section too, as we are not going to change any value here, but let's keep data with the data):

```
ftable   dd   1,\           ; 0!
              1,\           ; 1!
              2,\           ; 2!
              6,\           ; 3!
              24,\          ; 4!
              120,\         ; 5!
              720,\         ; 6!
              5040,\        ; 7!
              40320,\       ; 8!
              362880,\      ; 9!
              3628800,\     ; 10!
              39916800,\    ; 11!
              479001600     ; 12!
```

This is our lookup table containing 13 values of factorials for numbers in the range of 0 to 12, where each entry is double word (32 bit). Now, let's write a procedure that would use this table. The procedure will be implemented in accordance with the `stdcall` calling convention; it receives a single parameter, the number for which we need a factorial, and returns a factorial for the given number or 0 if the number is not in the allowed range (as 0 cannot be a value of factorial). Put the following code into the code section:

```
factorial:
    push   ebp
    mov    ebp, esp
    ;-------------
    virtual at ebp + 8          ; Assign a readable name to
        arg0  dd ?              ; a location on stack where
    end virtual                 ; the parameter is stored
    ;-------------
    mov    eax, [arg0]          ; Load parameter from the stack
    cmp    eax, 0x0c            ; Check whether it is in range
    ja     .oops                ; Go there if not
    mov    eax, [ftable + eax * 4]  ; Retrieve factorial from
                                    ; the lookup table
@@:
  leave
  ret    4

.oops:
  xor    eax, eax              ; Set return value to 0
  jmp    @b
```

The `virtual` directive lets us virtually define data at a specific address. In the preceding example, we defined a variable that points to the place on the stack where the parameter is stored. Everything we define within the `virtual` block is treated as a legal label by the assembler. In this case, the `arg0` translates to `ebp + 8`. If we had two or even more parameters passed to the procedure on stack, we could write the following:

```
virtual at ebp + 8
arg0 dd ?
arg1 dd ?
; the rest
end virtual
```

Here, `arg1` would be translated to `ebp+12`, `arg2` (if defined), `ebp+16`, and so on.

The procedure is indeed very simple as all it does is this:

- Checks whether the parameter fits the range
- Returns 0 if the parameter does not fit the range
- Uses the parameter as an index into the lookup table and returns a value referenced by the base address of the tables plus index (our parameter) times size of entries in the table

Structures

As a developer, I believe you would agree that most of the time we are not working with arrays of uniform data (I am definitely not underestimating the power of a regular array). Since data may be anything, starting with 8-bit numbers and ending with complex structures, we need a way to describe such data for the assembler, and the term *structure* is the key. Flat Assembler, just as any other assembler, lets us declare structures and treat them as additional types of data (similar to the `typedef` struct in C).

Let's declare a simple structure, an entry of a string table, and then see what is what:

```
struc strtabentry [s]
{
    .length dw  .pad - .string       ; Length of the string
    .string db  s, 0                 ; Bytes of the string
    .pad    rb  30 - (.pad - .string) ; Padding to fill 30 bytes
    .size = $ - .length              ; Size of the structure (valid
                                     ; in compile time only)

}
```

The dot (.) preceding the names of members of the struct denotes that they are part of a larger namespace. In this specific case, the name `.length` belongs to `strtabentry`.

Such a declaration would be equivalent to the following one in C:

```
typedef struct
{
    short           length;
    char            string[30];
}strtabentry;
```

However, while in C, we would have to initialize the variable of the type `strtabentry`, like this:

```
/* GCC (C99) */
strtabentry my_strtab_entry = {.length = sizeof("Hello!"), .string =
{"Hello!"} };

/* MSVC */
strtabentry my_strtab_entry = {sizeof("Hello!"), {"Hello!"} };
```

In Assembly, or to be more precise, when using Flat Assembler, we would initialize such a variable in a simpler way:

```
my_strtab_entry strtabentry "Hello!"
```

Either way, the structure is 32-bytes in size (as the string buffer is statically allocated and is 30 bytes) and has only two members:

- `length`: This is the word size integer containing the length of the string, plus 1 for a null terminator
- `string`: This is the actual text

Addressing structure members

A few words need to be said on how individual members of a structure may be addressed. When statically allocated, we may refer to a structure by its label/name, which is translated into its address. For example, if we have a `strtabentry` structure named `se` defined in our data section, and we need to read the *n*th byte from the string, all we have to do would be this:

```
mov  al, [se.string + n]    ; 0 <= n < 30
```

If, on the other hand, we cannot use a label (for example, we are in a procedure, and a pointer to a structure is its parameter), then we can use the mighty `virtual` directive. As a quick demonstration, here's a procedure that returns the length of the string, not including the terminating zero:

```
get_string_length:
    push    ebp
    mov     ebp, esp
    push    ebx
    ;=========
    virtual at ebp + 8      ; Give a name to the parameter on stack
        .structPtr dd 0     ; The parameter itself is not modified
    end virtual
    ;---------
    virtual at ebx          ; Give local name to the structure
        .s strtabentry 0    ; The structure is not really defined
    end virtual             ; so the string is not modified
    ;=========
    mov     ebx, [.structPtr] ; Load structure pointer to EBX
    mov     ax, [.s.length]   ; Load AX with the length
    movzx eax, ax             ; Upper 16 bits may still contain garbage
                              ; so we need to clean it
    dec     eax               ; Exclude null terminator
    pop     ebx
    leave
    ret     4
```

Just to keep things fresh in memory, let's take another look at the lines where we read the pointer from the stack and where we load AX with the length of the string. The first one is as follows:

```
mov     ebx, [.structPtr]
```

The preceding code loads the parameter from the stack. As we remember, declaring a virtual label lets us assign a readable name to the memory locations that cannot be named otherwise, and the stack is one of the examples. In this specific case, `.structPtr` is translated into `ebp + 8`, thus the line itself is equivalent to the following:

```
mov     ebx, [ebp + 8]
```

Similarly, had there be a second parameter, the virtual declaration would look like this:

```
virtual at ebp + 8
    .structPtr    dd 0
    .secondParam dd 0
end virtual
```

In that case, reading the second parameter would be done like this:

```
mov    ecx, [.secondParam]
```

Also, it would translate into the following:

```
mov    ecx, [ebp + 12]   ; Which is ebp + 8 + sizeof(.structPtr)
```

Here is the second line we are interested in:

```
mov    ax, [.s.length]
```

In this specific case, we are accessing the first member of the structure - `.length`, which means that the line is translated into this:

```
mov    ax, [ebx]
```

However, should we need to access the string itself, for example, if we need to load a register with the address of the string, the code would look like this:

```
lea    eax, [.s.string]
```

This would, in turn, translate into the following:

```
lea    eax, [ebx + 2]
```

Arrays of structures

By now, we are fine with everything regarding access to structures and members thereof, but what if we have more than one structure of the same type? We would naturally organize them into an array of structures. Looks simple, and partially so, it is.

In order to ease the process of accessing array members, we may use an array of pointers and access each structure in the array through a kind of lookup table. In this scenario, we would simply read a pointer from the lookup table with the following:

```
mov    ebx, [lookup_table + ecx * 4] ; ECX contains the index into array
                                      ; of pointers and 4 is the scale (size
                                      ; of pointer on 32-bit systems)
```

Having a pointer to the structure of interest, we continue the work as usual.

Our example structure is very convenient due to its size, which is only 32 bytes. Should we arrange many structures of this type into an array, we would be able to painlessly access them in an array of 134,217,727 members (on a 32-bit system), which is 4 GB in terms of occupied memory. While we would hardly need this number of strings with a maximum length of 30 bytes (or such a number of strings at all), the addressing in this specific case is very simple (again, due to the comfortable size of the structure). We still use the index in the array of structures, but, as we cannot use the scale part of SIB addressing to scale the index by 32 bytes, we need to multiply the index itself prior to accessing the array.

Let's define a macro instruction that would create such an array in the first place (building the pointer lookup table for demonstration purposes too):

```
macro make_strtab strtabName, [strings]
{
    common
    label strtabName#_ptr dword    ; The # operator concatenates strings
    local c                        ; resulting in strtabName_ptr
    c = 0

    forward
    c = c + 1                      ; Count number of structures

    common
    dd c                           ; Prepend the array of pointers with
                                   ; number of entries

    forward                        ; Build the pointer table
    local a
    dd a

    common                         ; Build the array of structures
    label strtabName dword

    forward
    a strtabentry strings
}
```

The invocation of the preceding macro, with the following parameters, is as follows:

```
make_strtab strtabName,\
            "string 0",\          ; Spaces are intentionally appended to
            "string 1 ",\         ; strings in order to provide us with
            "string 2   ",\       ; different lengths.
            "string 3     "
```

This would result in the following arrangement of data in memory:

```
.data:00402004    strtabName_ptr   dd 4                      ; Number of structure pointers in the array
.data:00402008                     dd offset strtabName
.data:0040200C                     dd offset structure_1
.data:00402010                     dd offset structure_2
.data:00402014                     dd offset structure_3
.data:00402018                     public strtabName
.data:00402018    strtabName       dw 9                      ; DATA XREF: start+2↑o
.data:00402018                                               ; .data:00402008↑o
.data:0040201A    aString0         db 'string 0',0
.data:00402023                     db 15h dup(0)             ; 0
.data:00402038    structure_1      dw 0Ah                    ; DATA XREF: .data:0040200C↑o
.data:0040203A    aString1         db 'string 1 ',0
.data:00402044                     db 14h dup(0)             ; 0
.data:00402058    structure_2      dw 0Bh                    ; DATA XREF: .data:00402010↑o
.data:0040205A    aString2         db 'string 2  ',0
.data:00402065                     db 13h dup(0)             ; 0
.data:00402078    structure_3      dw 0Ch                    ; DATA XREF: .data:00402014↑o
.data:0040207A    aString3         db 'string 3   ',0
```

As you can see, the `strtabName_ptr` variable contains the number of structures/pointers in the array followed by the array of four pointers. Next, at `strtabName`, (we can choose whatever name we want when invoking the macro as long as it fits the naming restrictions), we have the actual array of four structures.

Now, should we need to retrieve the length of a string in the structure at index 2 (indices are zero based), we would modify the `get_string_length` procedure so that it would accept two parameters (pointer to structure array and index) in the following way:

```
get_string_length:
    push    ebp,
    mov     ebp, esp
    push    ebx ecx

    virtual at ebp + 8
        .structPtr   dd ?      ; Assign label to first parameter
        .structIdx   dd ?      ; Assign label to second parameter
    end virtual

    virtual at ebx + ecx
        .s strtabentry ?       ; Assign label to structure pointer
    end virtual

    mov     ebx, [.structPtr]  ; Load pointer to array of structures
    mov     ecx, [.structIdx]  ; Load index of the structure of interest
    shl     ecx, 5             ; Multiply index by 32
    mov     ax, [.s.length]    ; Read the length
    movzx   eax, ax
```

```
dec    eax
pop    ecx ebx
leave
ret    8
```

The procedure call would be as follows:

```
push   2                    ; push index on stack
push   strtabName           ; push the address of the array
call   get_string_length
```

Arrays of pointers to structures

The previous subsection shows us how to approach arrays of uniform structures. As there is no particular reason to have string buffers of fixed size and, therefore, no reason for a fixed size structure, let's first of all make a tiny correction to the structure declaration:

```
struc strtabentry [s]
{
    .length dw   .pad - .string     ; Length of the string
    .string db   s, 0               ; Bytes of the string
    .size = $ - .length             ; Size of the structure (valid
                                    ; in compile time only)

}
```

We only removed the .pad member of the strtabentry structure, thus allowing it to be of variable size. Obviously, we may no longer use the same get_string_length procedure as we have no constant step to iterate through the array. But you might have definitely noticed the strtabName_ptr structure in the preceding image. This structure is there to help us solve the problem of lack of a fixed step. Let's rewrite the get_string_length procedure so that it would accept a pointer to an array of pointers to structures, rather than a pointer to the array itself and an index of the desired structure. The procedure would then look like this:

```
get_string_length:
    push    ebp,
    mov     ebp, esp
    push    ebx ecx

    virtual at ebp + 8
        .structPPtr   dd ?     ; Assign label to first parameter
        .structIdx    dd ?     ; Assign label to second parameter
    end virtual

    virtual at ebx
```

```
        .s strtabentry ?        ; Assign label to structure pointer
     end virtual

     mov    ebx, [.structPPtr]  ; Load pointer to array of structures
     mov    ecx, [.structIdx]   ; Load index of the structure of interest
     shl    ecx, 2              ; Multiply index by 4 (size of pointer
                                ; on a 32-bit platform
     cmp    ecx, [.structPPtr]  ; Check the index to fit the size of the
                                ; array of pointers
     jae    .idx_too_big        ; Return error if index exceeds the bounds
     mov    ebx, [ebx + ecx + 4]; We have to add 4 (the size of int), in
                                ; order to skip the number of structure
                                ; pointers in the array
     mov    ax, [.s.length]     ; Read the length
     movzx eax, ax

.return:
     dec    eax
     pop    ecx ebx
     leave
     ret    8

.idx_too_big:
     xor    eax, eax                 ; The value of EAX would be -1 upon return
     jmp    .return
```

Voila! We only had to make a few tiny modifications, add a line here and a line there, and now we are able to handle structures of variable sizes.

Nothing complicated thus far, nothing complicated to follow. While there are not too many types of data, there are more ways to arrange it. While the structure may be considered both a data type and a method of arrangement for non-uniform data, we will, for convenience, treat it as a type that we are free to define. By now, we have seen how data may be arranged in static memory when the arrangement thereof is not expected to change, but what if we are dealing with dynamic data when the amount of data is not known at the time of writing the code? In such case we should know how to deal with dynamic data. This leads us to the next stage in data arrangement-linked lists and their types.

Linked lists

Linked lists, as the name suggests, consists, of data items (nodes) that are linked to one another by means of pointers. Basically, there are two types of linked lists:

- **Linked list**: This is where each node has a pointer to the following node
- **Doubly linked list**: This is where each node has a pointer to the following and previous nodes

The following diagram illustrates the difference:

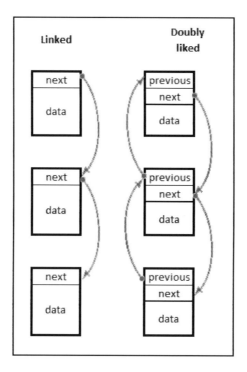

Linked lists of both types may be addressed in a few ways. Obviously, there is at least a pointer to the first node of the list (called `top`), which is optionally accompanied by a pointer to the last node of the list (called `tail`). There is, of course, no limit to the amount of auxiliary pointers, should there be a need for such. Pointer fields in the nodes are typically referred to as `next` and `previous`. As we can see in the diagram, the last node of a linked list and the first and the last nodes of a doubly linked list have `next`, `previous`, and `next` fields that point nowhere-such pointers are considered terminators denoting the end of the list and are typically populated with null values.

Before proceeding to the sample code, let's make a tiny change to the structure we've been using in this chapter and add the `next` and `previous` pointers. The structure should look like this:

```
struc strtabentry [s]
{
    .length    dw    .pad - .string
    .string    db    s, 0
    .pad       rb    30 - (.pad - .string)
    .previous dd    ?           ; Pointer to the next node
    .next      dd    ?           ; Pointer to the previous node
    .size = $ - .length
}
```

We will leave the `make_strtab` macro intact as we still need something to build a set of `strtabentry` structures; however, we will not consider it to be an array of structures any more. Also, we will add a variable (of type double word) to store the `top` pointer. Let's name it `list_top`.

Instead or writing a macro instruction that would link the four structures into a doubly linked list, we will write a procedure for adding new nodes to the list. The procedure requires two parameters--a pointer to the `list_top` variable and a pointer to the structure we want to add to the list. If we were writing in C, then the prototype of the corresponding function would be as follows:

```
void add_node(strtabentry** top, strtabentry* node);
```

However, since we are not writing in C, we will put down the following code:

```
add_node:
    push    ebp
    mov     ebp, esp
    push    eax ebx ecx

    virtual at ebp + 8
        .topPtr   dd ?
        .nodePtr dd ?
    end virtual
    virtual at ebx
        .scx strtabentry ?
    end virtual
    virtual at ecx
        .sbx strtabentry ?
    end virtual

    mov     eax, [.topPtr]      ; Load pointer to list_top
    mov     ebx, [.nodePtr]     ; Load pointer to new structure
```

```
        or      dword [eax], 0          ; Check whether list_top == NULL
        jz      @f                      ; Simply store the structure pointer
                                        ; to list_top if true

        mov     ecx, [eax]              ; Load ECX with pointer to current top
        mov     [.scx.next], ecx        ; node->next = top
        mov     [.sbx.previous], ebx    ; top->previous = node

@@:
        mov     [eax], ebx              ; top = node
        pop     ecx ebx eax
        leave
        ret     8
```

Now, having the procedure ready, we will call it from our main procedure:

```
_start:
        push strtabName + 40    ; Let the second structure be the first
        push list_top           ; in the list
        call add_node

        push strtabName + 120   ; Then we add fourth structure
        push list_top
        call add_node

        push strtabName + 80    ; Then third
        push list_top
        call add_node

        push strtabName         ; And first
        push list_top
        call add_node
```

The first, second, third, and fourth refers to positions of structures in memory, not to positions of nodes in the doubly linked list. Thus, after the last line of the preceding code is executed, we have a doubly linked list of strtabentry structures (shown by their position in the linked list) {0, 2, 3, 1}. Let's take a look at the following screenshot for a demonstration of the result:

```
.data:00402018 struct_0 dw 9                                          ; length
.data:00402018                                             ; DATA XREF: start+2D↑o
.data:00402018                                             ; .data:00402008↑o ...
.data:00402018 db 73h, 74h, 72h, 69h, 6Eh, 67h, 20h, 30h, 0, 0, 0, 0, 0, 0, 0, 0, 0, 0; string
.data:00402018 db 0, 0, 0, 0, 0, 0, 0, 0, 0, 0, 0, 0   ; string
.data:00402018 dd 0                                        ; previous
.data:00402018 dd offset struct_2                          ; next
.data:00402040 struct_1 dw 0Ah                             ; length ; DATA XREF: start↑o
.data:00402040                                             ; .data:0040200C↑o ...
.data:00402040 db 73h, 74h, 72h, 69h, 6Eh, 67h, 20h, 31h, 20h, 0, 0, 0, 0, 0, 0, 0; string
.data:00402040 db 0, 0, 0, 0, 0, 0, 0, 0, 0, 0, 0, 0, 0; string
.data:00402040 dd offset struct_3                          ; previous
.data:00402040 dd 0                                        ; next
.data:00402068 struct_2 dw 0Bh                             ; length
.data:00402068                                             ; DATA XREF: start+1E↑o
.data:00402068                                             ; .data:00402010↑o ...
.data:00402068 db 73h, 74h, 72h, 69h, 6Eh, 67h, 20h, 32h, 20h, 20h, 0, 0, 0, 0, 0, 0; string
.data:00402068 db 0, 0, 0, 0, 0, 0, 0, 0, 0, 0, 0, 0, 0, 0; string
.data:00402068 dd offset struct_0                          ; previous
.data:00402068 dd offset struct_3                          ; next
.data:00402090 struct_3 dw 0Ch                             ; length
.data:00402090                                             ; DATA XREF: start+F↑o
.data:00402090                                             ; .data:00402014↑o ...
.data:00402090 db 73h, 74h, 72h, 69h, 6Eh, 67h, 20h, 33h, 20h, 20h, 20h, 0, 0, 0, 0, 0; string
.data:00402090 db 0, 0, 0, 0, 0, 0, 0, 0, 0, 0, 0, 0, 0, 0; string
.data:00402090 dd offset struct_2                          ; previous
.data:00402090 dd offset struct_1                          ; next
.data:004020B8 list_top dd offset struct_0                 ; DATA XREF: start+5↑o
```

For the sake of convenience, the structures are named struct_0, struct_1, struct_2, and struct_3 in accordance with the order of their appearance in memory. The last line is the top pointer list_top. As we can see, it points to struct_0, which was the last we added to the list, and struct_0, in turn, only has a pointer to the next structure, while its previous pointer has a NULL value. The struct_0 structure's next pointer points to struct_2, struct_2 structure's next points to struct_3, and the previous pointers lead us back in the reverse order.

Obviously, linked lists (those with a single, either forward or backward), link are a bit simpler than doubly linked lists as we only have to take care of a single pointer member of a node. It may be a good idea to implement a separate structure that describes a linked list node (whether simple or doubly linked) and have a set of procedures for the creation/population of linked lists, search of a node, and removal of a node. The following structure would suffice:

```
; Structure for a simple linked list node
struc list_node32
{
    .next       dd ?    ; Pointer to the next node
    .data       dd ?    ; Pointer to data object, which
```

```
                        ; may be anything. In case data fits
                        ; in 32 bits, the .data member itself
                        ; may be used for storing the data.
    }

    ; Structure for a doubly linked list node
    struc dllist_node32
    {
        .next       dd ?
        .previous   dd ?    ; Pointer to the previous node
        .data       dd ?
    }
```

If, on the other hand, you are writing code for the long mode (64-bit), the only change you need to make is replacing dd (which stands for a 32-bit double word) with dq (which stands for a 64-bit quad word) in order to be able to store long mode pointers.

In addition to this, you may also want or need to implement a structure that will describe a linked list, as a whole, having all the required pointers, counters, and so on (in our example, it was the list_top variable; not quite a structure, but it did its job well enough). However, when it comes to an array of linked lists, it would be much more convenient to utilize an array of pointers to linked lists, as this would provide easier access to members of the array, thus making your code less error prone, simpler, and faster.

Special cases of linked lists

You have, most likely, heard a lot about different types of data structures other than arrays and linked lists in programming lessons, unless you are a self-taught developer, in which case you may still have heard or read about these a lot. By different types of data structures other than arrays and linked lists, I mean stacks, queues, deques, and priority queues. However, being a fan of the principle of Occam's Razor, I believe that we should face the truth and acknowledge that all of these are just special cases of linked lists, unless their implementation is based on arrays (which may sometimes be possible).

Stack

A stack is a **LIFO (Last In First Out)** arrangement of data. The simplest example would be the process/thread stack. Although such an implementation is rather array based, it fairly illustrates the mechanism.

However, most of the time, we would not know the size of the required stack in advance, maybe just a rough estimation. Not to mention the fact that we would hardly need to store only double or quad words; we'll mostly have more complex structures. The most common implementation of a stack would be a singly linked list addressed by a `top` pointer only. Ideally, only three operations are permitted on a stack:

- `push`: This is used to add a new member to the list
- `top`: This is used to view/read the last added member of the list
- `pop`: This is used to remove the last added member from the list

While the `push` and `pop` operations are equivalent to adding and removing a member from/to a singly linked list, the TOP operation basically means getting the value of the `top` pointer and so obtaining access to the topmost (added last) member of the list.

Queue and deque

Queues are, exactly as the name states, queues of elements. A linked list is addressed by two pointers-one for the `top` element and one for the `tail` element. By nature, queues are a **FIFO (First In First Out)** arrangement of data, meaning that the element that was pushed first is to be popped first, too. It is totally up to you to decide where the queue starts and where it ends-whether `top` is the beginning or the end of a queue, and the same for `tail`. Should we want to convert the example of a linked list we used in this chapter to a queue, we would only need to add a `list_tail` pointer.

Deques are double-ended queues, which means that elements may be pushed into the queue either at the `top` element or at the `tail` element depending on the algorithm. The same is true for popping elements from the queue.

Priority queues

A priority queue is a special case of a regular queue. The only difference is that elements added to it each have a certain priority, which is defined by the algorithm and depends on the needs. The idea is that elements with a higher priority are served first, then the elements with lower priorities. If two elements have the same priority, then the order they are served in is in accordance with their position in the queue, so there are at least two possible ways to implement such an arrangement.

One would be the implementation of a sorting algorithm, which would add new elements according to their priority. This merely converts deque into a sorted list.

The other would be combing a deque for elements with the highest priority and serving them first, which makes a deque not much different from a linked list. The only difference, probably, would be that elements may be added only to the `top` element or the `tail` element.

Cyclic linked list

A cyclic linked list is probably the easiest to implement following the singly linked list. The only difference between the two is that the last element of the list points to the first element of the list, instead of its `next` pointer having a `NULL` value.

Summary for special cases of linked lists

As we can see, the special cases of linked lists shown previously are simply different logical paradigms of the same idea. This is especially true in the case of Assembly, which, unlike higher-level languages (those higher than C), does not have any built-in implementation of the preceding approaches, thus performing the function of Occam's Razor, sweeping away redundant notions and showing how things are in low-level reality.

However, we'll consider what Albert Einstein said:

> *"Everything should be made as simple as possible, but not simpler."*

Having made the topic of linked lists and their special cases as simple as possible, we need to proceed to more complex, more powerful forms of data arrangement. In the next section of this chapter, we will meet trees-a very powerful and useful method to store data.

Trees

Sometimes, the data arrangement schemes we have already covered are not ideal for solving certain problems. For example, when having a set of data that is frequently being searched or modified, while having to maintain a sorted nature, we could place it into an array or a sorted linked list, but the search times could be non-satisfactory. In such a case, it would probably be best to arrange the data in the form of a tree. A binary search tree, for instance, is the best way to minimize the search time when searching dynamic (changing) data. In fact, the same applies to static data as well.

But, first of all, what are trees in computing? When talking about trees, one may imagine a special type of graph (graphs will be briefly covered later in this chapter), consisting of nodes which have a parent node (except the root node, which is called, well, root node) and zero or more child nodes. In Assembly, we would declare a structure for a tree node like this:

```
struc tnode dataPtr, leftChild, rightChild
{
    .left   dd  leftChild   ; Pointer to left node or 0
    .right  dd  rightChild  ; Pointer to right node or 0
    .data   dd  dataPtr     ; Pointer to data
}
```

So, we have a structure which has a pointer to the left child node (traditionally, nodes with a lower value), a pointer to the right child node (traditionally, nodes with a higher value), and a pointer to the data represented by the node. In general, it is not a bad idea to add a pointer to the parent node, which may ease the task of balancing a tree; however, we do not need that for the example that we will examine in this part of the chapter. The preceding node structure is sufficient for building a tree like this:

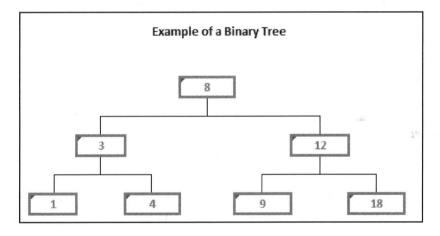

This figure demonstrates an ideal case of a balanced binary search tree. In reality, however, this happens not that often and depends on the balancing method. Unfortunately, methodologies of tree balancing slightly fall out of the scope of this book. The main idea, though, is to keep lower values to the left and higher values to the right, which may well involve a certain amount of rotation applied to subtrees, or even the whole tree.

A practical example

Enough with dry explanations. Being a developer, you are most likely familiar with tree-like structures and methods of balancing thereof, or you must have at least heard of them. Believing in learning by example as one of the most efficient ways of understanding something, I suggest we take a look at the following example.

Example - trivial cryptographic virtual machine

The idea behind this example is widely used and well known-a simple, not to say primitive, virtual machine. Imagine a situation where we have to implement a virtual machine that performs trivial string encryption with an XOR operation using a single byte key.

Virtual machine architecture

The architecture of the virtual processor is quite simple-it has a few registers that store the current execution state:

Register Name	Register function
register_a	An 8-bit general purpose register. The register is accessible to the VM code.
register_b	An 8-bit general purpose register. The register is accessible to the VM code.
register_key	An 8-bit register. This holds the encryption key byte.
register_cnt	An 8-bit register. This holds the counter for vm_loop instruction. The register is accessible to VM code.
data_base	A 32-bit (64-bit for the long mode) register. This holds the address of the data to be encrypted.
data_length	A 32-bit register. This holds the length of the data to be encrypted (only 8 bits are used, so the data cannot be longer than 256 bytes).

The virtual processor has a very limited instruction set, but they are not encoded sequentially:

Opcode	Mnemonic	Meaning
0x00	vm_load_key	This loads the key parameter of the VM procedure into the key register of the virtual processor.

0x01	`vm_nop`	This is the NOP instruction. No operation is performed.
0x02	`vm_load_data_length`	This loads the length of the string to be encrypted into the `data length` register of the virtual processor.
0x10	`vm_loop target`	This jumps to `target` if the `counter` register is less than the `data length` register.
0x11	`vm_jump target`	This unconditionally jumps to the `target` address.
0x12	`vm_exit`	This notifies the virtual processor that it should stop.
0x20	`vm_encrypt regId`	Performs the XOR operation on the content of `register[regId]` with the content of the key `register`.
0x21	`vm_decrement regId`	This decrements the content of `register[regId]`.
0x22	`vm_increment regId`	This increments the content of `register[regId]`.
0x30	`vm_load_data_byte regId`	Load byte from `data_base_address + counter_register` into `register[regId]`.
0x31	`vm_store_data_byte regId`	Store byte from `register[regId]` to `data_base_address + counter_register`.

Adding support for a virtual processor to the Flat Assembler

We will skip the declaration of a separate structure for the processor; instead, its state will be stored on a stack. However, we do need to make some preparations. First of all, we need to make the Flat Assembler understand our mnemonics and create a proper binary output. For this purpose, we will create an additional source file and name it `vm_code.asm`. As it will contain declarations of macro instructions and the VM code, which will be treated as data, the inclusion of the file in the main source would be done by adding the following:

```
include 'vm_code.asm'
```

Add this line somewhere in the data section. The next step-we have to define macro instructions that can be translated into a binary output that our virtual processor can understand. This is a very powerful feature of FASM, as one may add support for almost any architecture with a set of macro instructions (which, by the way, is the exact idea behind the Flat Assembler G):

```
macro vm_load_key
{
    db 0x00
}

macro vm_nop
{
    db 0x01
}

macro vm_load_data_length
{
    db 0x02
}

macro vm_loop loopTarget
{
    db 0x10
    dd loopTarget - ($ + 4)
}

macro vm_jump jumpTarget
{
    db 0x11
    dd loopTarget - ($ + 4)
}

macro vm_exit
{
    db 0x12
}

macro vm_encrypt regId
{
    db 0x20
    db regId
}

macro vm_decrement regId
{
    db 0x21
```

```
        db regId
    }

    macro vm_increment regId
    {
        db 0x22
        db regId
    }

    macro vm_load_data_byte regId
    {
        db 0x30
        db regId
    }

    macro vm_store_data_byte regId
    {
        db 0x31
        db regId
    }

    ; Let's give readable names to registers
    register_a   = 0
    register_b   = 1
    register_cnt = 2
```

Virtual code

Obviously, we did not write all of the preceding code just for fun; we need to write some code for the virtual processor. Since the architecture is very limited and restricted to a specific task, there are not too many options as to what the code may look like:

```
    ; Virtual code                      ; Binary output
    vm_code_start:
        vm_load_key                     ; 0x00
        vm_load_data_length             ; 0x02
        vm_nop                          ; 0x01
     .encryption_loop:
        vm_load_data_byte register_b    ; 0x30 0x01
        vm_encrypt register_b           ; 0x20 0x01
        vm_store_data_byte register_b   ; 0x31 0x01
        vm_loop .encryption_loop        ; 0x10 0xf5 0xff 0xff 0xff

        vm_exit                         ; 0x12
```

The virtual processor

Everything seems to be clear by now, except one thing-what does it all have to do with trees? We are almost there, as we have to implement the virtual processor itself, and that is what we are going to do here.

The easiest and probably the most common implementation of a virtual processor is a `while()` loop, which runs by reading instructions from the VM's memory and selects a proper execution path with the `switch()` statement implemented as the **indirect jump** and **jump table** (the table of jump target addresses). Although our example would probably run best when implemented this way, and the architecture described below would fit better for a complex instruction set, it was intentionally made simple in order to avoid the need to discuss certain aspects that are clearly unrelated to the topic-trees.

Our operation codes, as shown in the instruction/opcode table, are all 1 byte in size, plus a 1-byte or 4-byte operand (for instructions that require operand), and in range from `0x00` to `0x31`, with relatively large gaps. However, the amount of operation code allows us to arrange them in an almost perfect binary search tree:

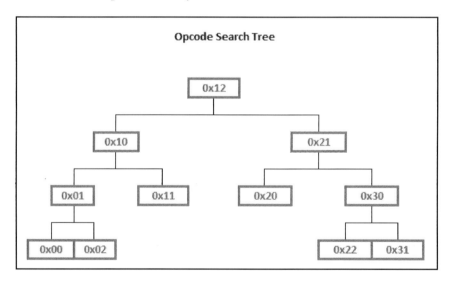

We say "almost" because if there were two child nodes for each of the nodes denoting opcodes `0x11` (vm_jump) and `0x20` (vm_encrypt), it would be an ideal binary search tree (but who says we cannot add four more instructions?).

Each node on the diagram represents a `tnode` structure containing all the necessary pointers, including a pointer to a small structure, which maps the operation code to real Assembly code in the virtual processor's loop:

```
struc instruction opcode, target
{
    .opcode dd opcode
    .target dd target
}
```

Thus, the first thing we do is build a table that maps all operation codes to Assembly code. The format of the table is rather simple. Each row contains the following:

- Double word operation code
- A pointer to the Assembly code (double word for the 32-bit mode or 64-bit for the long mode).

The implementation of the table in code is rather simple:

```
i_load_key          instruction 0x00,\
                                run_vm.load_key
i_nop               instruction 0x01,\
                                run_vm.nop
i_load_data_length  instruction 0x02,\
                                run_vm.load_data_length
i_loop              instruction 0x10,\
                                run_vm.loop
i_jump              instruction 0x11,\
                                run_vm.jmp
i_exit              instruction 0x12,\
                                run_vm.exit
i_encrypt           instruction 0x20,\
                                run_vm.encrypt
i_decrement         instruction 0x21,\
                                run_vm.decrement
i_increment         instruction 0x22,\
                                run_vm.increment
i_load_data_byte    instruction 0x30,\
                                run_vm.load_data_byte
i_store_data_byte   instruction 0x31,\
                                run_vm.store_data_byte
```

At last, we have reached the tree. Let's skip the tree building and balancing procedure, as the tree is statically allocated and as we are interested particularly in the structure itself. In the following code, we in fact create an array of `tnode` structures which, however, are not addressed by `base+index`, but are linked to a tree. The last line defines a pointer to the root node of the tree, `tree_root`, which refers to `t_exit`:

```
t_load_key               tnode i_load_key,\        ; 0x00  <-\
                               0,\                  ;          |
                               0                    ;          |
t_nop                    tnode i_nop,\             ; 0x01     | <-\
                               t_load_key,\        ; ---------/   |
                               t_load_data_length  ; ---------\   |
t_load_data_length tnode i_load_data_length,\      ; 0x02     <-/  |
                               0,\                  ;              |
                               0                    ;              |
t_loop                   tnode i_loop,\            ; 0x10          | <-\
                               t_nop,\             ; -------------/    |
                               t_jmp               ; --------\        |
t_jmp                    tnode i_jump,\            ; 0x11  <-/         |
                               0,\                  ;                 |
                               0                    ;                 |
t_exit                   tnode i_exit,\            ; 0x12             |
                               t_loop,\            ; -----------------/
                               t_decrement         ; --------\
t_encrypt                tnode i_encrypt,\         ; 0x20     | <-\
                               0,\                  ;          |   |
                               0                    ;          |   |
t_decrement              tnode i_decrement,\       ; 0x21  <-/    |
                               t_encrypt,\         ; -----------/
                               t_load_data_byte    ; --------\
t_increment              tnode i_increment,\       ; 0x22     | <-\
                               0,\                  ;          |   |
                               0                    ;          |   |
t_load_data_byte         tnode i_load_data_byte,\  ; 0x30  <-/    |
                               t_increment,\       ; -----------/
                               t_store_data_byte   ; --------\
t_store_data_byte        tnode i_store_data_byte,\ ; 0x31  <-/
                               0,\
                               0

tree_root dd t_exit
```

Once compiled, the data section of the executable would look like this:

```
.data:00402000 00                                  vm_code_start    db 0                            ; DATA XREF: _start+Cↄo
.data:00402001 02                                                   db 2
.data:00402002 01                                                   db 1
.data:00402003 30 01                                                dw 130h
.data:00402005 20 01                                                dw 120h
.data:00402007 31 01                                                dw 131h
.data:00402009 10                                                   db 10h
.data:0040200A F5 FF FF FF                                          dd 0FFFFFFF5h
.data:0040200E 12                                                   db 12h
.data:0040200F 00 00 00 00 00 00 00 00+  t_vm_load_key    tnode <0, 0, offset i_vm_load_key>
.data:0040200F 93 20 40 00                                                               ; DATA XREF: .data:t_vm_nopↄo
.data:0040201B 0F 20 40 00 27 20 40 00+  t_vm_nop         tnode <offset t_vm_load_key, offset t_vm_load_data_length, \
.data:0040201B 9B 20 40 00                                                               ; DATA XREF: .data:t_vm_loopↄo
.data:0040201B                                                               offset i_vm_nop>
.data:00402027 00 00 00 00 00 00 00 00+  t_vm_load_data_length tnode <0, 0, offset i_vm_load_data_length>
.data:00402027 A3 20 40 00                                                               ; DATA XREF: .data:t_vm_nopↄo
.data:00402033 1B 20 40 00 3F 20 40 00+  t_vm_loop        tnode <offset t_vm_nop, offset t_vm_jump, offset i_vm_loop>
.data:00402033 AB 20 40 00                                                               ; DATA XREF: .data:t_vm_exitↄo
.data:0040203F 00 00 00 00 00 00 00 00+  t_vm_jump        tnode <0, 0, offset i_vm_jump>
.data:0040203F B3 20 40 00                                                               ; DATA XREF: .data:t_vm_loopↄo
.data:00402048 33 20 40 00 63 20 40 00+  t_vm_exit        tnode <offset t_vm_loop, offset t_vm_decrement, offset i_vm_exit>
.data:0040204B BB 20 40 00                                                               ; DATA XREF: .data:tree_rootↄo
.data:00402057 00 00 00 00 00 00 00 00+  t_vm_encrypt     tnode <0, 0, offset i_vm_encrypt>
.data:00402057 C3 20 40 00                                                               ; DATA XREF: .data:t_vm_decrementↄo
.data:00402063 57 20 40 00 7B 20 40 00+  t_vm_decrement   tnode <offset t_vm_encrypt, offset t_vm_load_data_byte, \
.data:00402063 CB 20 40 00                                                               ; DATA XREF: .data:t_vm_exitↄo
.data:00402063                                                               offset i_vm_decrement>
.data:0040206F 00 00 00 00 00 00 00 00+  t_vm_increment   tnode <0, 0, offset i_vm_increment>
.data:0040206F D3 20 40 00                                                               ; DATA XREF: .data:t_vm_load_data_byteↄo
.data:0040207B 6F 20 40 00 87 20 40 00+  t_vm_load_data_byte tnode <offset t_vm_increment, offset t_vm_store_data_byte, \
.data:0040207B DB 20 40 00                                                               ; DATA XREF: .data:t_vm_decrementↄo
.data:0040207B                                                               offset i_vm_load_data_byte>
.data:00402087 00 00 00 00 00 00 00 00+  t_vm_store_data_byte tnode <0, 0, offset i_vm_store_data_byte>
.data:00402087 E3 20 40 00                                                               ; DATA XREF: .data:t_vm_load_data_byteↄo
.data:00402093 00 00 00 00 67 10 40 00  i_vm_load_key    instruction <0, offset vm_load_key>
.data:00402093                                                               ; DATA XREF: .data:t_vm_load_keyↄo
.data:0040209B 01 00 00 00 70 10 40 00  i_vm_nop         instruction <1, offset vm_nop>
.data:0040209B                                                               ; DATA XREF: .data:t_vm_nopↄo
.data:004020A3 02 00 00 00 73 10 40 00  i_vm_load_data_length instruction <2, offset vm_load_data_length>
.data:004020A3                                                               ; DATA XREF: .data:t_vm_load_data_lengthↄo
.data:004020AB 10 00 00 00 80 10 40 00  i_vm_loop        instruction <10h, offset vm_loop>
.data:004020AB                                                               ; DATA XREF: .data:t_vm_loopↄo
.data:004020B3 11 00 00 00 96 10 40 00  i_vm_jump        instruction <11h, offset vm_jump>
.data:004020B3                                                               ; DATA XREF: .data:t_vm_jumpↄo
.data:004020BB 12 00 00 00 A4 11 40 00  i_vm_exit        instruction <12h, offset vm_exit>
.data:004020BB                                                               ; DATA XREF: .data:t_vm_exitↄo
.data:004020C3 20 00 00 00 A2 10 40 00  i_vm_encrypt     instruction <20h, offset vm_encrypt>
.data:004020C3                                                               ; DATA XREF: .data:t_vm_encryptↄo
.data:004020CB 21 00 00 00 CA 10 40 00  i_vm_decrement   instruction <21h, offset vm_decrement>
.data:004020CB                                                               ; DATA XREF: .data:t_vm_decrementↄo
.data:004020D3 22 00 00 00 F9 10 40 00  i_vm_increment   instruction <22h, offset vm_increment>
.data:004020D3                                                               ; DATA XREF: .data:t_vm_incrementↄo
.data:004020DB 30 00 00 00 28 11 40 00  i_vm_load_data_byte instruction <30h, offset vm_load_data_byte>
.data:004020DB                                                               ; DATA XREF: .data:t_vm_load_data_byteↄo
.data:004020E3 31 00 00 00 66 11 40 00  i_vm_store_data_byte instruction <31h, offset vm_store_data_byte>
.data:004020E3                                                               ; DATA XREF: .data:t_vm_store_data_byteↄo
.data:004020EB                                  ; tnode *tree_root
.data:004020EB 4B 20 40 00              tree_root        dd offset t_vm_exit    ; DATA XREF: run_vm+1Eↄo
.data:004020EF 54 68 69 73 20 69 73 20+ aThisIsTheDataToEnc db 'This is the data to encrypt',0
```

Searching the tree

We need to take care of a procedure that would extract the correct address of the Assembly implementation of the virtual instruction from the tree prior to beginning the implementation of the virtual processor's loop.

The `tree_lookup` procedure requires two parameters:

- The address of the `tree_root` variable
- The byte opcode cast to double word

When this procedure is called, it "walks" the tree node by node (in accordance with the rule the tree was sorted by) and compares the opcode parameter to the opcode value of the instruction structure referred to by the current node. The procedure returns the address of the Assembly implementation of the operation code, or it returns a zero if no such opcode has been defined:

```
tree_lookup:
    push ebp
    mov  ebp, esp
    push ebx ecx

    virtual at ebp + 8
       .treePtr dd ?                  ; First parameter - pointer to tree_root
       .code dd ?                     ; Second parameter - opcode value
    end virtual
    virtual at ecx
       .node tnode ?,?,?              ; Lets us treat ECX as a pointer
                                      ; to tnode structure
    end virtual
    virtual at eax
       .instr instruction ?, ?        ; Lets us treat EAX as a pointer
                                      ; to instruction structure
    end virtual

    mov   ecx, [.treePtr]             ; Load the pointer to tree_root
    mov   ecx, [ecx]                  ; Load the pointer to root node
    mov   ebx, [.code]                ; Read current opcode
    movzx ebx, bl                     ; Cast to unsigned int

@@:
    or    ecx, 0                      ; Check whether ECX points to a node
    jz    .no_such_thing              ; and return zero if not

    mov   eax, [.node.data]           ; Load pointer to instruction structure
    cmp   ebx, [.instr.opcode]        ; Compare opcode value
    jz    @f
```

```
    ja    .go_right           ; If node contains lower opcode, then
                              ; continue searching the right subtree
    mov   ecx, [.node.left]   ; Otherwise continue searching the
    jmp   @b                  ; left subtree

.go_right:
    mov   ecx, [.node.right]
    jmp   @b

@@:
    mov   eax, [.instr.target] ; Relevant instruction structure has
                              ; been found, so return the address
                              ; of instruction implementation
@@:
    pop   ecx ebx             ; We are done
    leave
    ret   8

.no_such_thing:              ; Zero out EAX to denote an error
    xor   eax, eax
    jmp   @b
```

The loop

The implementation of the loop is a bit long, and we have many more interesting things to fill the space allocated for this chapter, so refer to the accompanying source code for the full version. Here, however, we will examine certain parts of the implementation:

- **Creating a stack frame and parameter markup**: The procedure's prolog code would be just as usual-we allocate some space on the stack and save registers that we want not to be affected by the procedure, and that means all the registers we use in the procedure:

```
run_vm:
    push  ebp
    mov   ebp, esp
    sub   esp, 4 * 3          ; We only need 12 bytes for storing
                              ; the state of virtual cpu
    push  eax ebx ecx edx esi ; We will use these registers
    virtual at ebp + 8        ; Assign local labels to parameters
        .p_cmd_buffer_ptr  dd ? ; Pointer to VM code
        .p_data_buffer_ptr dd ? ; Pointer to data we want to
                              ; encrypt
        .p_data_length     dd ? ; Length of data in bytes
        .p_key             dd ? ; Key value cast to double word
    end virtual
```

```
virtual at ebp - 0x0c       ; Assign local labels to stack
                            ; variables
    .register_a      db ? ; Register A of virtual processor
    .register_b      db ? ; Register B of virtual processor
    .register_key    db ? ; Register to hold the key
    .register_cnt    db ? ; Counter register
    .data_base       dd ? ; Pointer to data buffer
    .data_length     dd ? ; Size of the data buffer in size
end virtual
```

- **Preparing a virtual processor loop**: The loop itself begins with reading an opcode from the current position in the virtual code, then calls the `tree_lookup` procedure, and either jumps to the address returned by `tree_lookup` or to `.exit` if the procedure returns an error (zero):

```
virtual_loop:
    mov    al, [esi + ebx]   ; ESI - points to array of bytes
                             ; containing
                             ; virtual code
                             ; EBX - instruction pointer (offset
                             ; into virtual code)
    movzx eax, al            ; Cast opcode to double word
    push  eax
    push  tree_root
    call  tree_lookup        ; Get address of opcode emulation
                             ; code
    or    eax, 0             ; Check for error
    jz    .exit
    jmp   eax                ; Jump to emulation code
```

The preceding code is followed by a set of instructions emulating code fragments, as you can see in the accompanying source code.

The last few lines of the `run_vm` procedure are, in fact, the emulation of the `vm_exit` opcode:

```
.exit:
    pop   esi edx ecx ebx eax  ; Restore saved registers
    add   esp, 4 * 3           ; Destroy stack frame
    leave
    ret   4 * 4
```

Tree balancing

Now, when we know what a binary search tree looks like on the Assembly programming level, it would not be correct not to return to the question of binary search tree balancing. There are several approaches to this problem, however, we would only consider one-the Day-Stout-Warren algorithm (included in the accompanying code). The algorithm is simple:

1. Allocate a tree node and make it a "pseudo root" for the tree, making the original root the pseudo root's right child.
2. Convert the tree into a sorted linked list by means of an in-order traversal (this step also calculates the number of nodes in the original tree). No additional allocations are required, as the step reuses existing pointers in tree nodes.
3. Convert the list back into a complete binary tree (one in which the bottom layer is populated strictly from left to right).
4. Make pseudo root's right child the tree's root.
5. Dispose of the pseudo root node.

Applying this algorithm to our opcode tree will result in the following structure:

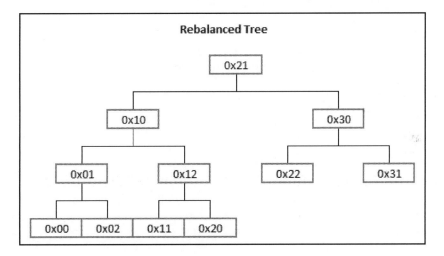

The structure remains almost the same-four levels, including the root node, and four nodes at the bottom-most layer. The order of opcodes has changed a bit, but this is not that important in the case of this particular example. However, should we design a more complex system that expects much more load, we could design the encoding of the operation code in such a way that the most frequently used opcodes would be encoded with values from the upper layers and the least frequently used opcodes, with values from the bottom layers.

Sparse matrices

Sparse matrices are rarely discussed, if at all, due to the relative complexity of implementation and maintenance; however, they may be a very convenient and useful instrument in certain cases. Basically, sparse matrices are conceptually very close to arrays, but they're much more efficient when working with sparse data as they allow memory savings, which in turn allows the processing of much larger amounts of data.

Let's take astrophotography as an example. For those of us not familiar with the subject, amateur astrophotography means plugging your digital camera into a telescope, selecting a region in the night sky, and taking pictures. However, since pictures are taken at night time without a flashlight or any other aid (it would be silly to try to light celestial objects with a flashlight anyway), one has to take dozens of pictures of the same object and then stack the images together using a specific algorithm. In this case, there are two major problems:

- Noise reduction
- Image alignment

Lacking professional equipment (meaning not having a huge telescope with a cooled CCD or CMOS matrix), one faces the problem of noise. The longer the exposition, the more noise in the final image. Of course, there are numerous algorithms for noise reduction, but sometimes, a real celestial object may mistakenly be treated as noise and be removed by the noise reduction algorithm. Therefore, it is a good idea to process each image and detect potential celestial objects. If certain "light", which otherwise may be considered as noise, is present in at least 80% of images (it is hard to believe that any noise would have survived for such a long time without any changes, unless we are talking about dead pixels), then its area needs different treatment.

However, in order to process an image, we need to make a decision on how to store the result. We, of course, may use an array of structures describing each and every pixel, but that would be too expensive by means of the memory required for such operation. On the other hand, even if we take a picture of the highly populated area of the night sky, the area occupied by celestial objects would be significantly smaller than the "empty" space. Instead, we may divide an image into smaller areas, analyze certain characteristics of those smaller regions, and only take into consideration those that seem to be populated. The following figure presents the idea:

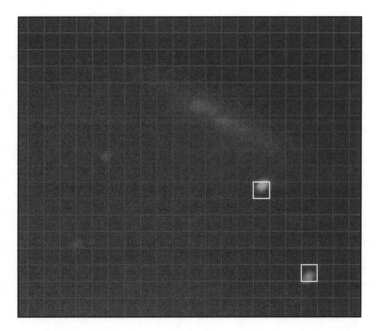

The figure (which shows the Messier 82 object, also known as *Cigar Galaxy*) is divided into 396 smaller regions (a matrix of 22 x 18 regions, 15 x 15 pixels each). Each region may be described by its luminosity, noise ratio, and many other aspects, including its location on the figure, meaning that it may occupy quite a sensible amount of memory. Having this data stored in a two-dimensional array with more than 30 images simultaneously may result in megabytes, of meaningless data. As the image shows, there are only two regions of interest, which together form about 0.5% (which fits the definition of sparse data more than perfectly), meaning that if we choose to use arrays, we waste 99.5% of the used memory.

Utilizing sparse matrices, we may reduce the usage of memory to the minimum required to store important data. In this particular case, we would have a linked list of 22 column header nodes, 18 row header nodes, and only 2 nodes for data. The following is a very rough example of such an arrangement:

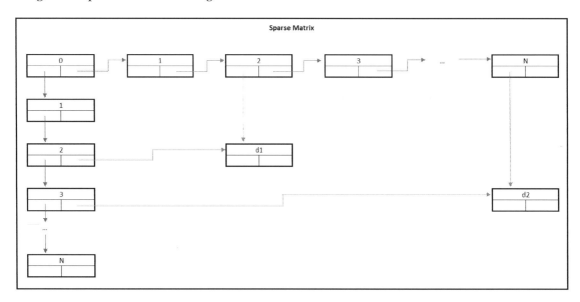

The preceding example is very rough; in reality, the implementation would contain a few other links. For example, empty column header nodes would have their `down` pointer point to themselves, and empty row headers would have their `right` pointers point to themselves, too. The last data node in a row would have its right pointer pointing to the row header node, and the same applies to the last data node in a column having its `down` pointer pointing to the column header node.

Graphs

The general definition of a graph states that a graph is a data structure consisting of a set of vertices (V) and edges (E). While the vertex may be anything (anything means any data structure), edge is defined by the two vertices it connects-*v* and *w*. Edges have a direction, meaning that the data flows from vertex *v* to vertex *w*, and *weight*, which indicates how difficult the flow is.

The easiest and probably the most common example of a graph structure is a perceptron-an artificial neural network paradigm:

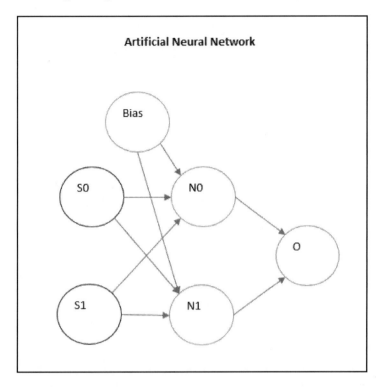

Traditionally, perceptrons are drawn from left to right, so we have three layers:

- The input layer (sensors)
- The hidden layer (where most of the processing takes place)
- The output layer (forms the output of a perceptron)

Although nodes of artificial neural network are called **neurons**, we will refer to them as vertices as we are discussing graphs, not ANNs.

In the preceding graph, we see a typical multilayer perceptron layout for an artificial neural network capable of solving the XOR problem.

An XOR problem in artificial neural networks is the problem of making an ANN implementation receiving two inputs in the range *{0, 1}* to produce a result, as if two inputs were XOR'ed. A single layer perceptron (where the hidden layer is also the output layer) is not able to find solutions for this problem, therefore an additional layer is added.

The vertices **S0** and **S1** do not perform any computations and serve as sources of data for vertices **N0** and **N1**. As it has been stated, edges have weights, and in this example, the data from **S0** and **S1** is multiplied with the weights of the edges *[s0, n0], [s0, n1], [s1, n0],* and *[s1, n1]*. The same applies to data being transferred via *[bias, n0], [bias, n1], [n0, o],* and *[n1, o]*.

However, graphs may be of any shape and edges may lead data in any direction (even to the same vertex), depending on the problem they intend to solve.

Summary

In this chapter, we have briefly covered several types of data structures (not to be confused with the Assembly struc[tures]) and reviewed a few of their possible applications. However, being very vast, the topic of data structures may require a separate chapter for each of the structures briefly described here, and their variations, which, unfortunately, falls out of the scope of this book.

Beginning with the next chapter (Chapter 8, *Mixing Modules Written in Assembly and Those Written in High-Level Languages*), we will approach more practical problems and will start applying the knowledge we have gathered thus far in an attempt to find an elegant solution.

In the next chapter, we will see how the Assembly code written for both 32-bit and 64-bit Windows and Linux operating systems may be linked with existing libraries written either in Assembly or in a high-level language. We will even cover the topic of interoperability of .NET and Assembly code (on both Linux and Windows).

8
Mixing Modules Written in Assembly and Those Written in High-Level Languages

We have come a long way and have covered almost every aspect of Assembly programming basics. In fact, we should be able to implement any algorithm in Assembly language by this time; however, there are a few important things left we have not touched yet, but they are nonetheless important to know.

Despite the fact that writing relatively large parts of a product (not to say writing a complete product) in Assembly language may not be the best idea when it comes to timelines, it may still be a very interesting and challenging task (educational as well). Sometimes it is more convenient to implement certain parts of an algorithm in Assembly, rather than using a high-level language. Remember the tiny virtual machine we used for XOR encryption of data? For the sake of an example, we will implement a simple encryption/decryption module in Assembly and see how it may be used with high-level languages.

In this chapter, we will cover the following topics:

- Implementing the core of a primitive cryptographic module
- Building object files for further linking with code written in high-level languages:
    - **OBJ**: Object files for Windows (32 and 64 bit);
    - **O**: Linkable ELF for Linux (32 and 64 bit);
- Building DLL (dynamic link libraries) and SO (shared objects) for Windows and Linux (32 and 64 bit) to be used with the .NET platform

Crypto Core

The main project of this chapter is a tiny, simple (not to say primitive) encryption/decryption module written entirely in Assembly. Since the topic of this chapter is interfacing Assembly modules and modules written in high-level languages, we will not delve into cryptography principles, but we will rather concentrate on the portability and interoperability of our code while using a slightly modified XOR algorithm. The idea behind the algorithm is to receive an array of bytes and do the following:

1. Take a byte and rotate it a certain number of bits to the left (the counter is randomly generated at compile time).
2. XOR the result with the 1-byte key (randomly generated at compile time as well).
3. Write the byte back to the array.
4. If there are more bytes to encrypt, go to step 1; otherwise break out of the loop.

The following screenshot is an example output of the algorithm we are about to implement:

Not the best encryption, but definitely enough for our needs.

Portability

Our intention is to write portable code that may be used on both 32-bit and 64-bit Windows and Linux platforms. This may either sound impossible or very tedious work, but it is quite simple. First of all, we have to define a few constants and macros, which will ease our further work, so let's begin by creating the `platform.inc` and `crypto.asm` source files where the latter is the main source file and the one we will compile.

Flat Assembler is capable of producing files in a variety of formats, beginning with raw binary output and DOS executables, through Windows-specific formats and up to Linux binaries (both executable and object). It is assumed that you are familiar with at least some of the following formats:

- 32-bit Windows object file (MS COFF format)
- 64-bit Windows object file (MS64 COFF format)
- 32-bit Windows DLL
- 64-bit Windows DLL
- 32-bit Linux object file (ELF)
- 64-bit Linux object file (ELF64)

There is no need to be deeply acquainted with them, as the Flat Assembler does all the hard work for us and all we have to do is tell it which format we are interested in (and format our code accordingly). We will use a compile time variable, ACTIVE_TARGET, for conditional compilation and use the following constants as possible values:

```
; Put this in the beginning of 'platform.inc'

type_dll        equ 0
type_obj        equ 1

platform_w32    equ 2
platform_w64    equ 4
platform_l32    equ 8
platform_l64    equ 16

TARGET_W32_DLL equ platform_w32 or type_dll
TARGET_W32_OBJ equ platform_w32 or type_obj
TARGET_W64_DLL equ platform_w64 or type_dll
TARGET_W64_OBJ equ platform_w64 or type_obj
TARGET_L32_O   equ platform_l32 or type_obj
TARGET_L64_O   equ platform_l64 or type_obj
```

Specifying the output format

As usual, the main source file (in our case, crypto.asm) should begin with the output format specification, thus telling the assembler how to treat the code and sections when creating the output file. As we have mentioned earlier, the compile-time variable, ACTIVE_TARGET, is the one to be used for the selection of the proper code for the assembler to process.

The next step would be defining a macro that would conditionally generate the proper code sequence. Let's call it `set_output_format`:

```
macro set_output_format
{
   if ACTIVE_TARGET = TARGET_W32_DLL
      include 'win32a.inc'
      format PE DLL
      entry DllMain

   else if ACTIVE_TARGET = TARGET_W32_OBJ
      format MS COFF

   else if ACTIVE_TARGET = TARGET_W64_DLL
      include 'win64a.inc'
      format PE64 DLL
      entry DllMain

   else if ACTIVE_TARGET = TARGET_W64_OBJ
      format MS64 COFF

   else if ACTIVE_TARGET = TARGET_L32_O
      format ELF

   else if ACTIVE_TARGET = TARGET_L64_O
      format ELF64
   end if
}
```

This macro would tell the assembler to evaluate the ACTIVE_TARGET compile-time variable and only use specific code. For example, when ACTIVE_TARGET equals TARGET_W64_OBJ, the assembler will only process the following line:

```
format MS64 COFF
```

Thus, it will generate a 64-bit Windows object file.

Conditional declaration of code and data sections

Having told the compiler what output format we are expecting, we need to declare the sections. Since we are writing portable code, we will use two macros to properly declare code and data sections for each of the formats mentioned earlier. As we are used to seeing a data section after the code section (at least in this book, as the order may vary), we will declare a macro responsible for the proper declaration of the beginning of the code section first:

```
macro begin_code_section
{
    if ACTIVE_TARGET = TARGET_W32_DLL
       section '.text' code readable executable
     ; This is not obligatory, but nice to have - the DllMain procedure
     DllMain:
       xor eax, eax
       inc eax
       ret 4 * 3

    else if ACTIVE_TARGET = TARGET_W32_OBJ
       section '.text' code readable executable

    else if ACTIVE_TARGET = TARGET_W64_DLL
       section '.text' code readable executable
     ; DllMain procedure for 64-bit Windows DLL
     DllMain:
       xor rax, rax
       inc eax
       ret

    else if ACTIVE_TARGET = TARGET_W64_OBJ
       section '.text' code readable executable

    else if ACTIVE_TARGET = TARGET_L32_O
       section '.text' executable

    else if ACTIVE_TARGET = TARGET_L64_O
       section '.text' executable

    end if
}
```

We will follow it by the macro declaring data section:

```
macro begin_data_section
{
    if ACTIVE_TARGET = TARGET_W32_DLL
        section '.data' data readable writeable

    else if ACTIVE_TARGET = TARGET_W32_OBJ
        section '.data' data readable writeable

    else if ACTIVE_TARGET = TARGET_W64_DLL
        section '.data' data readable writeable

    else if ACTIVE_TARGET = TARGET_W64_OBJ
        section '.data' data readable writeable align 16

    else if ACTIVE_TARGET = TARGET_L32_O
        section '.data' writeable

    else if ACTIVE_TARGET = TARGET_L64_O
        section '.data' writeable

    end if
}
```

Exporting symbols

The last macro in the series would be the one that makes it possible to export certain symbols. Our implementation of a cryptographic core would export just one symbol--the GetPointers() procedure--which, in turn, would return a pointer to a structure containing pointers to the rest of procedures. This macro follows the previously defined pattern:

```
; In this specific case, when the macro would be called
; at the end of the source, we may replace the
; "macro finalize" declaration with the "postpone" directive.
macro finalize
{
    if ACTIVE_TARGET = TARGET_W32_DLL
        section '.edata' export data readable
            export 'MA_CRYPTO.DLL',\
                GetPointers, 'GetPointers'

    else if ACTIVE_TARGET = TARGET_W32_OBJ
        public GetPointers as '_GetPointers'
```

```
    else if ACTIVE_TARGET = TARGET_W64_DLL
        section '.edata' export data readable
            export 'MA_CRYPTO.DLL',\
                GetPointers, 'GetPointers'

    else if ACTIVE_TARGET = TARGET_W64_OBJ
        public GetPointers as 'GetPointers'

    else if ACTIVE_TARGET = TARGET_L32_O
        public GetPointers as 'GetPointers'

    else if ACTIVE_TARGET = TARGET_L64_O
        public GetPointers as 'GetPointers'

    end if
}
```

The preceding macro would make the symbol visible to either a static or dynamic linker, depending on the target we are building. Alternatively, we could replace `macro finalize` with the `postpone` directive, which would force the body of the macro to be executed automatically once the end of the source is reached.

Now we may save the `platform.inc` file as we will not alter it in any way in the future.

Core procedures

Having taken care of all the output format specifics, we may safely proceed to the implementation of the core's code. As it has already been mentioned earlier, we are about to export only a single entry; however, we still need to implement the rest. There are only four procedures in our core:

- `f_set_data_pointer`: This procedure accepts a single parameter, which is a pointer to the data we want to process, and stores it to the `data_pointer` global variable
- `f_set_data_length`: This procedure accepts one parameter, which is the length of data we want to encrypt/decrypt, and stores it to the `data_length` global variable
- `f_encrypt`: This procedure implements the encryption loop
- `f_decrypt`: This is the inverse operation of `f_encrypt`

However, prior to implementing all of these, we first need to prepare the template or, to be more precise, the skeleton for our main source file. This template would look a tiny bit different from what we are used to due to the extensive usage of macroinstructions. However, don't let it confuse you. The structure is logically (and from an Assembler's point of view) the same as the one we have been dealing with earlier:

```
; First of all we need to include all that we have written this far
include 'platform.inc'

; The following variable and macro are used in compile time
; only for generation of pseudorandom sequences, where
; count specifies the amount of pseudorandom bytes to generate
seed = %t
macro fill_random count
{
    local a, b
    a = 0
    while a < count
        seed = ((seed shr 11) xor (seed * 12543)) and 0xffffffff
        b = seed and 0xff
        db   b
        a = a + 1
    end while
}

; ACTIVE_TARGET variable may be set to any of the
; TARGET* constants
ACTIVE_TARGET = TARGET_W32_DLL

; Tell the compiler which type of output is expected
; depending on the value of the ACTIVE_TARGET variable
set_output_format

; Create code section depending on selected target
begin_code_section

; We will insert our code here

; Create appropriate declaration of the data section
begin_data_section

    ; Tell the compiler whether we are expecting 32-bit
    ; or 64-bit output
    if(ACTIVE_TARGET = TARGET_W32_OBJ) |\
      (ACTIVE_TARGET = TARGET_W32_DLL) |\
      (ACTIVE_TARGET = TARGET_L32_O)
      use32
```

```
    else if(ACTIVE_TARGET = TARGET_W64_OBJ) |\
          (ACTIVE_TARGET = TARGET_W64_DLL) |\
          (ACTIVE_TARGET = TARGET_L64_O)
      use64
    end if

    ; This, in fact, is a structure which would be populated with
    ; addresses of our procedures
    pointers:
    fill_random 4 * 8
    ; Here the core stores the address of the data to be processed
    data_pointer:
    fill_random 8

    ; And here the core stores its length in bytes
    data_length:
    fill_random 8

    ; Pseudorandom encryption key
    key:
    fill_random 2

; The following line may be omitted if we used the postpone
; directive instead of "macro finalize"
finalize
```

Despite having a different look from what we are used to seeing, the preceding code is quite self-explanatory and there is not too much to add, if at all. All the hard work is being delegated to previously defined macroinstructions and the only aspect we still have to take care of is the bit capacity. As you can see, the size and addresses are given 8 bytes by default. The purpose of this is to make them fit both 32-bit and 64-bit needs. We could have inserted another if...else clause, but since we only have 3 bit capacity-dependent data items, spending another 4 bytes for each of them in 32-bit mode is not an issue.

Encryption/decryption

As we are developing a crypto core here, it is natural to begin with the implementation of the cryptographic functionality first. The following code performs the encryption of data according to the algorithm we previously defined:

```
f_encrypt:
    ; The if statement below, when the condition is TRUE, forces the
assembler to produce
    ; 32-bit code
    if (ACTIVE_TARGET = TARGET_W32_OBJ) |\
       (ACTIVE_TARGET = TARGET_W32_DLL) |\
```

```
        (ACTIVE_TARGET = TARGET_L32_O)
        push eax ebx esi edi ecx
        lea esi, [data_pointer]
        mov esi, [esi]
        mov edi, esi
        lea ebx, [data_length]
        mov ebx, [ebx]
        lea ecx, [key]
        mov cx, [ecx]
        and cl, 0x07

    ; Encryption loop
    @@:
        lodsb
        rol al, cl
        xor al, ch
        stosb
        dec ebx
        or ebx, 0
        jnz @b

        pop ecx edi esi ebx eax
        ret

; In general, we could have omitted the "if" statement here,
; but the assembler
; should not generate any code at all, if
; the value of ACTIVE_TARGET is not valid.
; In either case, the following block is processed only
; when we are expecting a 64-bit output
    else if (ACTIVE_TARGET = TARGET_W64_OBJ) |\
            (ACTIVE_TARGET = TARGET_W64_DLL) |\
            (ACTIVE_TARGET = TARGET_L64_O)
        push rax rbx rsi rdi rcx
        lea rsi, [data_pointer]
        mov rsi, [rsi]
        mov rdi, rsi
        lea rbx, [data_length]
        mov ebx, [rbx]
        lea rcx, [key]
        mov cx, [rcx]
        and cl, 0x07

    @@:
        lodsb
        rol al, cl
        xor al, ch
        stosb
```

```
        dec rbx
        or rbx, 0
        jnz @b

        pop rcx rdi rsi rbx rax
        ret

    end if
```

By now, you should be able to differentiate between different parts of a procedure yourself, seeing where the prolog ends, where the epilog begins, and where the core functionality resides. In this particular case, the majority of the code is dedicated to preserving/restoring registers and to accessing parameters/variables, while the core functionality may be narrowed down to this code:

```
; Encryption loop
    @@:
        lodsb
        rol al, cl
        xor al, ch
        stosb
        dec ebx
        or ebx, 0
        jnz @b
```

For 32-bit platform or to this code:

```
@@:
        lodsb
        rol al, cl
        xor al, ch
        stosb
        dec rbx
        or rbx, 0
        jnz @b
```

For its 64-bit platform.

It is quite obvious that the implementation of the decryption procedure would be 99% identical to the encryption one. The only change would be swapping the rotation and XOR instructions (while changing the direction of rotation, of course). Thus, the 32-bit version of f_decrypt would have the following:

```
    xor al, ch
    ror al, cl
```

Similarly, its 64-bit analog would be just the same two lines.

Setting the encryption/decryption parameters

As you may have noticed (I hope you have), the procedures discussed in the previous section do not receive any parameters at all. Therefore, we do need to supply two more procedures in order to make it possible to tell the core where data resides and how many bytes to process. As each of these procedures accepts one parameter, the code would be a bit more segmented in order to reflect the calling convention being used, which, in our case, is as follows:

- cdecl for 32-bit targets
- Microsoft x64 for Windows-based 64-bit targets
- AMD64 for Linux-based 64-bit targets

f_set_data_pointer

This procedure receives a parameter of the `void*` type . Of course, the assembler does not care about the type of parameter a certain procedure expects. To be more precise, the assembler, as a compiler, is not aware of the procedure parameters as a concept, not to mention that it has no concept of procedure at all. Let's take a look at the implementation of the `f_set_data_pointer` procedure:

```
f_set_data_pointer:
    if (ACTIVE_TARGET = TARGET_W32_OBJ) |\
       (ACTIVE_TARGET = TARGET_W32_DLL) |\
       (ACTIVE_TARGET = TARGET_L32_O)
       push eax
       lea eax, [esp + 8]
       push dword [eax]
       pop dword [data_pointer]
       pop eax
       ret

    else if (ACTIVE_TARGET = TARGET_W64_OBJ) |\
            (ACTIVE_TARGET = TARGET_W64_DLL)
       push rax
       lea rax, [data_pointer]
       mov [rax], rcx
       pop rax
       ret

    else if (ACTIVE_TARGET = TARGET_L64_O)
       push rax
       lea rax, [data_pointer]
       mov [rax], rdi
       pop rax
```

```
        ret

    end if
```

Nothing complicated in this code either. The parameter passed to this procedure is simply being written to the `data_pointer` location.

f_set_data_length

This procedure is identical to `f_set_data_pointer` with the only difference being the address where the parameter is written. Simply copy the preceding code and change `data_pointer` to `data_length`.

Another alternative is to implement a single procedure, thus getting rid of redundant code, which would accept two parameters:

- The actual parameter (either a pointer to data or its size) as the assembler does not care about types
- A selector, which will tell the procedure where the parameter value should be stored

Try to implement this yourself; it would be a good quick exercise.

GetPointers()

The `GetPointers()` procedure is the only one we make public, the only one that would be visible to a dynamic or static linker, depending on the selected output target. The logic behind this procedure is primitive. It creates a structure (in this example, the structure is statically allocated), filled with the addresses of core procedures, and returns the address of this structure:

```
GetPointers:

    if (ACTIVE_TARGET = TARGET_W32_OBJ) |\
       (ACTIVE_TARGET = TARGET_W32_DLL) |\
       (ACTIVE_TARGET = TARGET_L32_O)

    push dword pointers
    pop eax
    mov [eax], dword f_set_data_pointer
    mov [eax + 4], dword f_set_data_length
    mov [eax + 8], dword f_encrypt
    mov [eax + 12], dword f_decrypt
    ret
```

```
else if (ACTIVE_TARGET = TARGET_W64_OBJ) |\
        (ACTIVE_TARGET = TARGET_W64_DLL) |\
        (ACTIVE_TARGET = TARGET_L64_O)

    push rbx
    mov rbx, pointers
    mov rax, rbx
    mov rbx, f_set_data_pointer
    mov [rax], rbx
    mov rbx, f_set_data_length
    mov [rax + 8], rbx
    mov rbx, f_encrypt
    mov [rax + 16], rbx
    mov rbx, f_decrypt
    mov [rax + 24], rbx
    pop rbx
    ret

end if
```

Once all of the preceding procedures have been added to the main source file, you may safely compile it and see that an output of the selected output format is being generated. If you leave the target specified here, you should be able to see a 32-bit windows DLL being created.

Interfacing with C/C++

Let me take advantage of the topic of this chapter and say it once. Enough of the Assembly, let's do some C (for those willing to link Assembly code to C++, this C example should be easy to understand; if not--this is the wrong book). For the sake of an example, we will generate an object file out of our Assembly sources and link it with the code written in C for both 32-bit and 64-bit Windows and Linux.

Static linking - Visual Studio 2017

First of all, let's see how we generate an object file. I am quite sure you have already understood how to produce different targets in general and for this example in particular. Let's begin with a 32-bit MSCOFF object file by setting the ACTIVE_TARGET variable to TARGET_W32_OBJ and compiling the main source file.

Create a C/C++ project in Visual Studio and copy the object file into the project directory as shown in the following screenshot (the screenshot shows object files for both 32-bit and 64-bit):

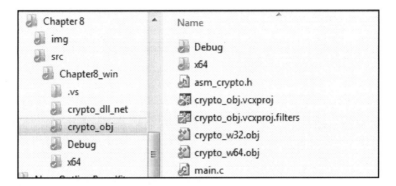

As you can see in the preceding screenshot, there is at least one more file we need, namely the header file. Since our crypto engine is fairly simple, we do not need any complicated header files. The one shown here would definitely suffice:

```
1      #pragma once
2
3      #ifdef __cplusplus
4       #define EXTERN
5       extern "C"
6       {
7      #else
8       #define EXTERN extern
9       #endif
10
11     typedef struct
12      {
13          void(*f_set_data_pointer)(void*);
14          void(*f_set_data_length)(int);
15          void(*f_encrypt)(void);
16          void(*f_decrypt)(void);
17      }crypto_functions_t, *pcrypto_functions_t;
18
19      EXTERN pcrypto_functions_t GetPointers(void);
20
21     #ifdef __cplusplus
22      }
23      #endif
```

There is a small catch in the preceding code. Try figuring out what isn't correct before you read the next paragraph.

Technically, the code is correct. It would compile and run without a problem, but there is one very important aspect of linking modules written in Assembly to other languages, very important and not quite obvious at the first glance:structure member alignment. In this example, we only used one structure (where we store procedure pointers) and we took proper care of it so that the pointers would be properly aligned depending on the platform. While we aligned our data on a byte boundary (stored it sequentially), Visual Studio's default structure member alignment value is, well, **Default**, which does not really tell us a lot. Assumptions may be made (in this case, we can assume that Default means the first option, which is a 1-byte alignment), but there is no guarantee of that and we have to explicitly specify the alignment, as assumptions not only do not always work in the case of Assembly, but they also pose a serious threat. It is important to mention that, despite the fact that we have been mentioning Visual Studio in this paragraph, the same applies to any C compiler.

One way to specify structure member alignment would be through the project settings, as follows:

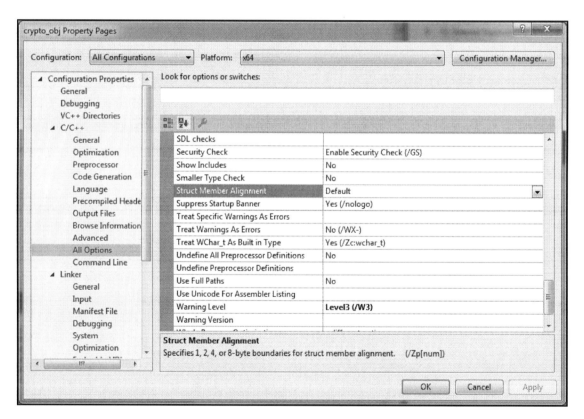

This is good enough for our example, but it may cause problems in the case of larger projects. It is highly recommended not to change the structure member alignment project-wide without any reasonable need for such a change. Instead, we may make a tiny modification to our header file, which would tell the compiler how to handle structure member alignment for this specific structure. Insert the following code right before the declaration of the `crypto_functions_t` structure:

```
#ifdef WIN32                    // For Windows platforms (MSVC)
#pragma pack(push, 1)           // set structure member alignment to 1
#define PACKED
#else                           // Do the same for Unix based platforms
(GCC)
#define PACKED  __attribute__((packed, aligned(1)))
#endif
```

Insert the following right after the declaration:

```
#ifdef WIN32                    // For Windows platforms
#pragma pack(pop)               // Restore previous alignment settings
#endif
```

Now, consider the following line:

```
}crypto_functions_t, *pcrypto_functions_t;
```

Change the preceding line to this:

```
}PACKED crypto_functions_t, *pcrypto_functions_t;
```

Then, add the `main.c` file as shown in the following screenshot:

```
1
2    #include "asm_crypto.h"
3    #include <stdio.h>
4
5    int main(void)
6    {
7        char testString[] = { "Hello, World!" };
8        pcrypto_functions_t funcs;
9
10       funcs = GetPointers();
11       funcs->f_set_data_pointer(testString);
12       funcs->f_set_data_length((int)sizeof testString);
13       funcs->f_encrypt();
14
15       funcs->f_decrypt();
16
17       return 0;
18   }
19
```

The code in the `main.c` file is more than self-explanatory. There are only two local variables; the `testString` variable represents the data we will process and `funcs` will store the pointer to the `pointers` structure in our Crypto Core.

Do not try to build the project yet as we have not told Visual Studio about our object file. Right-click on the project and select **Properties**. The following screenshot shows how to add our object file for a 64-bit platform project. The same should be done for a 32-bit project. You should just pay attention to which object file goes to which platform:

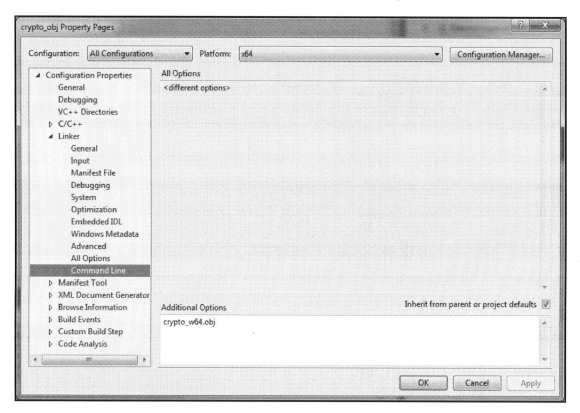

In the accompanying example project, the `crypto_w64.obj` file goes to the x64 platform, and `crypto_w32.obj` is for x86.

You are now free to build and run the project (either x86 or x64, given that the object files are specified correctly). I would suggest setting breakpoints at lines 13 and 15 of the `main.c` file in order to be able to spot the changes in memory pointed by `testString`. While running, you would get something similar to the following (similar because the key would be different with each build of our Crypto Core):

```
48 65 6c 6c 6f 2c 20 57 6f 72 6c 64 21 00 cc cc   Hello, World!.ÌÌ
cc cc cc cc a4 89 55 b1 14 f8 3a 00 0e 30 09 01   ÌÌÌÌ¤.U±.ø:..0..
```

The preceding screenshot shows the data supplied to the core prior to encryption. The following screenshot shows the same data after it has been encrypted:

```
59 ed c9 c9 c5 c8 f8 25 c5 b1 c9 e9 fc 78 cc cc   YíÉÉÅÈø%Å±ÉéüxÌÌ
cc cc cc cc a4 89 55 b1 14 f8 3a 00 0e 30 09 01   ÌÌÌÌ¤.U±.ø:..0..
```

The decryption of this encrypted data would take us back to the good old `Hello, World!`.

Static linking - GCC

There is not much difference between Visual Studio and GCC when it comes to linking object files built from Assembly sources to high-level language code. In fact, to be completely honest, we have to admit that an object file compiled from Assembly code is not different from an object file compiled from high-level languages. In the case of GCC, we have the high-level sources (the C source and the header; no need to modify the files) and two object files, which, for the sake of convenience, we name `crypto_32.o` and `crypto_64.o`. The commands used to build executables out of our source and object files would slightly differ depending on the platform in use. If you are running a 32-bit Linux system, then you would issue the following commands in order to build 32-bit and 64-bit executables, respectively:

```
gcc -o test32 main.c crypto_32.o
```

```
gcc -o test64 main.c crypto_64.o -m64
```

The second command would only work if you have 64-bit development tools/libraries installed.

If you are running a 64-bit system, then you make a slight change to the commands (and take care of the 32-bit development tools and libraries being installed):

```
gcc -o test32 main.c crypto_32.o -m32
```

And:

```
gcc -o test64 main.c crypto_64.o
```

Inspecting the memory content with GDB while running one of the `testxx` files would provide you with a picture similar to the following screenshot before encryption:

```
00000000  48 65 6c 6c 6f 2c 20 66  72 6f 6d 20 4c 69 6e 75  |Hello, from Linu|
00000010  78 21 0a 00 d0 97 04 08  c4 73 fa f7 70 d0 ff ff  |x!.......s..p...|
```

And after encryption, you will see something like the following:

```
00000000  4d 24 6c 6c 74 6e 0e 3c  9c 74 64 0e 6d 44 7c a4  |M$lltn.<.td.mD|.|
00000010  cc 06 5f 0f d0 97 04 08  c4 73 fa f7 70 d0 ff ff  |.._......s..p...|
```

Dynamic linking

Dynamic linking implies the use of dynamic link libraries (on Windows) or shared objects (on Linux) and is the same as with other DLLs/SOs. The mechanism of dynamic linking will be briefly covered in the next chapter.

We will, however, build dynamic link libraries and shared objects right now in order to be able to proceed further. Compile the `crypto.asm` file, setting the `ACTIVE_TARGET` compile-time variable to `TARGET_W32_DLL` in order to generate a 32-bit DLL for Windows, and then to `TARGET_W64_DLL` in order to generate a 64-bit DLL. Keep in mind the fact that changing `ACTIVE_TARGET` does not affect the name of the output, so we would have to rename the result of each compilation accordingly.

While on Windows you have to simply change the `ACTIVE_TARGET` compile-time variable and compile by going to **Run** | **Compile** in the GUI (or hit *Ctrl + F9* on the keyboard), you would have to build object files for Linux and then enter another command in a terminal when on Linux. The command would be one of these:

```
# For 64-bit output on 64-bit machine
gcc -shared crypto_64.o -o libcrypto_64.so

# For 64-bit output on 32-bit machine
gcc -shared crypto_64.o -o libcrypto_64.so -m64

# For 32-bit output on 64-bit machine
gcc -shared crypto_32.o -o libcrypto_32.so -m32

# For 32-bit output on 32-bit machine
gcc -shared crypto_32.o -o libcrypto_32.so
```

Having DLLs for Windows and shared objects for Linux, we are now safe to proceed further and see how modules written in Assembly may be integrated with frameworks such as .NET.

Assembly and managed code

As we have already seen, static or dynamic linking is not as difficult as it may seem, as long as we are dealing with native code, but what happens when we, for example, decide to use code written in Assembly with a program written in C#, which is a managed environment and is not run by the processor itself, but rather by a sort of a virtual machine? Many are afraid of mixing native modules and managed ones. Using native modules compiled from Assembly sources with managed code may seem to be even more frightening or even impossible. However, as we have seen earlier, there is no difference between modules initially written in Assembly and those written in other languages on the binary level. When it comes to managed code like, for example C#, things are just a bit more complex than linking to native object files or using a DLL/SO. The following does not apply to managed C++ code, in which case you may simply follow the steps discussed earlier in this chapter, in order to link a native object to managed code, as managed C++ is the only language supported by Visual Studio that provides such capability.

In the case of C#, however, we are limited to DLL/SO as C# is a pure managed environment without the ability to digest native code in the form of an object file. In such a case, there is a need for a sort of a shim code, an adapter. In our example, we will use a simple class, which imports our core's functionality from `crypto_wxx.dll` on Windows or from `libcrypto_xx.so` on Linux and exposes it through its methods to the rest of the code.

There is a common misbelief that the .NET platform is Windows-specific. Alas, this is too common. However, .NET platform is, in reality, almost as portable as Java and supports quite a selection of platforms. However, we will concentrate on Windows (32/64-bits) and Linux (32/64-bits).

Native structure versus managed structure

The first thing we would run into, when attempting to tie something similar to the implementation of our core's interface to a platform such as .NET, is the way data is passed between managed code and native code. There's hardly any possibility for managed and native code to access the same memory areas. It is not impossible, but definitely is not healthy, hence we would have to pass data between the two domains--the managed domain and native domain. Luckily, there is a class in the .NET framework that allows us to perform such operations relatively painlessly-- `System.Runtime.InteropServices.Marshal`. Since we are using a pointer to a structure containing pointers to exported procedures, we need to implement a managed structure to be used with our .NET crypto class and this is done in a rather simple manner:

```
// First of all, we tell the compiler how members of the
//struct are stored in memory and alignment thereof
[StructLayout(LayoutKind.Sequential, Pack=1)]

// Then we implement the structure itself
internal struct Funcs
{
    internal IntPtr f_set_data_pointer;
    internal IntPtr f_set_data_length;
    internal IntPtr f_encrypt;
    internal IntPtr f_decrypt;
}
```

The preceding code perfectly declares the type of structure we need and we may get to implement the crypto class. Although the implementation of misbelief C# class falls way beyond the scope of this book, it seems appropriate to dedicate a few lines to a definition of methods and delegates in this case.

Importing from DLL/SO and function pointers

Interoperability in .NET is an interesting topic, but it would be much better to refer to proper resources dedicated to it. Here, we will only consider .NET's analogs of function pointers and misbelief dynamic importing of functions exported by DLLs and shared objects. But, first, let's construct the class, import the `GetPointers()` procedure, and define function pointer delegates:

```
internal class Crypto
{
    Funcs   functions;
    IntPtr buffer;
```

```csharp
byte[] data;

// The following two lines make up the properties of the class
internal byte[] Data { get { return data; } }
internal int Length { get { return data.Length; } }
// Declare binding for GetPointers()
// The following line is written for 64-bit targets, you should
// change the file name to crypto_32.so when building for
// 32-bit systems.
// Change the name to crypto_wXX.dll when on Windows, where XX
// stands for 32 or 64.
[DllImport("crypto_64.so", CallingConvention = CallingConvention.Cdecl)]
internal static extern IntPtr GetPointers();

// Declare delegates (our function pointers)
[UnmanagedFunctionPointer(CallingConvention.Cdecl)]
internal delegate void dSetDataPointer(IntPtr p);

[UnmanagedFunctionPointer(CallingConvention.Cdecl)]
internal delegate void dSetDataSize(int s);

[UnmanagedFunctionPointer(CallingConvention.Cdecl)]
internal delegate void dEncrypt();

[UnmanagedFunctionPointer(CallingConvention.Cdecl)]
internal delegate void dDecrypt();

// Constructor
internal Crypto()
{
    // Luckily when we get a pointer to structure by calling
    // GetPointers() we do not have to do more than just let
    // the framework convert native structure to managed one
    functions = (Funcs)Marshal.PtrToStructure(
        GetPointers(),
        typeof(Funcs));

    // Set initial buffer ptr
    buffer = IntPtr.Zero;
}

// SetDataPointer() method is the most complex one in our class,
// as it includes invocation of SetDataLength()
internal void SetDataPointer(byte[] p)
{
    // If an unmanaged buffer has been previously allocated,
    // then we need to free it first.
    if(IntPtr.Zero != buffer)
```

```
        Marshal.FreeHGlobal(buffer);
     buffer = Marshal.AllocHGlobal(p.Length);

     // Copy data to both the local storage and unmanaged buffer
     data = new byte[p.Length];
     Array.Copy(p, data, p.Length);
     Marshal.Copy(p, 0, buffer, p.Length);

     // Call f_set_data_pointer with a pointer to unmanaged buffer
     ((dSetDataPointer) Marshal.GetDelegateFromFunctionPointer(
        functions.f_set_data_pointer,
        typeof(dSetDataPointer)))(buffer);

     // Tell the core what the length of the data buffer is
     ((dSetDataSize) Marshal.GetDelegateFromFunctionPointer(
        functions.f_set_data_length,
        typeof(dSetDataSize)))(p.Length);
  }

  // The remaining two methods are more than simple
  internal void Encrypt()
  {
     // Encrypt the data in the unmanaged buffer and copy it
     // to local storage
     ((dEncrypt)Marshal.GetDelegateFromFunctionPointer(
        functions.f_encrypt,
        typeof(dEncrypt)))();
     Marshal.Copy(buffer, data, 0, data.Length);
  }

  internal void Decrypt()
  {
     // Decrypt the data in the unmanaged buffer and copy it
     // to local storage
     ((dDecrypt)Marshal.GetDelegateFromFunctionPointer(
        functions.f_decrypt,
        typeof(dDecrypt)))();
     Marshal.Copy(buffer, data, 0, data.Length);
  }
}
```

The preceding code is for the Linux version; however, it may easily be changed to the Windows version by changing the name of the shared object to the name of a DLL. With this class, working with our Crypto Core is rather simple and may be summarized by the following code:

```
Crypto c = new Crypto();
string message = "This program uses \"Crypto Engine\" written in Assembly
language.";
c.SetDataPointer(ASCIIEncoding.ASCII.GetBytes(message));
c.Encrypt();
c.Decrypt();
```

However, despite the fact that, if we implement the preceding class and try to use it in our code, it would compile well, we are still unable to actually run it. This is because we need to supply the DLL or shared object, depending on the platform of our choice. The easiest way to supply the libraries is to copy them into the solution folder and tell the IDE (Visual Studio or Monodevelop) to handle them properly.

The first step is to copy the libraries (DLLs on Windows and SOs on Linux) into the project folder. The following screenshot shows the Monodevelop project folder on Linux, but the procedure is just the same for both Linux and Windows:

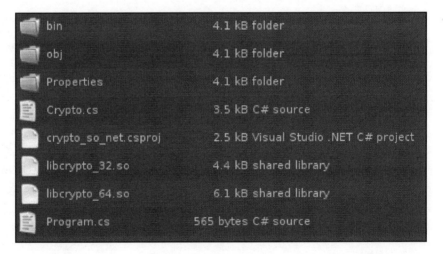

The next step would be to actually tell the IDE how to treat these files. First, add them to the project by right-clicking on the project and then navigating to **Add** | **Existing Item** for Visual Studio or **Add** | **Add Files** for Monodevelop, and then set the properties for each of the libraries as shown in the following screenshots.

To set the properties in Visual Studio:

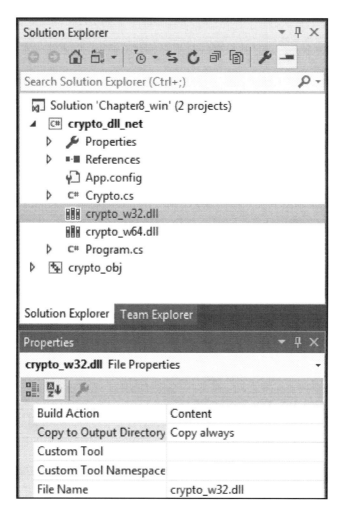

To set the properties in Monodevelop:

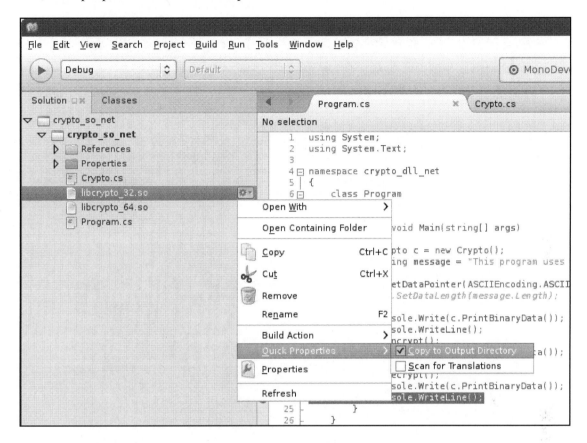

Although the GUI is different, both need to have **Build Action** set to **Content** and **Copy to Output Directory** set to **Copy always** in Visual Studio and checked in Monodevelop.

Now we can build out project (either on Windows or Linux) and run it. We may either watch the data being encrypted/decrypted in memory or add a tiny function that would print out the content of memory within a specific range.

If everything is set up correctly, then the output should be similar to the following when on Windows:

```
54 68 69 73 20 70 72 6f 67 72 61 6d 20 75 73 65     This program use
73 20 22 43 72 79 70 74 6f 20 45 6e 67 69 6e 65     s "Crypto Engine
22 20 77 72 69 74 74 65 6e 20 69 6e 20 41 73 73     " written in Ass
65 6d 62 6c 79 20 6c 61 6e 67 75 61 67 65 2e        embly language.

a0 d8 da ee 48 e8 ec d6 c6 ec ca d2 48 e2 ee c2     ????H???????H???
ee 48 4c 8e ec fa e8 e0 d6 48 82 d4 c6 da d4 c2     ?HL??????H??????
4c 48 e6 ec da e0 e0 c2 d4 48 da d4 48 8a ee ee     LH???????H??H???
c2 d2 cc d0 fa 48 d0 ca d4 c6 e2 ca c6 c2 54        ?????H????????T

54 68 69 73 20 70 72 6f 67 72 61 6d 20 75 73 65     This program use
73 20 22 43 72 79 70 74 6f 20 45 6e 67 69 6e 65     s "Crypto Engine
22 20 77 72 69 74 74 65 6e 20 69 6e 20 41 73 73     " written in Ass
65 6d 62 6c 79 20 6c 61 6e 67 75 61 67 65 2e        embly language.
```

The output on Linux would be similar to this:

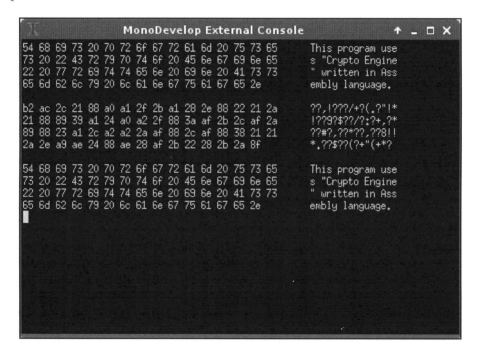

Summary

In this chapter, we covered just a few aspects of interfacing your Assembly code to the outer world. There are numerous programming languages out there; however, a decision was taken to concentrate on C/C++ and the .NET platform as the best way to illustrate how modules written in Assembly language may be bound to the code written in high-level languages. To put it simply, any language that is compiled into native code would use the same mechanism as C and C++; on the other hand, any .NET-like platform, although, having a platform-specific binding mechanism, would use the same approach on a low level.

However, I assume that there is one question hanging in the air. How about linking third-party code to our Assembly program? Although the title of this chapter may have implied that this topic is included, it would make much more sense to cover it in the next chapter as the only thing we will be dealing with is using third-party code with our programs written in the Assembly language.

9

Operating System Interface

While preparing to write this chapter, I remembered a real-time systems course in college. Not the whole course, of course, but one of the tasks we were given --one of the most interesting ones, if not the most interesting. We had to write a small program that would display a text string that should move from left to right and back again on the screen until a certain key was pressed on the keyboard. Two additional keys would make it possible to control the speed of the string's movement. It was 2001 or 2002, we were still using DOS for Assembly-related exercises and the task appeared to be quite simple.

I personally found it extremely boring to use DOS interrupts for this purpose (I had no idea of Occam's Razor principle at the time, besides, I wanted to look smart), so I decided not to use any OS at all. My laptop had a floppy drive, so the only thing I was missing was a program to write raw sectors to a floppy diskette, which I wrote myself (guess what programming language).

The program consisted of two parts:

- **Bootloader**: This was a tiny piece of code (it had to fit into a 512-bytes sector after compilation) responsible for one thing only --loading my program from a floppy and setting it up for running
- **The program**: This is actually the program for displaying a moving string

Having proper documentation was not a big deal to implement the whole package. However, I had to take care of things we usually do not deal with. One of them was a primitive video driver, which would have handled switching to graphic mode, displaying the string at the proper location, and switching back to the text mode before the program terminated. The other one was writing a primitive keyboard driver, basically an interrupt handler to listen to the keyboard and make proper adjustments to the speed of the string's movement, or tell the program to terminate. To put it simply, I had to interface hardware myself (oh, the good old times of the real mode... everything was so simple and so complicated).

In modern days, unless you are a driver developer, you are completely free from accessing hardware directly --the operating system does all the dirty work for us and we may concentrate purely on the implementation of our ideas.

We are able to implement any algorithm in Assembly language thus far, we may even, provided that we have proper documentation, write our own drivers, however, doing so only introduces redundant work when trying to write a user-space application. Not to mention the fact that there are already drivers for all your hardware provided by hardware vendors, and Occam's Razor principle tells us not to multiply things without need. Modern operating systems are good at managing these drivers and providing easier and seamless access to hardware, thus allowing us to concentrate on the process of creation.

In this chapter, we will see how to easily and painlessly use the power given to us by the operating system and numerous libraries already created by others. We will begin by linking third-party object files to our code, proceed through importing API from DLL/SO and finish with dynamically loading DLL/SO, and importing the API at runtime.

The rings

Almost all modern platforms, except a few embedded ones, utilize the same security principle --the division of execution environments by security levels and privileges; in this case, this means the ability to access certain resources. On Intel-based platforms, there are four security levels known as **protection rings**. These rings are numbered 0 through 3, where the greater the number, the less privileged the ring. Obviously, the code running at a less privileged level cannot access memory with a higher privilege level directly. We will shortly see how data is transferred between different privilege levels.

The following figure illustrates the concept of protection rings:

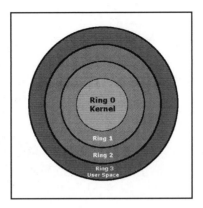

Here's a description of the different privileges of protection rings:

- **Ring 0** is the most privileged level where all instructions are available and all hardware is accessible. This is the grey area where the kernel resides, accompanied by kernel space drivers.
- **Ring 1** and **Ring 2** are intended to serve as the driver execution environment, but are hardly used at all.
- **Ring 3** is the user space. It is the privilege level regular software is granted, and it is the only privilege level we are interested in. Although getting deeper may be very interesting, it would not be practical for the purpose of this book, as all our code requires privilege level 3 only.

System call

The user-space application is of no value if it cannot make service requests to the kernel, as it is not able to even terminate properly without asking the kernel to terminate the process it is running in. All system calls may be categorized as follows:

- **Process control**: System calls that fall into this category are responsible for the creation of processes/threads and their management, as well as memory allocation/deallocation
- **File management**: These system calls are responsible for file creation, deletion, and IO
- **Device management**: This category contains system calls used for device administration/access

- **Maintenance**: This category contains system calls for management of date, time, and files or device attributes
- **Communication**: Management of communication channels and remote devices

System call hardware interface

On the hardware level, the processor provides us with several ways to invoke a kernel procedure to handle a system call:

- **Through an interrupt (INT instruction on 32-bit systems)**: The operating system allocates a descriptor for an interrupt with a specific number, which points to a procedure in the kernel space that handles the interrupt in accordance with its parameters (parameters are passed via registers). One of the parameters is the index into system call table (roughly speaking, the table of pointers to specific system call handlers).
- **Using the SYSENTER instruction (32-bit systems excluding WOW64 processes)**: Beginning with Pentium II, we are able to use the SYSENTER instruction to perform fast calls to a ring 0 procedure. This instruction is accompanied by the SYSEXIT instruction, which returns from a system call.
- **Using the SYSCALL instruction (64-bit systems)**: This instruction was introduced by the x86_64 architecture and is only available in the long mode. This instruction allows faster transfer to a system call handler and does not access the interrupt descriptor table.

Direct system calls

Using one of the preceding instructions would mean making a direct system call and bypassing all system libraries as shown in the following figure. However, this is not the best practice and we will see why in a moment:

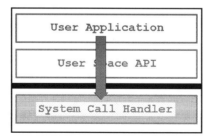

Using the direct system call approach on Linux would, most likely, work, as Linux system calls are well documented and their numbers are well known (they may be found in /usr/include/asm/unistd_32.h for a 32-bit system and in /usr/include/asm/unistd_64.h for a 64-bit one), and those numbers do not tend to change. For example, the following code prints a msg string to the standard output on a 32-bit Linux system:

```
mov    eax, 4        ; 4 is the number of sys_write system call
mov    ebx, 1        ; 1 is the stdout file number
lea    ecx, [msg]    ; msg is the label (address) of the string to write
mov    edx, len      ; length of msg in bytes
int    0x80          ; make syscall
```

Here is its 64-bit counterpart:

```
mov    rax, 1        ; 1 is the number of sys_write on 64-bit Linux
mov    rdi, 1        ; 1 is the stdout file number
mov    rsi, msg      ; msg is the label (address) of the string
mov    rdx, len      ; length of msg in bytes
syscall              ; make the system call
```

On Windows, however, despite the fact that the idea is the same, the implementation is different. To begin with, there is no publicly available official documentation of Windows system calls, which not only requires a certain portion of reverse engineering, but also gives no guarantee that the information found through reversing ntdll.dll would remain intact after the next update, not to mention the fact that system call numbers tend to change from version to version. However, for the sake of common education, here is the system call invocation procedure from the 32-bit ntdll.dll:

```
_KiIntSystemCall:
    lea    edx, [esp + 8]    ; Load EDX with pointer to the parameter block
    int    0x2e              ; make system call
```

Also, if the SYSENTER instruction is available, then we have the following:

```
_KiFastSystemCall:
    mov    edx, esp          ; Load EDX with stack pointer so that kernel
                             ; may access the parameter block on stack
    sysenter                 ; make system call
```

Although the second variant is more promising, there is still no guarantee that the format of the parameter block would not change (though, this is not likely). In conclusion of this subsection, it is important to say that it is much advised not to make use of direct system calls unless absolutely necessary.

Indirect system calls

A more common way of making use of system services is through supporting libraries, whether system DLLs on Windows or libc on Linux, which provide a more convenient API than the raw system call interface. The process is depicted in the following diagram:

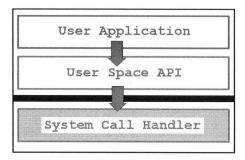

Although it may seem like another layer may introduce redundant complications, in reality, it is exactly the opposite, not to mention that in such cases our code would become much more portable.

Using libraries

As it has been stated earlier, the best way to interact with the operating system from a program written in Assembly is through the system API --system DLLs on Windows and libc on Linux, and the rest of the chapter is dedicated to this topic, as it will significantly make your life easier as an Assembly developer.

The rest of the chapter is dedicated to the use of external libraries and DLLs if on Windows, or external libraries and shared objects if on Linux. We will try to kill two rabbits in one shot, meaning that we will not only learn how to link DLLs or system lib files to our code, but we will also cover the linking of other object files with our code.

For the sake of an example, we will create a small program that prints a message to the standard output and uses the module we developed in Chapter 8, *Mixing Modules Written in Assembly and Those Written in High-Level Languages*, for the encryption and decryption of the message.

Windows

There are two options for how to gain access to external functionality on Windows; one would be compiling our code to an object file and linking it against other object files or libraries, and the other would be creating executable and importing functions exported by different DLLs. We will examine them both so that you will be able to select the most suitable approach when the need arises.

Linking against object and/or library files

An object file is a file that contains billets of executable code and/or data. It cannot be executed by itself (even if it contains all the code for an executable), as the information stored in such files is only used by a linker when building the final executable; otherwise, all the code and data within the file is not bound to any address, and only hints are provided. Detailed information on the Microsoft object file format, as well as the PE executable format specifications, may be obtained at `http://www.microsoft.com/whdc/system/platform/firmware/PECOFF.mspx`. Visit this URL, click on the **Download** button, and select `pecoff.docx`.

Object file

Let's get to business and write the code for our object file, `obj_win.asm`:

```
; First we need to tell the assembler that
; we expect an object file compatible with MS linker
format MS COFF

; Then specify the external API we need
; extrn means that the procedure is not in this file
; the 4 after the '@' specifies size of procedure parameters
; in bytes
; ExitProcess is a label and dword is its size
extrn '__imp__ExitProcess@4' as ExitProcess:dword
extrn '__imp__GetStdHandle@4' as GetStdHandle:dword
extrn '__imp__WriteConsoleA@20' as WriteConsole:dword

; And, of course, our "crypto API"
extrn '_GetPointers' as GetPointers:dword

; Define a constant for GetStdHandle()
STD_OUTPUT_HANDLE    equal -11

; and a structure to ease the access to "crypto functions"
struc crypto_functions
```

```
{
    .f_set_data_pointer   dd ?
    .f_set_data_length    dd ?
    .f_encrypt            dd ?
    .f_decrypt            dd ?
}

; The following structure makes it a bit easier
; to manipulate strings and sizes thereof
struc string [s]
{
    common
    .          db s
    .length = $ - .
}
```

Before we implement our code, let's create the data section so that the code is easier to understand:

```
section '.data' data readable writeable
    ; We will store the STDOUT handle here
    stdout        dd ?

    ; This buffer contains the message we will operate on
    buffer        string 'Hello from object file!', 0x0a, 0x0d

    ; Progress messages
    msg1          string 'Encrypted', 0x0a, 0x0d
    msg2          string 'Decrypted', 0x0a, 0x0d

    ; This one is required by the WriteConsole procedure
    bytesWritten  dd ?
```

The data section is quite self-explanatory and we are now ready to write the code at last:

```
section '.text' code readable executable
    ; We need the entry point to be accessible to the linker,
    ; therefore make it "public"
    public _start

_start:
    ; The first step would be obtaining the STDOUT handle
    push  STD_OUTPUT_HANDLE
    ; Since we are linking against a DLL, the GetStdHandle
    ; label would refer to a location in the import section
    ; which the linker will create for us. Hence we make an
    ; indirect call
    call  [GetStdHandle]
```

```
; Store the handle
mov    [stdout], eax

; Print the message
push   0 bytesWritten buffer.length buffer eax
call   [WriteConsole]

; Let's play with encryption a bit
; First get the procedure pointers. Since the GetPointers()
; is in another object file, it would be statically linked,
; therefore we make a direct call
call   GetPointers
; Store the pointer to the crypto_functions structure in EBX
mov    ebx, eax
```

Remember the `virtual` directive?

We, programmers, are sometimes lazy people and like things to be convenient, especially when it comes to reading our own code a week after it was written, therefore, we would prefer to address our cryptographic procedures by name, rather than by an offset from the address of the `crypto_functions` structure, and this is when the `virtual` directive comes in handy allowing us to label the location pointed by the EBX register as shown in the following code snippet:

```
virtual at ebx
    funcs   crypto_functions
end virtual
```

The `funcs` is a virtual label that refers to the location pointed to by the `ebx` register, and it will be replaced with `ebx` in compile time. Any member of the `crypto_functions` structure referred by `funcs` will be replaced by its offset within the structure. Let's now set up the crypto engine and encrypt and then decrypt the message stored at `buffer`:

```
; Set the pointer to data and its length
push   buffer
call   [funcs.f_set_data_pointer] ; Equivalent to 'call [ebx]'
push   buffer.length
call   [funcs.f_set_data_length]

; We have to restore the stack pointer due to the
; fact that the above two procedures are in accordance
; with the cdecl calling convention
add    esp, 8

; Encrypt the content of the buffer
call   [funcs.f_encrypt]
; Print progress message
```

```
push    0 bytesWritten msg1.length msg1 [stdout]
call    [WriteConsole]

; Decrypt the content of the buffer
call    [funcs.f_decrypt]

; Print another progress message
push    0 bytesWritten msg2.length msg2 [stdout]
call    [WriteConsole]

; Print the content of the buffer in order to verify
; decryption
push    0 bytesWritten buffer.length buffer [stdout]
call    [WriteConsole]

; All is fine and we are free to exit
push    0
call    [ExitProcess]
```

Producing the executable

Compiling this source file will produce the `obj_win.obj` file, which we will link to `kernel32.lib` and `crypto_w32.obj`. But where do we find the `kernel32.lib` file? This task may not be such a simple one sometimes, although not a difficult one. All system libraries may be found at `c:\Program Files\Microsoft SDKs\Windows\vX.X\Lib`, where `vX.X` stands for the version (there will, most likely, be more than one). For 64-bit Windows, the directory would be `c:\Program Files (x86)\Microsoft SDKs\Windows\vX.X\Lib`. So, let's copy the `crypto_w32.obj` file to our working directory and try to link it. Open the **Developer Command Prompt for VS 2017** command window, as shown in the following screenshot, and navigate to your working directory:

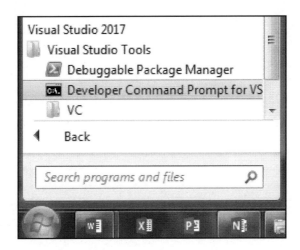

Type the following command:

```
link /entry:start /subsystem:console obj_win.obj "c:\Program
Files\Microsoft SDKs\Windows\v7.0A\Lib\kernel32.lib" crypto_w32.obj
```

Once you press enter, if all went well, the Microsoft (R) Incremental Linker logo message will appear in the console followed by a new prompt, and the obj_win.exe file will be generated. Try to run it and you should get this output:

```
Hello from object file!
Encrypted
Decrypted
Hello from object file!
```

Voila! We have just used external functionality in our Assembly code.

Importing procedures from DLL

The Flat Assembler provides us with yet another option for using external functionality. While with other assemblers we need a linker in order to link against DLLs, Flat Assembler makes it possible to produce an executable with all the imports defined in source code, which allows us to simply compile the source code and run the executable.

The process of runtime linking dynamic link libraries to our code is fairly simple and may be illustrated with the following diagram:

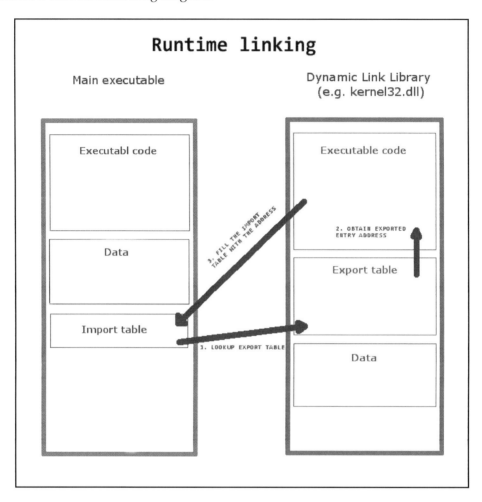

Once the loader has loaded an executable, it parses its import table (if present) and identifies the requested libraries (refer to PECOFF.docx for the import table format specifications). For each library reference found in the import section, the loader attempts to load the library, then parses the executable's import section for the names of procedures exported by the library in question, and scans the library's export section for a match. Once a matching entry is found, the loader calculates the virtual address of the entry and writes it back to the import section of the executable. This sequence is repeated for every imported entry of every requested library.

For our example, we will use the same code as with linking objects (just rename it to `dll_win.asm`) with just a few tiny modifications, and `crypto_w32.dll` instead of `crypto_w32.obj`. First of all, remove all the `extrn` and `public` declarations and then tell the assembler that this time we are expecting a console executable, rather than an object file, by changing `format MS COFF` to `format PE CONSOLE`.

As we will create our own import table, we need to include the `win32a.inc` file that contains all the macros we may need for our purpose. Add this line after the format declaration:

```
include 'win32a.inc'
```

We are almost there; append the following code to the source file:

```
section '.idata' import data readable writeable

    ; Tell the assembler which libraries we are interested in
    library kernel,'kernel32.dll',\
            crypto,'crypto_w32.dll'

    ; Specify procedures we need from kernel32.dll
    import kernel,\
        GetStdHandle, 'GetStdHandle',\
        WriteConsole, 'WriteConsoleA',\
        ExitProcess, 'ExitProcess'

    ; And, finally, tell the assembler we are also
    ; interested in our crypto engine
    import crypto,\
        GetPointers, 'GetPointers'
```

The last modification that we have to make is change `call GetPointers` to `call [GetPointers]`, as this time, the `GetPointers`; procedure will not be statically linked to our executable, but it will be imported from a dynamic link library, meaning that the `GetPointers` label will refer to an address in memory where the address of the `GerPointers` procedure will be stored.

Try to compile the file and run it in the console. You should get the same output as the one with the executable we linked from multiple objects.

If you get an error message saying that the executable failed to launch instead of the expected output, try adding the `section '.reloc'` `fixups data readable discardable` line to the `TARGET_W32_DLL` section of the `finalize` macro in the `platform.inc` file, and recompile `crypto_w32.dll`. This is correct for building a DLL in general, although it may work without this in certain circumstances.

It is, of course, possible to load DLLs manually with the `LoadLibrary()` Windows API, and resolve addresses of needed procedures with `GetProcAddress()`, but that does not differ from linking against a DLL or importing APIs, as we still do need to import these two APIs. There is, however, a method that allows us to import API addresses in the so-called stealthy way.

The exact same rules apply when it comes to building 64-bit executables. The only difference is the location of `kernel32.lib`, which will be `c:\Program Files\Microsoft SDKs\Windows\vX.X\Lib\x64`, and the size of pointers. Also, it is very important to remember that the calling convention used on x86_64 Windows is neither `cdecl` nor `stdcall`!

Linux

In Linux, just like in Windows, we have the same support for both static and dynamic linking (and support for manual import too). The main difference is that in Linux (and this is my sole opinion), building software is much easier as all the development tools are integrated into the system. Well, except Flat Assembler, but its integration is not a problem -- we simply copy the `fasm` executable to one of the `bin` directories that are included in the user's PATH environment variable.

Fortunately for us, Flat Assembler has built-in support for generation of both object files and executables, which imports procedures from libraries on Linux just as well as it supports such methods on Windows. We will shortly see that these approaches on Linux are almost identical to those on Windows, as long as we do not start diving into the depth of the ELF specifications and format.

If you want to explore the ELF format in-depth, specifications are available at
`http://refspecs.linuxbase.org/elf/elf.pdf` for specifications of 32-bit ELF
and
`http://ftp.openwatcom.org/devel/docs/elf-64-gen.pdf` for specifications of 64-bit ELF.

You may also find these specifications with Google or any other search engine, if these links appear broken.

Just like we did in the case of Windows, we will begin by linking several object files to a single executable and then proceed to create an executable ELF file with dynamic dependency linking.

Linking against object and/or library files

The structure of the **Microsoft Common Object File Format (MS COFF)** and that of **ELF (Executable and Linkable Format**, previously known as **Extensible Linking Format)** are very different, but for us, this difference does not matter at all. The ELF was developed by UNIX System Laboratories and was published in 1997. It was later selected as a portable object file format for the 32-bit Intel architecture. As of today, there is ELF for 32-bit systems and ELF64 for 64-bit systems.

From our perspective, however, the code for Linux is very similar to the code for Windows. To be more precise, FASM is what makes it quite similar.

Object file

Just as with the object file source code for Windows, as always we will begin by telling the assembler what kind of output we are expecting, which procedures are public, and which are external:

```
format ELF

; As we want GCC to take care of all the startup code
; we will call our procedure "main" instead of _start,
; otherwise we would be using LD instead of GCC and
; would have to specify all runtime libraries manually.
public main

; The following function is linked from libc
extrn printf
```

```
; And this one is from our crypto library
extrn GetPointers
```

Then we proceed with convenience macro definition, and the suggestion is to put convenience macros into a separate include file so that they may be painlessly used with different code without the need to rewrite them:

```
struc crypto_functions
{
    .f_set_data_pointer dd ?
    .f_set_data_length  dd ?
    .f_encrypt          dd ?
    .f_decrypt          dd ?
}

struc string [s]
{
    common
    .                   db s
    .length = $ - .
    .terminator         db 0
}
```

The data section is almost the same as in the case of the object file for Windows, except that we do not need a variable to hold the stdout handle:

```
section '.data' writeable
    buffer  string  'Hello from ELF linked from objects!', 0x0a
    msg1    string  'Encrypted', 0x0a
    msg2    string  'Decrypted', 0x0a
```

And, at last, the code section. It is logically the same code with the only difference being the use of printf() instead of WriteConsoleA(), in which case the printf() implementation in libc will make all the arrangements and invoke a SYS_write Linux system call for us. As we are, from GCC's point of view, only implementing the main() function, we do not have to terminate the process ourselves, hence there is no exit() procedure imported --the runtime code is automatically added and linked, and GCC will do all the rest, while we simply return from main():

```
section '.text' executable

; Remember that we are using GCC for linking, hence the name is
; main, rather than _start
main:
    ; Print the content of the buffer to stdout
    ; As all procedures (except crypto procedures) would be
    ; statically linked, we are using direct calls
```

```
push   buffer
call   printf
; Restore stack as printf() is a cdecl function
add    esp, 4


; Get pointers to cryptographic procedures
call   GetPointers
mov    ebx, eax
; We will use the same trick to ease our access to cryptography
; procedures by defining a virtual structure
virtual at ebx
   funds   crypto_functions
end virtual


; Right now we will push parameters for all subsequent procedure
; calls onto the stack in reverse order (parameter for the last
; call is pushed first
push   0 buffer msg2 msg1 buffer.length buffer


; Set crypto library's data pointer
; Crypto procedures are not available at link time, hence not
; statically linked. Instead we obtain pointers thereof and this
; is the reason for indirect call
call   [funcs.f_set_data_pointer]
; Restore stack
add    esp, 4


; Set size of the data buffer
call   [funcs.f_set_data_length]
add    esp, 4


; Encrypt the buffer. As this procedure has no parameter, there
; is no reason to do anything to stack following this call
call   [funcs.f_encrypt]


; Print msg1
call   printf
add    esp, 4


; Decrypt the buffer back
call   [funcs.f_decrypt]


; Print msg2
call   printf
add    esp, 4


; Print the content of the buffer to ensure correct decryption
call   printf
```

```
add     esp, 4

; All is done, so we may safely exit
pop     eax
ret
```

Producing the executable

Save the file as `o_lin.asm` and compile it into an object file with the `fasm o_lin.asm` command in the terminal. The next step will be linking `o_lin.o` with `crypto_32.o` with the following command:

```
gcc -o o_lin o_lin.o crypto_32.o
# If you are on a 64-bit system then
gcc -o o_lin o_lin.o crypto_32.o -m32
```

This will result in a `5KB` `o_lin` executable --quite a heavy one in relation to the size of code we used to produce. Such a huge size is due to the GCC linking C runtime into it. Try to run it and you should see this in the terminal:

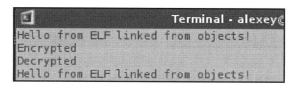

Dynamic linking of ELF

It is not always suitable to statically link object files into a single executable, and Linux provides us with a mechanism to produce an ELF executable that would be linked with the required libraries (shared objects) dynamically at runtime. The Flat Assembler used to have relatively basic support for ELF, meaning one could only create an executable that would use system calls directly, or create an object file to be linked with others (exactly in the manner we did).

Flat Assembler's support for ELF was extended with the release of version 1.69.05 --a few segment attributes were added along with several convenience macros, which let us manually create the import table in an ELF executable. These macros are in the Linux package under the `examples/elfexe/dynamic` directory (underlined in the following screenshot):

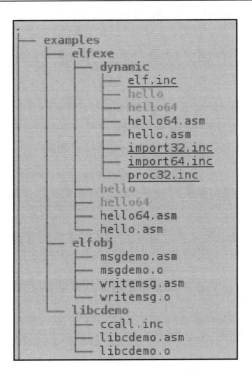

```
— examples
  — elfexe
    — dynamic
      — elf.inc
      — hello
      — hello64
      — hello64.asm
      — hello.asm
      — import32.inc
      — import64.inc
      — proc32.inc
    — hello
    — hello64
    — hello64.asm
    — hello.asm
  — elfobj
    — msgdemo.asm
    — msgdemo.o
    — writemsg.asm
    — writemsg.o
  — libcdemo
    — ccall.inc
    — libcdemo.asm
    — libcdemo.o
```

These macros may be found under the linux_include folder in the accompanying code
for this chapter.

The code

The code for dynamically linked ELF is almost the same as for an ELF object file, with a few
tiny differences. First of all, the formatter directive must tell the assembler to produce an
executable, rather than an object file:

```
format ELF executable 3     ; The 3 may be omitted if on Linux

; Include this in order to be able to create import section
include 'linux_include/import32.inc'

; We have to specify the entry point for the executable
entry _start
```

The convenience structures we used in this chapter (`crypto_functions` and `string`) are still intact and should be placed in the file too. There is no strict definition as to where they should be placed exactly, but they should appear before they are used:

```
; The content of the data section is the same as in object file
; source. The section itself is declared in a different way (in
; fact, although, an ELF file is divided into sections, it is
; treated a bit differently when in memory - it is divided into
; segments)
segment readable writeable
    buffe   string 'Hello from dynamically linked ELF!', 0x0a
    msg1    string 'Encrypted', 0x0a
    msg2    string 'Decrypted', 0x0a
```

A new segment is introduced in order to improve the Flat Assembler's ELF support; one is the **interpreter** that contains the name of the loader to be used with the executable:

```
segment interpreter writeable
    db '/lib/ld-linux.so.2',0
```

Another one is **dynamic** and serves as an import index. However, we are not going to declare this segment ourselves; instead, we will use two macros --one of them will create a list of the needed libraries and the other specifies procedures to be imported. In our case, it will look like this:

```
; In our example we only need to libraries - libc for
; printf() and exit() (and we will use exit() this time)
; and crypto_32.so for our cryptographic core.
needed\
    'libc-2.19.so',\
    'crypto_32.so'

; Then we specify requested procedures
import\
    printf,\
    exit,\
    GetPointers
```

The rest of the code has only a few changes. First of all, the code section is declared as follows:

```
segment executable readable
_start:
```

This time all procedures are called indirectly:

```
push   buffer
call   [printf]
add    esp, 4

call   [GetPointers]
mov    ebx, eax

virtual at ebx
    funcs  crypto_functions
end virtual

push   0 buffer msg2 msg1 buffer.length buffer

; All procedures are cdecl, so we have to adjust
; the stack pointer upon return from procedures
; with parameters

call   [funcs.f_set_data_pointer]
add    esp, 4

call   [funcs.f_set_data_length]
add    esp, 4

call   [funcs.f_encrypt]

call   [printf]
add    esp, 4

call   [funcs.f_decrypt]

call   [printf]
add    esp, 4

call   [printf]
add    esp, 4

call   [exit]
```

The last two instructions we replace the two lines:

```
pop    eax
ret
```

with:

```
cal  [exit]
```

Save the file as so_lin.asm.

Now, you may build and run the newly created executable:

```
fasm  so_lin.asm
./so_lin
```

If everything is done right, then you should see this:

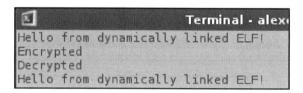

Summary

In this chapter, you got acquainted with system calls --an operating system's service gateway. You learned that it is much more practical and convenient to use existing libraries in order to invoke system calls indirectly, and in a much more convenient and secure way.

This chapter was intentionally left without 64-bit examples, as I would like you to try and write 64-bit versions of these simple executables yourself as a small exercise to test yourself.

Now we are masters. We have a firm base and are able to implement any algorithm in pure Intel Assembly, and we are even able to invoke system calls directly (on Linux at least, as it is strongly discouraged on Windows). However, as real masters, we know that there is much more to learn and explore, as a base alone is not enough.

10
Patching Legacy Code

A few years ago, I had an opportunity to work on an interesting project--I was contacted by a business owner who was left with an unusable executable, locked by a disgraceful developer who took the money and disappeared. Having no source code, the only option was to patch the executable in order to change the execution flow and bypass the lock.

Unfortunately, this is not an isolated case. It happens quite often that an old tool, which has been around for years (if not decades), needs to be slightly changed and then... well, then there are at least two options:

- The source code has been lost and there is no way to rebuild the executable after applying changes.
- The source code is there, but it appears to be so old that it cannot even be compiled with modern compilers without rewriting it almost from scratch. In this case, even if rewriting is not a big issue, the possibility of libraries used with the software being incompatible with modern compilers or their output, which would make the whole project significantly more complicated, is still there.

Depending on the complexity of changes that are needed to be applied, simply patching the binary executable file with new code may be a sufficient option as it is definitely simpler to put a few bytes in a hex editor rather than reverse-engineer a tool (either its binary form or old source code, which may no longer be supported by compilers) and rewrite it from scratch.

In this chapter, we will consider a very simplistic example of an executable that needs a security fix. We will create the executable ourselves for both Windows and Linux, and we'll, first of all, examine the options and then apply a binary patch. As we will be targeting two platforms, we will address the formats of PE and ELF files where needed.

The executable

As was mentioned earlier, we have to create the executable first. It appeared to be a relatively hard task to find a real-life example simple enough to fit the chapter, so the decision was made to take a real-life problem and wrap it with simplistic code. We will write the code for our executable in C and compile with Visual Studio 2017 when on Windows and GCC when on Linux. The code will be as simple as this:

```c
#include <stdio.h>
#include <stdlib.h>
#include <string.h>
int main()
{
    /*
        This buffer is used for IO interactions with
        a user.
    */
    char    ioBuffer[128];

    /*
        This would be a dynamically allocated buffer
        for internal storage of user's input.
    */
    char*   stringBuffer;

    /* Prompt for user input. */
    printf("Enter your name: ");

    /* This is the core of the problem */
    gets(ioBuffer);

    /*
        Copy user's input into dynamically allocated
        buffer.
    */
    stringBuffer = (char*)malloc(strlen(ioBuffer) + 1);
    strcpy(stringBuffer, ioBuffer);

    /*
        Show user's input and free local buffer.
    */
    printf("\n\nYour name is: %s", stringBuffer);
    free(stringBuffer);
    return 0;
}
```

As we may see, the only thing this code is capable of is reading user input as a string into a 128-byte buffer, allocating an internal buffer specifically for the input string, copying the input string there, and printing it from the internal buffer.

Create a new solution in Visual Studio 2017, name it `Legacy`, and fill the preceding illustrated code to its `main.cpp` file. Personally, I prefer to use the `.c` extension when writing in C and set the **Compile As** option (which can be found by navigating to **Configuration Properties | C/C++ | Advanced** in the project properties window) to **C**.

The process of building the executable out of the preceding code is quite straightforward, except for one detail with Visual Studio 2017. As we are attempting to fake a `Legacy` executable, we need to disable Linker's **Dynamic Base** option. While in Visual Studio, right-click on the project and select **Properties**. The following screenshot illustrates where the **Dynamic Base** option may be found:

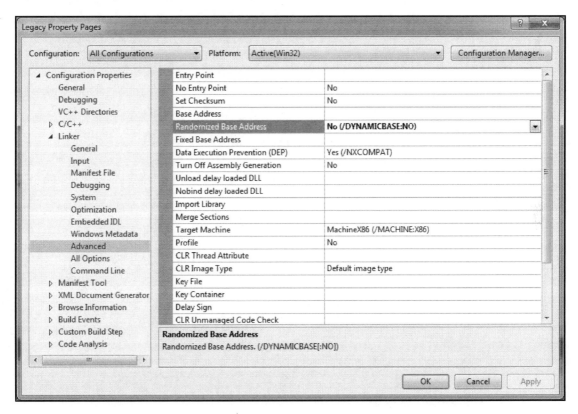

Once this option has been disabled, simply click on **Build** or **Build All**.

On Linux, however, we may simply build the executable the usual way by entering one of the following commands in the terminal (ignore the warning for now):

```
# As we are interested in 32-bit executable
# on a 32-bit platform we will type:
gcc -o legacy legacy.c

# and on a 64-bit platform we will type:
gcc -o legacy legacy.c -m32
```

In this chapter, we will begin by patching the Windows executable first, then we will proceed to the Linux executable and see how the problem may be solved in the case of ELF. Oh, and most importantly; forget about the C sources and pretend that we do not have them.

The issue

Whether we try to run our executables on Windows or on Linux, we would hardly notice any problem, as the program asks for our name and then prints it back. This will keep working in a stable manner as long as the program does not encounter a name longer than 127 ASCII characters (the 128th character is the terminating NULL value) and such names exist. Let's try to run this executable (we are referring to the one built for Windows, but the same idea applies to the Linux executable too) and feed it with a long line of text, much longer than 127 characters. This is what will happen:

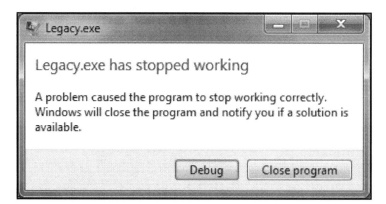

The reason for this message is the gets() function. If C is not your language of choice, you may be unaware of the fact that this function does not check the length of the input, which may lead to stack corruption in the best case (just like what caused the preceding message to appear) and is a vulnerability inviting specially crafted exploits in the worst case. Luckily, the solution for the gets() problem is quite simple; the call to gets() has to be replaced by a call to the fgets() function. Should we have sources, this would be a one minute fix, but we don't (at least we are pretending we don't have them).

However, the solution we will shortly implement is not complex. All we need is a disassembler (preferably IDA Pro), a hex editor, and, of course, Flat Assembler.

PE files

In order to successfully implement a patch, we need to understand the PE file format (PE stands for portable executable). While a detailed specification may be obtained at this URL, http://www.microsoft.com/whdc/system/platform/firmware/PECOFF.mspx, we only need to understand a few things about the format and be able to manually parse its basic structure.

Headers

A PE file contains several headers and the first one we encounter is the DOS header, which only contains two things that are interesting for us; the first is the MZ signature and the second is the offset of the file header, also known as the PE header (as it is preceded by the PE\x0\x0 signature). The file header contains basic information about the file such as, for example, the number of sections.

Following the PE header is the optional header, which, in turn, contains even more interesting information such as ImageBase, --the address at which the image (file) should preferably be loaded, --and NumberOfRvaAndSizes, and the latter is of special interest for us. The NumberOfRvaAndSizes field denotes the number of entries in the array of IMAGE_DATA_DIRECTORY entries immediately following the optional header. The IMAGE_DATA_DIRECTORY structure is defined as follows:

```
struct IMAGE_DATA_DIRECTORY
{
    DWORD VirtualAddress;
    DWORD Size;
}
```

Each of these structures describes certain areas of the PE file. For example, Import IMAGE_DATA_DIRECTORY, the one we are particularly interested in, refers to information about functions not present in this file, but imported from dynamic link libraries.

The next would be an array of IMAGE_SECTION_HEADER structures, where each of the PE sections is described (we are given a section's file offset and size as well as its virtual address and virtual size, the size in memory, which may and most likely will be different from its size in the file).

While I strongly encourage you to read the official specification, I would also suggest downloading and installing the best hex editor I have ever seen, --010 Editor (available at https://www.sweetscape.com/010Editor/). This powerful application, in addition to having builds for Windows, mac OS X, and Linux, supports templates for easier parsing of different binary formats and has a template for parsing of PE files. Take a look at the template's output; --it makes understanding the PE format much easier. Here is how a PE file is displayed in 010 Editor:

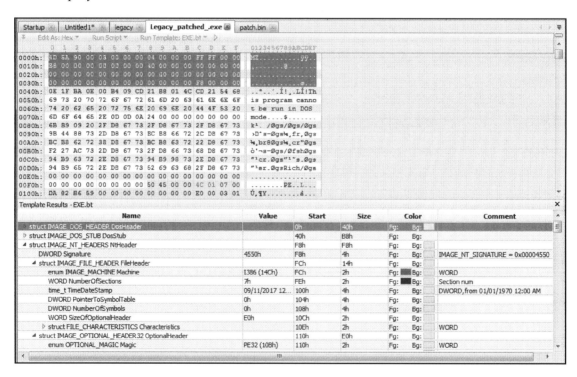

Imports

The `gets()` function we are hunting for is dynamically linked from the `ucrtbased.dll` file, therefore we should check the import table for it. Using the 010 Editor to find and parse the import table, as we see in the following screenshot, is not difficult:

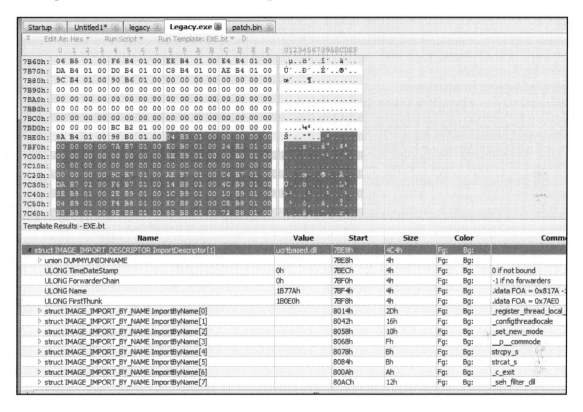

Although it may be (and in fact is) an interesting process to manually parse a PE executable, it is much more convenient and easy to use one of the tools available out there. For example, IDA Pro would do all the dirty work for us.

Gathering information

Load the `Legacy.exe` file into IDA Pro or any other disassembler of your choice as we will now start gathering information about what we have to do in order to patch the `Legacy.exe` file and force it to use `fgets()` instead of `gets()`.

Locating calls to gets()

We are lucky, in our case, that there is only one call to `gets()`, and we know that it should be somewhere around the call to `printf`, which prints the `Enter your name:` string. However, let's take a look at the **Strings** window in IDA Pro:

Address	Length	Type	String
[s] .rdata:00417B30	00000012	C	Enter your name:
[s] .rdata:00417B48	00000013	C	\n\nYour name is: %s
[s] .rdata:00417B90	0000001C	C	Stack around the variable '
[s] .rdata:00417BAC	00000011	C	' was corrupted.
[s] .rdata:00417BC0	0000000F	C	The variable '

Finding the string of interest takes a second in the worst case, and once found, we simply double-click on it and get to the `.rdata` section of the executable where we see the following:

```
.rdata:00417B2C 00                              db    0
.rdata:00417B2D 00                              db    0
.rdata:00417B2E 00                              db    0
.rdata:00417B2F 00                              db    0
.rdata:00417B30 45 6E 74 65 72 20 79 6F+ aEnterYourName db 'Enter your name: ',0
.rdata:00417B30 75 72 20 6E 61 6D 65 3A+                             ; DATA XREF: sub_411780+28↑o
.rdata:00417B42 00 00 00 00 00 00              align 8
.rdata:00417B48 0A 0A 59 6F 75 72 20 6E+ aYourNameIsS db 0Ah        ; DATA XREF: sub_4117B0+8C↑o
.rdata:00417B48 61 6D 65 20 69 73 3A 20+              db 0Ah
.rdata:00417B48 25 73 00                              db 'Your name is: %s',0
.rdata:00417B5B 00 00 00 00 00                align 10h
.rdata:00417B60                        ; LPCSTR lpMultiByteStr
.rdata:00417B60 20 7C 41 00            lpMultiByteStr dd offset aTheValueOfEspW
```

Double-clicking on `DATA XREF:` takes us to the place in the code where the string is being accessed from:

```
.text:004117D5 168 89 45 FC                         mov     [ebp+var_4], eax
.text:004117D8 168 68 30 7B 41 00                   push    offset aEnterYourName ; "Enter your name: "
.text:004117DD 16C E8 57 FB FF FF                   call    sub_411339
.text:004117E2 16C 83 C4 04                          add     esp, 4
.text:004117E5 168 8D 85 78 FF FF FF                 lea     eax, [ebp+Buffer]
.text:004117EB 168 50                                push    eax               ; Buffer
.text:004117EC 16C E8 F3 FA FF FF                   call    j_gets
.text:004117F1 16C 83 C4 04                          add     esp, 4
.text:004117F4 168 8D 85 78 FF FF FF                 lea     eax, [ebp+Buffer]
```

Going down just five lines, we see the call to `j_gets`... Why `j_gets`, you may ask; aren't we looking for the `gets()` function's address and not for jumps to it? Of course we are looking for `gets()`; however, since there may have been more than one call to `gets()`, the compiler created a single "call hub" for this function so that any other code calling `gets()` would, in fact, call `j_gets` and then be directed to the real `gets()` function's address in the import table. And this is what we see at the address of `j_gets`:

```
.text:004112E4                     ; char *__cdecl j_gets(char *Buffer)
.text:004112E4                     j_gets          proc near            ; CODE XREF: sub_411780+3C↓p
.text:004112E4 000 E9 EF 38 00 00                   jmp     gets
.text:004112E4                     j_gets          endp
.text:004112E4
```

For now, we only have to take note of the address of the `call j_gets` instruction, which is `0x4117Ec`.

Preparing for the patch

Unfortunately, we cannot simply redirect the call to `fgets()` instead of `j_gets`, because we do not have `fgets()` imported at all (as we are not using it in our C source) as well as due to the fact that `gets()` takes only one argument (as we see at the address `0x4117EB`- cdecl passing of a parameter), while `fgets()` expects three. Trying to patch the code in place so that it would pass three parameters is not possible without damaging the executable and rendering it unusable. This means that we need to find a place for shim code, which would add the two additional parameters and actually call `fgets()` (once we add it as an imported function).

Fortunately for us, PE sections in memory (and, in fact, in files too) occupy much more space than their actual content. This is true in our case as well and we need to find where the content of the `.text` section ends; for this reason we, first of all, look at where the next section begins, as shown in the following screenshot:

Name	Value	Start	Size
▷ struct IMAGE_DOS_HEADER DosHeader		0h	40h
▷ struct IMAGE_DOS_STUB DosStub		40h	B8h
▷ struct IMAGE_NT_HEADERS NtHeader		F8h	F8h
▷ struct IMAGE_SECTION_HEADER SectionHeaders[7]		1F0h	118h
▷ struct IMAGE_SECTION_DATA Section[0]	.text	400h	5200h
struct IMAGE_SECTION_DATA Section[1]	.rdata	5600h	2200h
▷ struct IMAGE_SECTION_DATA Section[2]	.data	7800h	200h
▷ struct IMAGE_SECTION_DATA Section[3]	.idata	7A00h	C00h

As we see in the preceding screenshot, the next section is `.rdata` and the beginning of its content is highlighted. Once we are there, we begin to scroll up, till we see content other than zeros or `0xcc` bytes, as shown in the following screenshot:

```
   Edit As: Hex ▼    Run Script ▼    Run Template: EXE.bt ▼  ▷
         0  1  2  3  4  5  6  7  8  9  A  B  C  D  E  F   0123456789ABCDEF
40C0h:  41 00 FF 25 08 B0 41 00 FF 25 0C B0 41 00 FF 25   A.ÿ%.°A.ÿ%.°A.ÿ%
40D0h:  10 B0 41 00 FF 25 14 B0 41 00 FF 25 54 B0 41 00   .°A.ÿ%.°A.ÿ%T°A.
40E0h:  FF 25 50 B0 41 00 FF 25 4C B0 41 00 FF 25 48 B0   ÿ%P°A.ÿ%L°A.ÿ%H°
40F0h:  41 00 FF 25 44 B0 41 00 FF 25 40 B0 41 00 FF 25   A.ÿ%D°A.ÿ%@°A.ÿ%
4100h:  3C B0 41 00 FF 25 38 B0 41 00 FF 25 34 B0 41 00   <°A.ÿ%8°A.ÿ%4°A.
4110h:  FF 25 30 B0 41 00 FF 25 2C B0 41 00 FF 25 28 B0   ÿ%0°A.ÿ%,°A.ÿ%(°
4120h:  41 00 FF 25 24 B0 41 00 FF 25 20 B0 41 00 FF 25   A.ÿ%$°A.ÿ% °A.ÿ%
4130h:  1C B0 41 00 FF 25 18 B0 41 00 CC CC CC CC CC CC   .°A.ÿ%.°A.ÌÌÌÌÌÌ
4140h:  55 8B EC B0 01 5D C3 CC CC CC CC CC CC CC CC CC   U‹ì°.]ÃÌÌÌÌÌÌÌÌÌ
4150h:  55 8B EC B0 01 5D C3 CC CC CC CC CC CC CC CC CC   U‹ì°.]ÃÌÌÌÌÌÌÌÌÌ
4160h:  55 8B EC B0 01 5D C3 CC CC CC CC CC CC CC CC CC   U‹ì°.]ÃÌÌÌÌÌÌÌÌÌ
4170h:  55 8B EC B0 01 5D C3 CC CC CC CC CC CC CC CC CC   U‹ì°.]ÃÌÌÌÌÌÌÌÌÌ
4180h:  55 8B EC B0 01 5D C3 CC CC CC CC CC CC CC CC CC   U‹ì°.]ÃÌÌÌÌÌÌÌÌÌ
4190h:  55 8B EC 33 C0 5D C3 CC CC CC CC CC CC CC CC CC   U‹ì3À]ÃÌÌÌÌÌÌÌÌÌ
41A0h:  CC CC CC CC CC CC CC CC CC CC CC CC CC CC CC CC   ÌÌÌÌÌÌÌÌÌÌÌÌÌÌÌÌ
41B0h:  CC CC CC CC CC CC CC CC CC CC CC CC CC CC CC CC   ÌÌÌÌÌÌÌÌÌÌÌÌÌÌÌÌ
41C0h:  CC CC CC CC CC CC CC CC CC CC CC CC CC CC CC CC   ÌÌÌÌÌÌÌÌÌÌÌÌÌÌÌÌ
41D0h:  CC CC CC CC CC CC CC CC CC CC CC CC CC CC CC CC   ÌÌÌÌÌÌÌÌÌÌÌÌÌÌÌÌ
41E0h:  CC CC CC CC CC CC CC CC CC CC CC CC CC CC CC CC   ÌÌÌÌÌÌÌÌÌÌÌÌÌÌÌÌ
41F0h:  CC CC CC CC CC CC CC CC CC CC CC CC CC CC CC CC   ÌÌÌÌÌÌÌÌÌÌÌÌÌÌÌÌ
4200h:  CC CC CC CC CC CC CC CC CC CC CC CC CC CC CC CC   ÌÌÌÌÌÌÌÌÌÌÌÌÌÌÌÌ
4210h:  CC CC CC CC CC CC CC CC CC CC CC CC CC CC CC CC   ÌÌÌÌÌÌÌÌÌÌÌÌÌÌÌÌ
```

We see that as the actual content's last byte is at file offset `0x4196`, we have some spare space beginning with the file offset `0x4197`; however, it does not seem right to begin a procedure at an unaligned address, so let's begin with the file offset `0x4198`. Just to be sure that we are at the right place, let's compare the bytes with what we see in IDA Pro:

```
  .text:00414D90
  .text:00414D90                     sub_414D90      proc near           ; CODE XREF: sub_4112CB↑j
  .text:00414D90                                                         ; .text:0041131B↑j
▶•.text:00414D90 000 55                             push    ebp
 •.text:00414D91 004 8B EC                           mov     ebp, esp
 •.text:00414D93 004 33 C0                           xor     eax, eax
 •.text:00414D95 004 5D                              pop     ebp
 •.text:00414D96 000 C3                              retn
  .text:00414D96                     sub_414D90      endp
  .text:00414D96
  .text:00414D96
  .text:00414D96                     ; ---------------------------------------
 •.text:00414D97 CC CC CC CC CC CC CC CC CC+         db 1347h dup(0CCh)
 •.text:004160DE 00 00 00 00 00 00 00 00 00+         align 200h
 •.text:00416200 ?? ?? ?? ?? ?? ?? ?? ??+           dd 380h dup(?)
  .text:00416200 ?? ?? ?? ?? ?? ?? ?? ??+   _text     ends
  .text:00416200 ?? ?? ?? ?? ?? ?? ?? ??+
```

Eventually, we see that the bytes are the same and we may use the file offset `0x4198` (virtual address `0x414d98`) for our shim code.

Importing fgets()

Before we begin the implementation of our patch, we still need to make the executable import `fgets()` instead of `gets()`. This appears to be quite easy. Let's take a look at the content of the import table where the `gets()` function is imported:

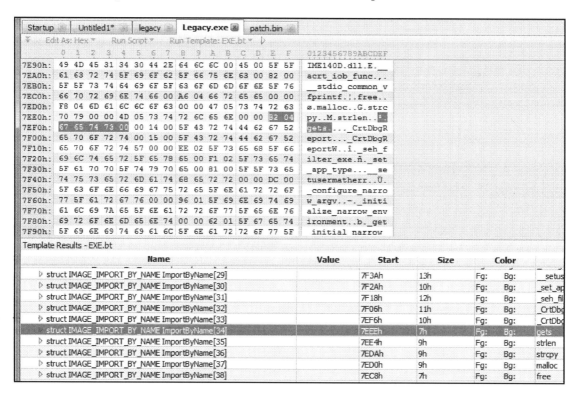

Having located the string, we may safely overwrite it with `fgets`. The explanation, looking at the following screenshot, makes it clear why such overwriting is safe in this specific case:

	0	1	2	3	4	5	6	7	8	9	A	B	C	D	E	F	0123456789ABCDEF
7E90h:	49	4D	45	31	34	30	44	2E	64	6C	6C	00	45	00	5F	5F	IME140D.dll.E.__
7EA0h:	61	63	72	74	5F	69	6F	62	5F	66	75	6E	63	00	82	00	acrt_iob_func.,.
7EB0h:	5F	5F	73	74	64	69	6F	5F	63	6F	6D	6D	6F	6E	5F	76	__stdio_common_v
7EC0h:	66	70	72	69	6E	74	66	00	A6	04	66	72	65	65	00	00	fprintf.¦.free..
7ED0h:	F8	04	6D	61	6C	6C	6F	63	00	00	47	05	73	74	72	63	ø.malloc..G.strc
7EE0h:	70	79	00	00	4D	05	73	74	72	6C	65	6E	00	00	B2	04	py..M.strlen..².
7EF0h:	66	67	65	74	73	00	14	00	5F	43	72	74	44	62	67	52	fgets.._CrtDbgR
7F00h:	65	70	6F	72	74	00	15	00	5F	43	72	74	44	62	67	52	eport..._CrtDbgR
7F10h:	65	70	6F	72	74	57	00	00	EE	02	5F	73	65	68	5F	66	eportW..î._seh_f
7F20h:	69	6C	74	65	72	5F	65	78	65	00	F1	02	5F	73	65	74	ilter_exe.ñ._set
7F30h:	5F	61	70	70	5F	74	79	70	65	00	81	00	5F	5F	73	65	_app_type..._se
7F40h:	74	75	73	65	72	6D	61	74	68	65	72	72	00	00	DC	00	tusermatherr..Ü.
7F50h:	5F	63	6F	6E	66	69	67	75	72	65	5F	6E	61	72	72	6F	_configure_narro
7F60h:	77	5F	61	72	67	76	00	00	96	01	5F	69	6E	69	74	69	w_argv..-._initi
7F70h:	61	6C	69	7A	65	5F	6E	61	72	72	6F	77	5F	65	6E	76	alize_narrow_env
7F80h:	69	72	6F	6E	6D	65	6E	74	00	00	62	01	5F	67	65	74	ironment..b._get
7F90h:	5F	69	6E	69	74	69	61	6C	5F	6E	61	72	72	6F	77	5F	initial_narrow_

The preceding screenshot shows `gets` being replaced by `fgets` already. We are lucky once more here because the `gets` string, which started at the file offset `0x7EF0`, did not end on an even boundary, so we had an extra zero at `0x7EF5`, thus leaving us enough space to overwrite `gets` with `fgets` and have the terminating `NULL` intact.

Patching calls

The next step would be patching calls to `gets()` and redirecting them to our shim. As we only have a single call to `gets()` (which is now a call to `fgets()` with an invalid number of parameters), we will patch the call itself. If we had multiple calls to `fgets()`, we would then patch the `jmp fgets` instruction rather than patching each and every call.

As we have already seen, the call is relative to `EIP`, so we have to calculate a new offset for the call so that it would call our shim code located at `0x414d98`. The formula is rather simple:

new_offset = 0x414d98 - 0x4117EC - 5

Here, `0x4117EC` is the address of the call instruction and `5` is its length in bytes. We need to use this length of the call instruction as, at the time it is executed, the `EIP` already points at the instruction immediately following the call. The resulting offset would be `0x35A7`.

However, before we can apply this patch, we have to find the right place in the hex editor and we use a few bytes representing this call instruction and a few bytes that follow as shown in the following screenshot:

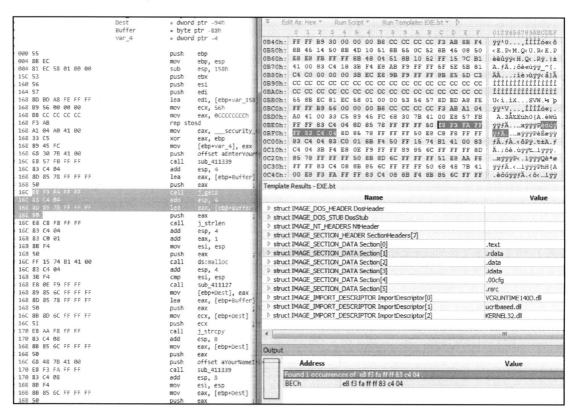

We used the `0xe8 0xf3 0xfa 0xff 0xff 0x83 0xc4 0x04` bytes for our search. Doing this, one has to make sure such a sequence of bytes appears only once in the search result. Here the `0xe8` is the call instruction and the `0xf3 0xfa 0xff 0xff` bytes are the offset from the next instruction --`0xfffffaf3`. The following screenshot shows the offset patch being applied:

	0	1	2	3	4	5	6	7	8	9	A	B	C	D	E	F	0123456789ABCDEF
0BC0h:	FF	FF	B9	56	00	00	00	B8	CC	CC	CC	CC	F3	AB	A1	04	ÿÿ¹V...¸ÌÌÌÌó«¡.
0BD0h:	A0	41	00	33	C5	89	45	FC	68	30	7B	41	00	E8	57	FB	A.3Å‰Eüh0{A.èWû
0BE0h:	FF	FF	83	C4	04	8D	85	78	FF	FF	FF	50	E8	A7	35	00	ÿÿƒÄ...…xÿÿÿPè§5.
0BF0h:	00	83	C4	04	8D	85	78	FF	FF	FF	50	E8	C8	F8	FF	FF	.ƒÄ...…xÿÿÿPèÈøÿÿ
0C00h:	83	C4	04	83	C0	01	8B	F4	50	FF	15	74	B1	41	00	83	ƒÄ.ƒÀ.‹ôPÿ.t±A.ƒ
0C10h:	C4	04	3B	F4	E8	0E	F9	FF	FF	89	85	6C	FF	FF	FF	8D	Ä.;ôè.ùÿÿ‰…lÿÿÿ.
0C20h:	85	78	FF	FF	FF	50	8B	8D	6C	FF	FF	FF	51	E8	AA	F8	…xÿÿÿP‹.lÿÿÿQèªø
0C30h:	FF	FF	83	C4	08	8B	85	6C	FF	FF	FF	50	68	48	7B	41	ÿÿƒÄ.‹…lÿÿÿPhH{A
0C40h:	00	E8	F3	FA	FF	FF	83	C4	08	8B	F4	8B	85	6C	FF	FF	.èóúÿÿƒÄ.‹ô‹…lÿÿ
0C50h:	FF	50	FF	15	78	B1	41	00	83	C4	04	3B	F4	E8	C5	F8	ÿPÿ.x±A.ƒÄ.;ôèÅø
0C60h:	FF	FF	33	C0	52	8B	CD	50	8D	15	94	18	41	00	E8	F9	ÿÿ3ÀR‹ÍP..".A.èù
0C70h:	F9	FF	FF	58	5A	5F	5E	5B	8B	4D	FC	33	CD	E8	FE	F9	ùÿÿXZ_^[‹Mü3Íèþù
0C80h:	FF	FF	81	C4	58	01	00	00	3B	EC	E8	98	F8	FF	FF	8B	ÿÿ.ÄX...;ìè˜øÿÿ‹
0C90h:	E5	5D	C3	90	01	00	00	00	9C	18	41	00	78	FF	FF	FF	å]Ã....œ.A.xÿÿÿ
0CA0h:	80	00	00	00	A8	18	41	00	69	6F	42	75	66	66	65	72	€...¨.A.ioBuffer
0CB0h:	00	CC	CC	CC	CC	CC	CC	CC	CC	CC	CC	CC	CC	CC	CC	CC	.ÌÌÌÌÌÌÌÌÌÌÌÌÌÌÌ
0CC0h:	CC	CC	CC	CC	CC	CC	CC	CC	CC	CC	CC	CC	CC	CC	CC	CC	ÌÌÌÌÌÌÌÌÌÌÌÌÌÌÌÌ

The offset is overwritten with `0x000035a7`. Now, the instruction at `0x4117ec` would call our shim code. But we still have to implement the shim code.

Shim code

The code we are about to write will look a tiny bit different from the code we are used to as we are not expecting an executable file to be generated out of it; instead, we will generate a binary file containing a 32-bit procedure assumed to be loaded at a specific address, and that is what we are going to tell the compiler in the first two lines of our `patch.asm` source file:

```
; Tell the assembler we are writing 32-bit code
use32

; Then specify the address where the procedure
; is expected to be loaded at
org 0x414d98
```

Then we will define two labels pointing at addresses outside our procedure. Fortunately, Flat Assembler allows us to define a label at an arbitrary address, like this:

```
; Assign label to the code where jump
; to fgets is performed
```

```
label fgets at 0x414bd8

; We will discuss this label in just a few seconds
label __acrt_iob_func at 0x41b180
```

After this, we are ready to begin our implementation of the actual shim code as a regular `cdecl` procedure:

```
fgets_patch:
    ; Standard cdecl prolog
    push  ebp
    mov   ebp, esp

    ; Ooops... We need to pass a pointer to
    ; the stdin as one of the fgets' parameters,
    ; but we have no idea what this pointer is...
```

The implementation of the standard C library on Windows provides us with a function for determining pointers to streams based on their number. The function is `__iob_func(int)`. Luckily for us, our victim executable is importing this function from `ucrtbased.dll` as we can see in the **Imports** tab of IDA Pro (or in the 010 Editor too):

0041B170	strcpy	ucrtbased
0041B174	malloc	ucrtbased
0041B178	free	ucrtbased
0041B17C	__stdio_common_vfprintf	ucrtbased
0041B180	__acrt_iob_func	ucrtbased
0041B184	__stdio_common_vsprintf_s	ucrtbased
Line 70 of 71		

Although the name differs a bit (prepended with __acrt_), this is the function we are interested in and it is located at the virtual address `0x41b180`. This is why we added the `__acrt_iob_func` label a few moments ago. Visiting that address, we may see that the address of the real `__acrt_iob_func` would be placed there after dynamic linking:

```
.idata:0041B17C ?? ?? ?? ??                 extrn __stdio_common_vfprintf:dword
.idata:0041B17C                                         ; CODE XREF: sub_411730+3C↑p
.idata:0041B17C                                         ; DATA XREF: sub_411730+3C↑r ...
.idata:0041B180 ?? ?? ?? ??                 extrn __acrt_iob_func:dword
.idata:0041B180                                         ; CODE XREF: sub_411900+32↑p
.idata:0041B180                                         ; DATA XREF: sub_411900+32↑r ...
.idata:0041B184 ?? ?? ?? ??                 extrn __imp___stdio_common_vsprintf_s:dword
.idata:0041B184                                         ; DATA XREF: __stdio_common_vspri
.idata:0041B188
```

In order to call this external function for getting the pointer to the `stdin` stream, we must remember that the `stdin` number is 0 and that imported functions are called indirectly:

```
; Get the stdin stream pointer
push   0
call   dword[__acrt_iob_func]
; The result is in the EAX register
; Do not forget to fix the stack pointer
; after calling a cdecl procedure
add    esp, 4
```

Now, we are ready to forward the execution flow to `fgets()` and we do that in the following way:

```
; Forward the call to fgets()
push   eax              ; stdin
push   128              ; max input length
push   dword [ebp + 8]  ; forward pointer to the
                        ; input buffer
call   fgets
add    esp, 12

; Standard cdecl epilog
mov    esp, ebp
pop    ebp
ret
```

The code for the patch is ready. As simple as that (in this particular case). Compiling this code would generate a 35-bytes binary file containing raw binary code. This is the code seen in the hex editor:

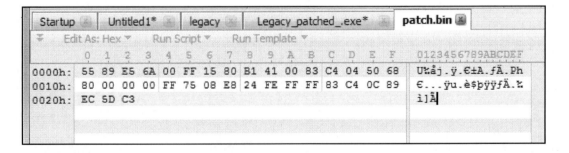

Applying the patch

In the *Preparing for the patch* subsection of this chapter, we have already located the place where the patch should be applied in the hex editor, which is at the file offset `0x4198`. The application of the patch is rather simple --we copy the bytes from the `patch.bin` file into the executable at the aforementioned location and get the following:

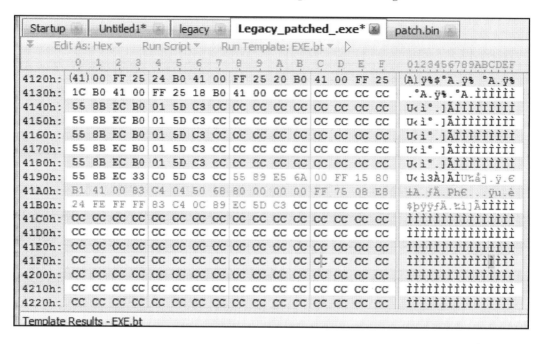

Now save the file and we are done. The executable has been patched and would use `fgets()` instead of `gets()` from now on. We may check this by running the executable and feeding a very long string instead of a name:

```
Enter your name: njduryffvnkr'qor pqerwf nonv onrvowl;ajserjfwerghiuqh[ewfkkldskcdp kwpu309u4ton23;p54otn24p5gh-28 90ejhv[njduryffvnkr'qor pqerwf nonv onrvowl;ajserjfwerghiuqh[ewfkkldskcdp kwpu309u4ton23;p54otn24p5gh-28 90ejhv[njduryffvnkr'qor pqerwf nonv onrvowl;ajserjfwerghiuqh[ewfkkldskcdp kwpu309u4ton23;p54otn24p5gh-28 90ejhv[

Your name is: njduryffvnkr'qor pqerwf nonv onrvowl;ajserjfwerghiuqh[ewfkkldskcdp kwpu309u4ton23;p54otn24p5gh-28 90ejhv[njduryffvnkr'qor pqerw
```

As we see, such input no longer causes any error as with `fgets()` at most 127 characters are read, thus keeping our stack safe, and we see the result in the preceding screenshot; -- the output is truncated.

A complex scenario

We have just gone through a simplistic scenario of patching a PE executable; alas, real-life situations are rarely that simple and modifications are usually much more complex than simply importing a different function. Is there a way to statically patch executables in such cases? Of course there is. In fact, there are more than one. For example, one may patch a certain procedure within the file, thus altering the algorithm it implements. This is, however, only possible when the existing procedure occupies enough space for the new code. Another option is to add an executable section to a PE file, which is rather simple and deserves being examined here. The whole process contains five easy steps (six, --if modifying the `patch.asm` file counts) and we are going to cover them one by one.

Preparing the patch

This is the easiest step as we hardly have to do anything here. We already have a working patch code and the only important difference from the Assembly point of view is where the code is going to be placed in memory. We will be adding a new section right at the end of the victim executable, thus the loading address for the code (the `Virtual Address`) is calculated by the summation of `Virtual Address` and `Virtual Size` of the currently last section and rounding it up to the nearest multiple of `SectionAlignment`, which, in our case, would be `0x1D000 + 0x43C = 0x1d43C`, rounded up to `0x1e000`. However, despite being called a virtual address, this value is in fact an offset from `ImageBase`, which is `0x400000`, thus the real virtual address would be `0x41e000`.

To put it simply, we only have to modify one line of `patch.asm`, --line number 2, so that `org 0x414d98` would become `org 0x41e000`. The rest of the code remains the same.

Adjusting file headers

Since we are about to append the section to an executable file, we need to make some changes to its headers so that they reflect the new reality. Let's open the `Legacy.exe` file in either the 010 Editor or any other hex editor you prefer and go through all its headers making modifications where necessary.

Before we proceed to update the file, we have to decide what would be the size of the new section in file (`SizeOfRawData`) and in memory (`VirtualSize`) in accordance with the `FileAlignment` and `SectionAlignment` values, respectively. Checking this values in the `IMAGE_OPTIONAL_HEADER32` structure, we see that the `FileAlignment` value is `0x200` and `SectionAlignment` is `0x1000`. Since the code we want to insert into the new section is tiny (only 35 bytes), we may proceed with minimum sizes, making the section's `SizeOfRawData = 0x200` and `VirtualSize = 0x1000`.

However, let's proceed step by step and, as the first modification, adjust the `NumberOfSections` field of `IMAGE_FILE_HEADER` under `IMAGE_NT_HEADERS`, as shown in the following screenshot:

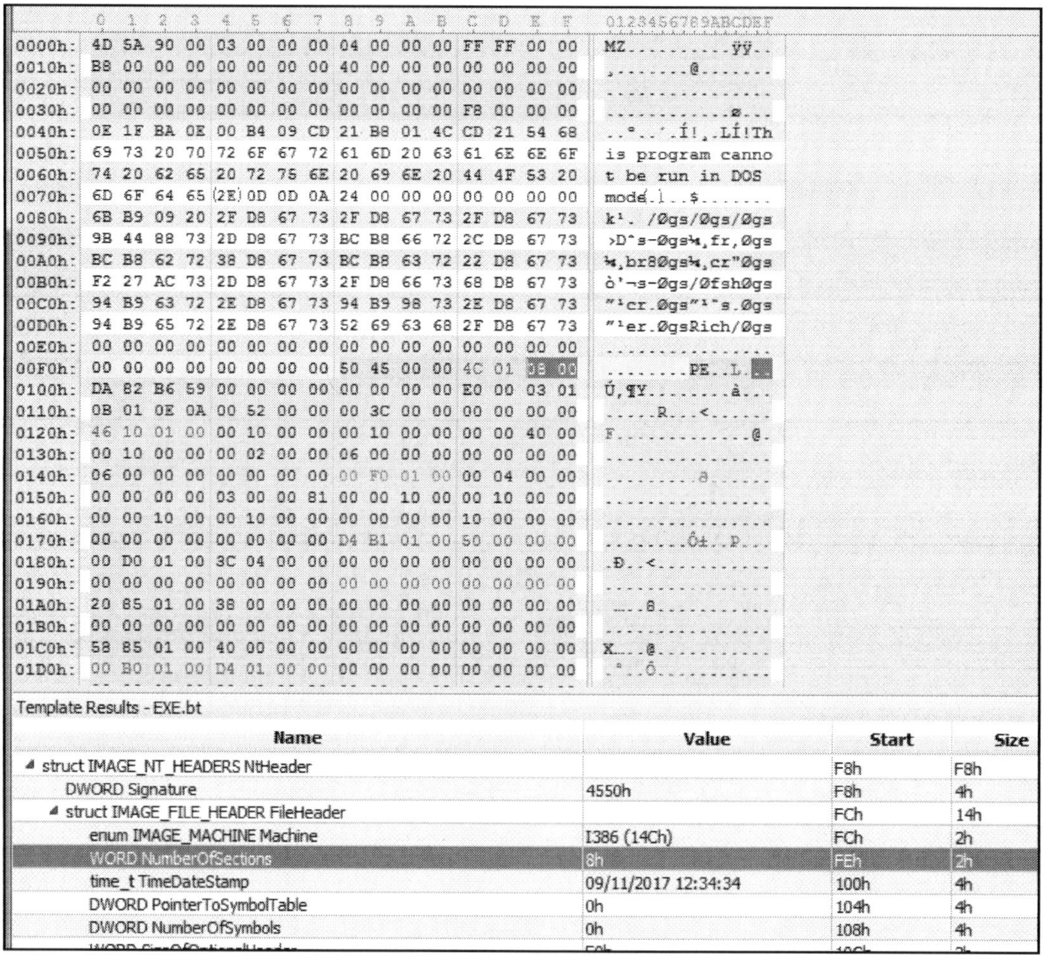

Originally, the file had seven sections and, as we are going to add another section, we change the WORD NumberOfSections value to 8h.

Once the NumberOfSections field has been updated, we proceed with updating the SizeOfImage field (which is the size of the executable image in memory) of the IMAGE_OPTIONAL_HEADER32 header. The original value of the SizeOfImage field is 0x1E000 and, as our new section should occupy 0x1000 bytes in memory, we simply set SizeOfImage to 0x1F000, as shown in the following screenshot:

Template Results - EXE.bt

Name	Value	Start
WORD MajorSubsystemVersion	6h	140h
WORD MinorSubsystemVersion	0h	142h
DWORD Win32VersionValue	0h	144h
DWORD SizeOfImage	1F000h	148h
DWORD SizeOfHeaders	400h	14Ch
DWORD CheckSum	0h	150h
enum IMAGE_SUBSYSTEM Subsystem	WINDOWS_CUI (3h)	154h
▷ struct DLL_CHARACTERISTICS DllCharacteristics		156h
DWORD SizeOfStackReserve	100000h	158h
DWORD SizeOfStackCommit	1000h	15Ch
DWORD SizeOfHeapReserve	100000h	160h
DWORD SizeOfHeapCommit	1000h	164h

Now comes a rather more interesting part --adding a section header. Section headers are located right after the array of IMAGE_DATA_DIRECTORY entries, which, in our case, is at the file offset of 0x1F0. The last section header (for the .rsrc section) is located at the file offset 0x2E0 and we are going to insert our header right after starting at file offset 0x308. In the case of this executable, we have plenty of spare bytes, so we may safely proceed.

The first eight bytes of the section header contain the section's name and we will name our section .patch. The interesting fact about the section name field is that the name does not have to end with 0 (the NULL string terminator) and may occupy all eight bytes.

The next four byte are integers describing the virtual size of a section (how many bytes it would occupy in memory), which, as we have previously decided, is 0x1000 bytes (another interesting fact--we may set this field to 0 and it would still work well).

The next field is a four bytes integer describing the VirtualAddress field of a section (where the section should be loaded at). The value for this field is the previous value of the SizeOfImage field, which was 0x1E000.

Following the VirtualAddress field, there is the SizeOfRawData field (4 bytes as well), which we set to 0x200, --the size of the new section in the file, --and PointerToRawData, which we set to the previous size of the file --0x8E00.

The remaining fields are filled with zeros, except the last field, Characteristics, which we set to 0x60000020, denoting the section as containing code and being executable.

The section header you added should look like the one shown in the following screenshot:

```
          0  1  2  3  4  5  6  7  8  9  A  B  C  D  E  F   0123456789ABCDEF
01F0h:   2E 74 65 78 74 62 73 73 00 00 01 00 00 10 00 00   .textbss........
0200h:   00 00 00 00 00 00 00 00 00 00 00 00 00 00 00 00   ................
0210h:   00 00 00 00 A0 00 00 E0 2E 74 65 78 74 00 00 00   .... ..à.text...
0220h:   DE 50 00 00 00 10 01 00 00 52 00 00 00 04 00 00   ÞP.......R......
0230h:   00 00 00 00 00 00 00 00 00 00 00 00 20 00 00 60   ............ ..`
0240h:   2E 72 64 61 74 61 00 00 75 20 00 00 00 70 01 00   .rdata..u ...p..
0250h:   00 22 00 00 00 56 00 00 00 00 00 00 00 00 00 00   ."...V..........
0260h:   00 00 00 00 40 00 00 40 2E 64 61 74 61 00 00 00   ....@..@.data...
0270h:   A4 05 00 00 00 A0 01 00 00 02 00 00 00 78 00 00   ¤.... .......x..
0280h:   00 00 00 00 00 00 00 00 00 00 00 00 40 00 00 C0   ............@..À
0290h:   2E 69 64 61 74 61 00 00 F7 0A 00 00 00 B0 01 00   .idata..÷....°..
02A0h:   00 0C 00 00 00 7A 00 00 00 00 00 00 00 00 00 00   .....z..........
02B0h:   00 00 00 00 40 00 00 40 2E 30 30 63 66 67 00 00   ....@..@.00cfg..
02C0h:   04 01 00 00 00 C0 01 00 00 02 00 00 00 86 00 00   .....À.......†..
02D0h:   00 00 00 00 00 00 00 00 00 00 00 00 40 00 00 40   ............@..@
02E0h:   2E 72 73 72 63 00 00 00 3C 04 00 00 00 D0 01 00   .rsrc...<....Ð..
02F0h:   00 06 00 00 00 88 00 00 00 00 00 00 00 00 00 00   .....^..........
0300h:   00 00 00 00 40 00 00 40 2E 70 61 74 63 68 00 00   ....@..@.patch..
0310h:   00 02 00 00 00 E0 01 00 00 02 00 00 00 8E 00 00   .....à.......Ž..
0320h:   00 00 00 00 00 00 00 00 00 00 00 00 20 00 00 60   ............ ..`
0330h:   00 00 00 00 00 00 00 00 00 00 00 00 00 00 00 00   ................
0340h:   00 00 00 00 00 00 00 00 00 00 00 00 00 00 00 00   ................
0350h:   00 00 00 00 00 00 00 00 00 00 00 00 00 00 00 00   ................
0360h:   00 00 00 00 00 00 00 00 00 00 00 00 00 00 00 00   ................
0370h:   00 00 00 00 00 00 00 00 00 00 00 00 00 00 00 00   ................
0380h:   00 00 00 00 00 00 00 00 00 00 00 00 00 00 00 00   ................
0390h:   00 00 00 00 00 00 00 00 00 00 00 00 00 00 00 00   ................
03A0h:   00 00 00 00 00 00 00 00 00 00 00 00 00 00 00 00   ................
```

Template Results - EXE.bt

Name	Value	Start
◢ struct IMAGE_SECTION_HEADER SectionHeaders[7]	.patch	308h
▷ BYTE Name[8]	.patch	308h
◢ union Misc		310h
DWORD PhysicalAddress	200h	310h
DWORD VirtualSize	200h	310h
DWORD VirtualAddress	1E000h	314h
DWORD SizeOfRawData	200h	318h
DWORD PointerToRawData	8E00h	31Ch
DWORD PointerToRelocations	0h	320h
DWORD PointerToLinenumbers	0h	324h
WORD NumberOfRelocations	0h	328h
WORD NumberOfLinenumbers	0h	32Ah
▷ struct SECTION_CHARACTERISTICS Characteristics		32Ch

Appending a new section

There are just two more steps to take and the first of them would be appending the actual section data to the file. Scrolling the file to the end in a hex editor, we will see that the first available file offset to add bytes to is `0x8e00`, which is exactly the value we set the `PointerToRawData` field to.

We should append `0x200` bytes to the file, thus setting its size to `0x9000`, and fill the first 35 bytes of those `0x200` bytes with our code, as shown on the following screenshot:

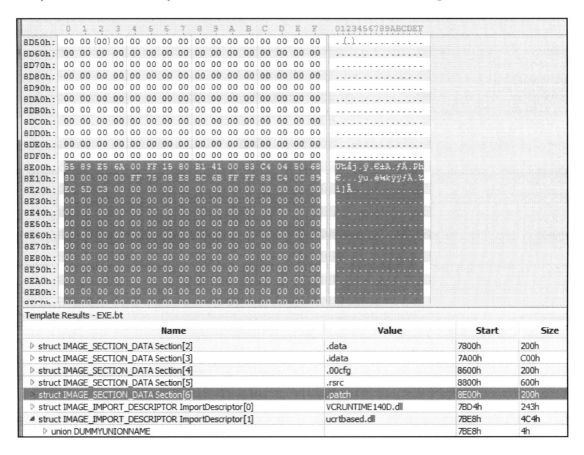

Just one more step to take before we can actually run the executable, so let's not hesitate.

Fixing the call instruction

All that is left to do is to fix the `call gets()` instruction so that it would point to our new code. We use the same binary string `0xE8 0xF3 0xFA 0xFF 0xFF 0x83 0xC4 0x04` in order to locate the call we are interested in and replace the `0xF3 0xFA 0xFF 0xFF` bytes with `0x0F 0xC8 0x00 0x00`, which is the exact offset from the instruction following the call to our new section. The following screenshot illustrates precisely this:

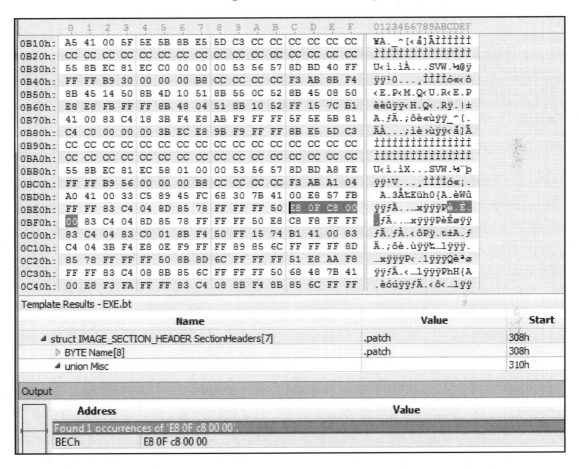

At last, save the file and try to launch it. If the patching has been done correctly, then you will see the same result as with the previous approach.

ELF executables

Patching ELF executables is a bit more difficult than patching their PE counterparts as ELF files tend to have no spare space in their sections, thus leaving no other choice but to either add a section, which is not as simple as with PE files, or inject a shared object.

Adding a section requires a good knowledge of the ELF format (specifications can be found at `http://www.skyfree.org/linux/references/ELF_Format.pdf`), which, although quite interesting, resides, in its fullness, outside the scope of this book. The most noticeable problem is in the way sections and headers are arranged within an ELF executable and in the way an ELF structure is treated by Linux, which makes it hard to append data as we did in the case of PE patching.

Injection of a shared object, on the other hand, is much simpler to implement and easy to use, so let's proceed this way.

LD_PRELOAD

The `LD_PRELOAD` environment variable is used by the Linux dynamic linker/loader `ld.so` and, if set, contains a list of shared objects to be loaded with the executable before any other shared object is loaded, including `libc.so`. This means that we may create a shared object, which would export a symbol named `gets`, and specify this shared object in `LD_PRELOAD`, which would guarantee, that if the executable we are attempting to run imports a symbol with the same name, our implementation of `gets` would be linked instead of the one from `libc.so`, which would be loaded afterward.

A shared object

Right now, we are going to implement our own `gets()` procedure, which would, in fact, forward calls to `fgets()` just as our PE patch did. Unfortunately, Flat Assembler's support for ELF does not allow us to create shared objects in a simple way yet; therefore, we will create an object file and later link it with GCC as a shared object for a 32-bit system.

The source code is, as usual, quite simple and intuitive:

```
; First the formatter directive to tell
; the assembler to generate ELF object file
format ELF

; We want to export our procedure under
; the name "gets"
```

```
    public gets as 'gets'

    ; And we need the following symbols to be
    ; imported from libc
    ; As you may notice, unlike Windows, the
    ; "stdin" is exported by libc
    extrn fgets
    extrn stdin

    ; As we want to create a shared object
    ; we better create our own PLT (Procedure
    ; Linkage Table)
    section '.idata' writeable
      _fgets  dd  fgets
      _stdin  dd  stdin


    section '.text' executable

    ; At last, the procedure
    gets:
        ; Standard cdecl prolog
        push  ebp
        mov   ebp, esp

        ; Forward the call to fgets()
        mov   eax, [_stdin]
        push  dword [eax]           ; FILE*
        push  127                   ; len
        push  dword [ebp + 8]       ; Buff*
        call  [_fgets]
        add   esp, 12

        ; Standard cdecl epilog
        mov   esp, ebp
        pop   ebp
        ret
```

Save the preceding code as `fgets_patch.asm` and compile it with `fasm` or `fasm.x64`; this will result in the `fgets_patch.o` object file. Building a shared object out of this object file is as simple as running one of the following commands in the terminal:

```
# On a 32-bit system
gcc -o fgets_patch.so fgets_patch.o -shared

# and on a 64-bit system
gcc -o fgets_patch.so fgets_patch.o -shared -m32
```

Let's now test and run the legacy executable without the patch and feed it with a long string (140 bytes). Here is the result:

```
Enter your name: tw2qrq3gq[wpoi]-=0iwreotjgewrt[q0jgf][0-oergjk'qwtjm[asv09jca[rjtg qija ijfdn
gvironj gijsadviu0er9ugp0i4jno3irnvoszifvjhpo jhrpsoihnvreingns

Your name is: tw2qrq3gq[wpoi]-=0iwreotjgewrt[q0jgf][0-oergjk'qwtjm[asv09jca[rjtg qija ijfdngvi
ronj gijsadviu0er9ugp0i4jno3irnvoszifvjhpo jhrp00        vreingns
Segmentation fault
```

As we can see, the stack was corrupted, which caused a segmentation fault (invalid memory access). Now we may try to run the same executable but set the `LD_PRELOAD` environment variable to `"./fgets_patch.so"`, thus forcing our shared object to be loaded before anything else when launching the `legacy` executable. The command line would then be as follows:

```
LD_PRELOAD=./fgets_patch.so ./legacy
```

This time, we get the output just as expected, --truncated to 127 characters, --meaning that our implementation of `gets()` was linked by the dynamic linking process:

```
+ LD_PRELOAD=./fgets_patch.so
+ ./legacy
Enter your name: tw2qrq3gq[wpoi]-=0iwreotjgewrt[q0jgf][0-oergjk'qwtjm[asv09jca[rjtg qija ijfdn
gvironj gijsadviu0er9ugp0i4jno3irnvoszifvjhpo jhrpsoihnvreingns

Your name is: tw2qrq3gq[wpoi]-=0iwreotjgewrt[q0jgf][0-oergjk'qwtjm[asv09jca[rjtg qija ijfdngvi
ronj gijsadviu0er9ugp0i4jno3irnvoszifvjhpo jhr
```

Summary

Modification of existing executable code and/or running processes is a rather broad theme, which is very difficult to fit into a single chapter as it may itself deserve a separate book. It is, however, much more relevant to programming techniques, and operating systems in general, while we were trying to concentrate on the Assembly language.

This chapter hardly covers the tip of the iceberg called modification of binary code (known as patching). The purpose was to demonstrate how easy and interesting the process may be, rather then covering each and every method in much detail. We have, however, acquired a general indication of where to go to when it comes to modification of code that cannot be simply rebuilt.

The method of code analysis was covered very superficially just to provide you with the general idea, just as the most part of the process of patching an application too, as the emphasis was on the implementation of patches themselves. My personal suggestion is --go and get acquainted with the format specs for both Windows PE executables and object files and Linux ELF. Even if you would never have to patch a single executable, you would then understand what happens on lower levels when you are coding in a higher-level languages.

11
Oh, Almost Forgot

Our journey approaches its end. However, it is important to make it clear that this book only covers the tip of the iceberg called Assembly programming and there is much more to learn ahead of you. The main idea of this book is to show you how powerful and easy it is to create software in Assembly language and how portable and convenient it may be.

There are a few topics that we have not touched over the course of the book, but which, nevertheless, deserve attention. One such topic is how we can keep our code protected from sneaky eyes. We will shortly see how some of the methods of protecting our code may be implemented by means of the Flat Assembler, without the need for third-party software.

Another topic, which in my eyes, is interesting and deserves some coverage, is how to write code that would be executed in kernel space. We will implement a small loadable kernel module for Linux.

Protecting the code

There are numerous books, articles, and blog posts on how to better protect your code. Some of them are even useful and practical; however, most of them are dedicated to certain third-party tools or combinations thereof. We are not going to review any of those, neither books nor tools. Instead, we are about to see what we are able to do ourselves with the tools we already have.

First of all, we have to assimilate the fact that there is no such thing as 100% protection for our code. No matter what we do, the more valuable our code is, the higher is the possibility that it will be reverse engineered. We may use packers, protectors, and whatever other tools we may come up with, but at the end, they are all well known and will be bypassed one way or another. Thus, the final frontier is the code itself. To put it correctly, it is the way the code appears to a potential attacker. This is where the obfuscation comes into play.

The dictionary definition of the word *obfuscation* is the action of making something obscure, unclear, or unintelligible. It may be quite a powerful technique, whether in conjunction with other approaches or alone. I once had a chance to reverse engineer a program that used encryption extensively. This program was not protected with any third-party tool, instead there was a very nice and unclear (at first glance) game of bits and I have to admit--it was much more difficult to reverse engineer than it could have been if any tool like **Themida** was in place.

In this part of the chapter, we will see a primitive example of what obfuscation may look like by slightly enhancing the patch we made for our Windows-based executable with `gets()`. As obfuscation is not the primary topic of the book; we will not dive into much detail, but show how simple and tiny changes may make it a bit harder to understand the underlying logic of the code without dynamically watching it in a debugger.

The original code

Let's begin by taking a quick look at the original code of the procedure we planted into the executable as part of our patch. The code is quite straightforward and, knowing what we already know, is easy to read:

```
; First of all we tell the assembler
; that this is a 32-bit code
use32

; Tell the assembler that we are expecting
; this code to appear at 0x41e000
org 0x41e000

; Define labels for "external" procedures
; we are about to use
label fgets at 0x414bd8
label __acrt_iob_func at 0x41b180

; Implement the procedure
fgets_patch:
```

```
; We begin the procedure with the standard
; prolog for cdecl calling convention
push   ebp
mov    ebp, esp

; As we need the pointer to the stdin stream
; we call the __acrt_iob_func procedure
push   0                       ; This is the number of the stream
call   dword[__acrt_iob_func]
add    esp, 4                  ; Restore the stack pointer

; Forward the parameter (char*) and
; invoke fgets()
push   eax                     ; Contains pointer to the stdin stream
push   128                     ; Maximum input length
push   dword[ebp + 8]          ; Pointer to the receiving buffer
call   fgets
add    esp, 4 * 3              ; Restore the stack pointer

; Standard epilog for procedures using cdecl
; calling convention
mov    esp, ebp
pop    ebp
ret
```

The code is rather simple and it is fairly difficult to find anything valuable to protect here. Since this is the situation, we will use this example to show how simply a `call` instruction may be implemented with other instructions in such a way that it would neither point to the callee nor resemble a procedure call at all.

The call

There are several ways to replace the `call` instruction with a sequence of instructions that would perform exactly the same action but would be treated by decompilers in a different manner. For example, the following code would do exactly what the `call` instruction does:

```
; Preceding code
push   .return_address    ; Push the return address on stack
push   .callee            ; Redirect the execution flow to
ret                       ; callee
.return_address:
; the rest of the code
```

We may, as well, replace the following sequence:

```
push   callee
ret
```

with, for example:

```
lea   eax, [callee]
jmp eax
```

This would still yield the same result. However, we want our obfuscation to be a bit stronger; therefore, we proceed and create a macro.

The call obfuscation macro

Prior to beginning with the obfuscation of the `call` instruction itself, we will define a utility macro called `random`:

```
; The %t below stands for the current
; timestamp (at the compile time)
random_seed = %t

; This macro sets 'r' to current random_seed
macro random r
{
    random_seed = ((random_seed *\
               214013 +\
               2531011) shr 16) and 0xffffffff
    r = random_seed
}
```

The `random` macro generates a pseudo-random integer and returns it in the parameter variable. We will need this tiny portion of randomization in order to add some diversity to our `call` implementation occurrences. The macro itself (let us call it `f_call`) makes use of the EAX register; therefore, we would either take care of preserving this register before the `f_call` invocation or only use this macro with procedures returning a value in the EAX register as, otherwise, the value of the register would be lost. Also, it is only suitable for direct calls due to the way it handles the parameter.

At last, we come to the macro itself. As the best way to understand the code is to look at the code, let's peer into the macro:

```
; This macro has a parameter - the label (address)
; of the procedure to call
macro   f_call callee
{
    ; First we declare a few local labels
    ; We need them to be local as this macro may be
    ; used more than once in a procedure
    local .reference_addr,\
          .out,\
          .ret_addr,\
          .z,\
          .call


    ; Now we need to calculate the reference address
    ; for all further address calculations
    call   .call
.call:
    add    dword[esp], .reference_addr - .call
    ; Now the address or the .reference_addr label
    ; is at [esp]
    ; Jump to the .reference_addr
    ret


    ; Add some randomness
    random .z
    dd     .z


    ; The ret instruction above returns to this address
.reference_addr:
    ; Calculate the address of the callee:
    ; We load the previously generated random bytes into
    ; the .z compile time variable
    load .z dword from .reference_addr - 4

    mov  eax, [esp - 4]      ; EAX now contains the address
                             ; of the .reference_addr label
    mov  eax, [eax - 4]      ; And now it contains the four
                             ; random bytes
    xor  eax, callee xor .z  ; EAX is set to the address of
                             ; the callee


    ; We need to set up return address for the callee
    ; before we jump to it
    sub  esp, 4              ; This may be written as
                             ; 'add esp, -4' for a bit of
```

```
                            ; additional obfuscation
      add   dword[esp], .ret_addr - .reference_addr
      ; Now the value stored on stack is the address of
      ; the .ret_addr label
      ; At last - jump to the callee
      jmp   eax

      ; Add even more randomness
      random .z
      dd     .z
      random .z
      dd     .z

      ; When the callee returns, it falls to this address
   .ret_addr:
      ; However, we want to obfuscate further execution
      ; flow, so we add the following code, which sets
      ; the value still present on stack (address of the
      ; .ret_addr) to the address of the .out label
      sub   dword[esp - 4], -(.out - .ret_addr)
      sub   esp, 4
      ret
      ; The above two lines are, in fact, an equivalent
      ; of 'jmp dword[esp - 4]'

      ; Some more randomness
      random .z
      dd     .z

   .out:
   }
```

As we may see, there are no complex computations involved in this particular obfuscation attempt and, even more, the code is still readable and understandable, but let's replace the line `call fgets` in our `patch_section.asm` file with `f_call fgets`, recompile, and re-apply the patch to the executable.

The new patch is significantly bigger--86 bytes instead of 35 bytes:

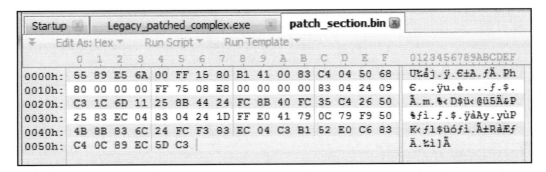

Copy these bytes and paste them into the `Legacy.exe` file at the `0x8e00` offset, as shown in the following screenshot:

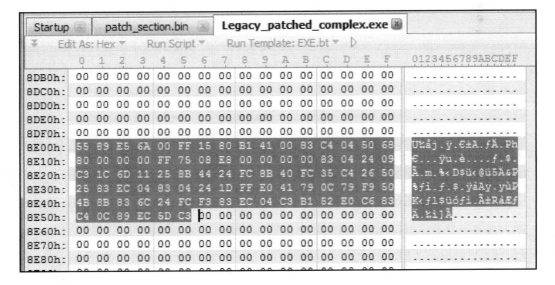

Running the executable, we will obtain the same result as we did in the previous chapter, so no visible difference at this stage. However, let's take a look at what the code looks like in the disassembler:

```
.patch:0041E000
.patch:0041E000                              sub_41E000      proc near               ; CODE XREF: sub_4117B0+3C↑p
.patch:0041E000
.patch:0041E000                              var_10          = dword ptr -10h
.patch:0041E000                              arg_0           = dword ptr  8
.patch:0041E000
.patch:0041E000 000 55                                       push    ebp
.patch:0041E001 004 89 E5                                    mov     ebp, esp
.patch:0041E003 004 6A 00                                    push    0
.patch:0041E005 008 FF 15 80 B1 41 00                        call    ds:__acrt_iob_func
.patch:0041E00B 008 83 C4 04                                 add     esp, 4
.patch:0041E00E 004 50                                       push    eax
.patch:0041E00F 008 68 80 00 00 00                           push    80h
.patch:0041E014 00C FF 75 08                                 push    [ebp+arg_0]
.patch:0041E017 010 E8 00 00 00 00                           call    $+5
.patch:0041E01C 014 83 04 24 09                              add     [esp+10h+var_10], 9
.patch:0041E020 014 C3                                       retn
.patch:0041E020                              sub_41E000      endp ; sp-analysis failed
.patch:0041E020
.patch:0041E021                              ; ---------------------------------------------
.patch:0041E021 1C 6D                                        sbb     al, 6Dh
.patch:0041E023 11 25 8B 44 24 FC                            adc     ds:0FC244488h, esp
.patch:0041E029 8B 40 FC                                     mov     eax, [eax-4]
.patch:0041E02C 35 C4 26 50 25                               xor     eax, 255026C4h
.patch:0041E031 83 EC 04                                     sub     esp, 4
.patch:0041E034 83 04 24 1D                                  add     dword ptr [esp], 1Dh
.patch:0041E038 FF E0                                        jmp     eax
.patch:0041E038                              ; ---------------------------------------------
.patch:0041E03A 41 79                                        dw 7941h
.patch:0041E03C                              ; ---------------------------------------------
.patch:0041E03C 0C 79                                        or      al, 79h
.patch:0041E03E F9                                           stc
.patch:0041E03F 50                                           push    eax
.patch:0041E040 4B                                           dec     ebx
.patch:0041E041 8B 83 6C 24 FC F3                            mov     eax, [ebx-0C03DB94h]
.patch:0041E047 83 EC 04                                     sub     esp, 4
.patch:0041E04A C3                                           retn
.patch:0041E04A                              ; ---------------------------------------------
.patch:0041E04A B1                                           db 0B1h
.patch:0041E04C 52 E0 C6 83 C4 0C 89 EC+                     dd 83C6E052h, 0EC890CC4h, 0C35Dh, 6Ah dup(0)
.patch:0041E200 ?? ?? ?? ?? ?? ?? ?? ??+                     dd 380h dup(?)
.patch:0041E200 ?? ?? ?? ?? ?? ?? ?? ??+     _patch          ends
```

We can't say that the code is heavily obfuscated here, but it should give you an idea of what may be done with the aid of relatively simple macros used with the Flat Assembler. The preceding example may still be read with a tiny effort, but the application of a few more obfuscation tricks would render it literally unreadable and almost irreversible without a debugger.

A bit of kernel space

Until this very moment, we were only working with user-space code, writing small applications. In this part of the chapter, however, we will implement a small and very simple **loadable kernel module (LKM)** for Linux.

A few years ago, I was engaged in an interesting project, where the objective was to spot the data processed by certain kernel module. The project was even more challenging due to the fact that, not only did I not have access to the kernel sources, I had no access to the kernel itself, not to mention that it was not an Intel platform. All I knew was the version of the kernel in question and the name and address of the target module.

I had to go a long and interesting way until I was able to build an LKM that was capable of doing the work I needed it to do. At the end, I was able to build an LKM written in C, but I would not have been myself if I did not try to write one in Assembly. It was an unforgettable experience, I have to admit. However, once the project was completed, I decided to try to implement a simple LKM on my development machine. Since the first module was written for a different platform and for a kernel of a different version and taking into account that I decided to pretend like I had no sources for my running kernel, I had to perform almost as much research and reverse engineering, even though I was writing a module for my own system.

LKM structure

Let me save you from going the same long way of digging for information, reversing the structure of other kernel modules and examining kernel sources in order to see how exactly a module is loaded. Instead, let us proceed directly to the structure of an LKM.

A loadable kernel module is, in fact, an ELF object file with a few additional sections and some information, which we neither meet in object files nor in executables created for user-space. We should point out at least five sections that we do not usually have in regular files:

- `.init.text`: This section contains all the code required for module initialization. In terms of Windows, for example, the content of this section may be compared to the `DllMain()` function and all the functions that it references. In terms of Linux, it may be considered a section containing constructors (Windows executables may have that too).
- `.exit.text`: This section contains all the code needed to be executed before the module is unloaded.

- `.modinfo`: This section contains information about the module itself, the version of kernel it is written for, and so on.
- `.gnu.linkonce.this_module`: This section contains the `this_module` structure, which, in turn, contains the name of the module and pointers to module initialization and de-initialization procedures. While the structure itself is a bit obscure for us in this case, we are interested in certain offsets only, which, in case of lack of sources, may be found with a reverse engineering tool such as IDA Pro. We may, however, check for offsets of the `.init.text` and `.exit.text` pointers within the structure, by running the `readelf` command in the terminal, as follows:

  - **readelf- sr name_of_the_mofule.ko**

Then, we see the offsets in the output:

```
Relocation section '.rela.gnu.linkonce.this_module' at offset 0x3c8 contains 2 entries:
   Offset          Info            Type            Sym. Value      Sym. Name + Addend
000000000150  000100000001 R_X86_64_64          0000000000000000 .init.text + 0
000000000248  000200000001 R_X86_64_64          0000000000000000 .exit.text + 0
```

As we see, the pointer to `.init.text` is at the offset `0x150` and the pointer to `.exit.text` is at the offset `0x248` into the `this_module` structure.

- `__versions`: This section contains the names of external symbols prepended with their version numbers. This table is used by the kernel in order to verify compatibility of the module in question.

LKM source

The structure of an LKM is not a secret. It may be retrieved from Linux kernel sources, which are freely available and, therefore, we have no need to dig any deeper into it; instead, following Occam's Razor principle, let's move on to the implementation of the module.

As has been mentioned already, an LKM is an object file; therefore, we begin by creating a `lkm.asm` file and entering our code like this:

```
format ELF64       ; 64-bit ELF object file
extrn printk       ; We are going to use this symbol,
                   ; exported by the kernel, in order to
                   ; have an indication of the module being
                   ; loaded without problems
```

Right after this, we are free to begin creating sections of an LKM.

.init.text

This section contains the code required for successful initialization of an LKM. In our case, as we are not adding any functionality to the module, it could simply return, but as we need an indication of our LKM having loaded successfully, we will implement a tiny procedure, which will print a string into the system log:

```
section '.init.text' executable

module_init:
    push  rdi         ; We are going to use this register
    mov   rdi, str1   ; Load RDI with the address of the string
                      ; we want to print to system log (we will
                      ; add it to the data section in a few moments)
    xor   eax, eax
    call  printk      ; Write the string to the system log

    xor   eax, eax    ; Prepare return value
    pop   rdi         ; Restore the RDI register
    ret
```

Rather simple, isn't it? We just print the string and return from this procedure.

.exit.text

The content of this section is going to be even simpler (in our specific case). We simply return from the procedure:

```
section '.exit.text' executable
module_cleanup:
    xor   eax, eax
    ret
```

Since we did not allocate any resources nor load any modules or open any files, we simply return 0.

.rodata.str1.1

This is a read-only data section and the only thing we have to put in it, is the string we are going to write to the system log:

```
section '.rodata.str1.1'
    str1  db  '<0> Here I am, gentlemen!', 0x0a, 0
```

.modinfo

In this section, we have to put certain information about the module of ours, such as license, dependencies, as well as the version of the kernel and supported options:

```
section '.modinfo'
    ; It is possible to specify another license here,
    ; however, some kernel symbols would not be
    ; available for license other than GPL
    db  'license=GPL', 0

    ; Our LKM has no dependencies, therefore, we leave
    ; this blank
    db  'depends=', 0

    ; Version of the kernel and supported options
    db  'vermagic=3.16.0-4-amd64 SMP mod_unload modversions ', 0
```

If you are unsure about what to specify as `vermagic`, you may run the `modinfo` command on any of the modules found in the `/lib/modules/`uname -r`/` directory. For example, I run the following command on my system:

`/sbin/modinfo /lib/modules/`uname -r`/kernel/arch/x86/crypto/aesni-intel.ko`

The output will be as shown in the following screenshot:

```
filename:      /lib/modules/3.16.0-4-amd64/kernel/arch/x86/crypto/aesni-intel.ko
alias:         crypto-aes
alias:         aes
license:       GPL
description:   Rijndael (AES) Cipher Algorithm, Intel AES-NI instructions optimized
alias:         crypto-fpu
alias:         fpu
alias:         cpu:type:x86,ven*fam*mod*:feature:*0099*
depends:       glue_helper,aes-x86_64,lrw,cryptd,ablk_helper
intree:        Y
vermagic:      3.16.0-4-amd64 SMP mod_unload modversions
```

Once you have this information, you may simply copy the `vermagic` string and paste it into your code.

.gnu.linkonce.this_module

There's nothing special to say here. This section contains only one structure--`this_module`, which is mostly filled with zeroes (as it is used by the LKM loader internally) except three fields:

- Name of the module
- A pointer to the initialization procedure--`module_init`
- A pointer to the de-initialization procedure--`module_cleanup`

These fields, in the case of this kernel version and this Linux distro, are located at offsets `0x18`, `0x150`, and `0x248`, respectively; therefore, the code would be as follows:

```
section '.gnu.linkonce.this_module' writeable

this_module:
    ; Reserve 0x18 bytes
    rb  0x18
    ; String representation of the name of the module
    db  'simple_module',0

    ; Reserve bytes till the offset 0x150
    rb  0x150 - ($ - this_module)
    ; The address of the module_init procedure
    dq  module_init

    ; Reserve bytes till the offset 0x248
    rb  0x248 - ($ - this_module)
    ; The address of the module_cleanup procedure
    dq  module_cleanup
    dq  0
```

This is all we had to take care of in this section.

__versions

The information in this section describes external symbols by version numbers and names thereof, and is used by the loader in order to ensure that the kernel and the LKM are using symbols of the same version, so there would not be any surprises. You may try to build a module without this section and it may even be loaded, but it is not suggested to do so. The loader refuses to load modules with invalid symbol versions, thus telling us that this information is not just for fun, but is used in order to prevent failures.

At the time, I could not find reliable information on where to obtain version numbers for certain symbols, but it may be a good workaround, which is definitely sufficient for our small LKM, to simply search for symbol names prepended with the 8-byte version value (4 bytes on 32-bit systems), as shown in the following screenshot:

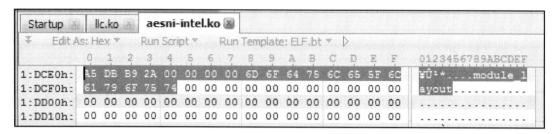

We only need two external symbols for our LKM, which are module_layout and printk. As you see in the preceding screenshot, the version of the module_layout symbol is 0x2AB9DBA5. Taking the same approach for obtaining the version of the printk symbol, we get (so it is on my system, but it may differ on yours) 0x27E1A049.

These entries are stored as an array of structures, where each structure contains two fields:

- version number: This is the 8-byte version identifier (4 bytes on 32-bit systems)
- symbol name: This is the variable length string (<u>up to 56 bytes</u>) representing the name of the symbol

Since we are talking about fixed-size fields here, it is natural to define a structure; however, since we do not want to name each and every structure for each and every symbol, we will use a macro:

```
macro __version ver, name
{
    local .version, .name
    .version   dq   ver
    .name      db   name, 0
    .name_len = $ - .name
             rb   56 - .name_len
}
```

Having defined the `__version` macro, we are ready to conveniently implement the `__versions` section:

```
section '__versions'
    __version  0x2AB9DBA5, 'module_layout'
    __version  0x27E1A049, 'printk'
```

That is it. Save the file and let's try to compile it and load.

Testing the LKM

Testing the module is much more simple than writing one. The compilation is not different from the usual; we simply compile it with the Flat Assembler:

```
# It is just the name of the output file that differs
# The extension would be 'ko' - kernel object, instead
# of 'o' for regular object
fasm lkm.asm lkm.ko
```

Once our kernel module is compiled, we need to ensure that it has the executable attribute set by running the `chmod +x lkm.ko` command in the Terminal.

In order to load the LKM into the currently running kernel, we use the `insmode` command in the following way:

```
sudo /sbin/insmode ./lkm.ko
```

We will not be given any error unless there is a serious problem with the format of the LKM (for example, invalid symbol version(s)). If all went well, try to run the `dmesg` command in the terminal, like this:

```
dmesg | tail -n 10
```

You should see the `"<0> Here I am, gentlemen!"` string appearing at the end of the system log. If the string is not there, then, most likely, you have to reboot your system, but first try to unload the module by running the `rmmod` command in the Terminal, like this:

```
sudo /sbin/rmmod simple_module
```

If all went well, then we will now be able to create Linux LKMs using pure Assembly.

Summary

We have gone a long way. Beginning with an overview of the Intel architecture, we went through the implementation of different algorithms, although mostly simplified for the sake of understandability, and we finished with the implementation of a loadable kernel module for Linux.

The intention behind this final chapter was to draw your interest toward a couple of topics that lie outside the scope of the book and therefore could not get enough attention, but are still important one way or another. Although the obfuscation given in the beginning of the chapter is rather simple, it should have given you the general idea of how more complicated obfuscation schemes may be brought up with the basic tool provided by the Flat Assembler, the macro engine.

We dedicated some time to kernel programming in the second part of the chapter and, although the kernel module we have implemented is, perhaps, the most basic one possible, we have shown that even such aspects of programming as kernel development, aspects that many people consider very complicated even when viewed from a high-level language perspective, include nothing to be afraid of even when viewed from the top of the solid rock called Assembly language.

By now, you should have a strong enough base to let you keep going on easily and improving your Assembly programming skills and abilities, and I would like to wish you good luck in doing this.

Thank you!

Index

92000998R00161

Made in the USA
Middletown, DE
04 October 2018